W0038419

A BENCHMARK SERIES BOOK

The Dachshund

An Owner's Survival Guide

Diane Morgan

Published by Doral Publishing, Phoenix, Arizona
Printed in the United States of America.

Edited by Amanda Pisani
Interior Design by The Printed Page
Cover Design by 1106 Design
Cover photo courtesy of Joella Maser, Ch. Von Maser's Caramel Nougat

Library of Congress Card Number: 2003100548
ISBN: 0-944875-92-0

*This book is dedicated to Melinda Brown
and in memory of her Chloe*

Contents

Introduction

The Delight of Dachshunds

The Dachshund is not one dog but many. His coat may be sleek and smooth, long and silky, or wiry and tough. He may weigh ten pounds, or more than thirty. As for color, a Dachshund may be solid, or he may be a mix of shades of red, cream, black, chocolate, fawn, and gray-blue. He can be dappled or double dappled, brindled or piebald.

What other breed offers such a variety? Irish setters and Weimaraners all look alike. Poodles come in a variety of sizes, but only one coat type. Labradors come in three colors but only one size and coat type. Collies and St. Bernards can be shorthaired or longhaired, but their size standard remains the same. Only the Dachshund provides such a glorious mélange.

Yet, magically, beneath this delightful multiplicity lurks a paradox. The Dachshund is not many dogs but one. Beneath the Smooth, Longhair or Wirehair coat, packaged small or large, painted black or fawn or a mixture, is one spirit, one heart, and one soul. It is the spirit of courage, the heart of loyalty, and the soul of nobility. Roger Caras, late president emeritus of the American Society for Prevention of Cruelty to Animals, once said: "Dogs are not our whole lives, but they can make out lives whole." This is undoubtedly even truer of the Dachshund than of most breeds.

Dachshund Devotees

Famous Doxie fans have included Queen Victoria to Clark Gable, and everyone in between. Some of those in between are Errol Flynn, Noel Coward, E.B. White, Pablo Picasso, and William Randolph Hearst. Not bad for a dog "two dogs long and half a dog high."

Welcome to the world of the Dachshund. You'll never go home again.

Annie, All Tangled Up

Photo Courtesy of Daisy Buchignani
Owners: Frank & Renee Renwick

Chapter 1

The Development of the Dachshund

It may be hard to imagine, but Dachshunds didn't start out looking anything like Dachshunds. They looked like wolves, and for a very good reason—they were. Thousands of years of close association with people turned some wolves gradually into dogs, and thousands more years of selective breeding turned generic dogs into the countless canine varieties that exist today. Some breeds, like German Shepherds and Alaskan Malamutes, retain many of the physical features of the wolf. Others, of which the Dachshund is a prime example, differ so much from their wolfish forebears that you wouldn't know they were even related. Yet they are.

Dachshunds and wolves are different members of the same species—*Canis lupus*. They have the same genetic code and could interbreed successfully, producing fertile young, although one hesitates to say just what they might look like. The wolf is *Canis lupus lupus*, and the Dachshund is *Canis lupus familiaris*—the familiar wolf. This is something we should never forget. For although a Dachshund may look nothing like a wolf, he retains some of the wolf's behavior patterns: a powerful prey drive, a strong sense of pack loyalty, and undaunted courage. In these respects, and certain others, a Dachshund may be more true to his ancestry than some larger, more superficially imposing breeds of dog.

Barney, a red smooth miniature guards the property   *Photo courtesy of Phyllis Grilli*

Between the wolf and the Dachshund lies a fascinating history of breeding—although unfortunately our knowledge about most of it is lost forever. Some people believe the ancestry of the breed can be traced to ancient Egypt, although this is said of so many dog breeds that it's not very helpful, even if it's true.

A Member of the Hound Family

The Dachshund is a hound. This means that he was designed to search unrelentingly and independently for game, taking his human helper along behind him. The Dachshund's small size (and even the largest Doxies are not large dogs) did not come about as an attempt to produce a "toy" dog. Dachshunds were bred by the Germans with a specific and deadly purpose. They had a job to do: to find and hunt badgers, one of the most ferocious and difficult to catch of all prey. To this end, the Dachshund was developed with a shape and a size to enable him to enter badger tunnels. (I've never been quite sure what the Germans had against badgers—they're not very tasty from what I understand. One source I consulted mentioned that badgers ruined hunting parties, but didn't say how they accomplished this. Perhaps just digging holes in the ground was enough to irritate the Germans. Groundhogs affect many people that way.)

Badger Busters

Dachshunds were bred to catch the European badger *(Meles meles)*, a larger, but less carnivorous and more social relative of our American badger *(Taxidea taxus)*. Neither variety of badger is anything to fool around with, by the way. These things have long teeth, sharp claws, and can weigh up to forty pounds. And they don't enjoy being ripped out of their homes and killed to amuse hunters.

However, most historians of the Dachshund believe that it is something more than a hound—a "hound-plus," if you will. Since the Dachshund is the only hound breed that goes to ground after its prey, some experts think that they were bred with terriers along the way, even the Smooth and Longhaired versions. This makes sense, because Dachshunds do have a terrier-like quality in their personalities. So those enjoying the companionship of a Dachshund are getting the determination, firmness, and steady nature of the hound, combined with the vivacity, spunk, and charm of the terrier.

Teaching the youngster...   *Photo courtesy of Karen Wheeler Gray*

Since the German word for badger is *dachs* and the word for dog is *hund*, a Dachshund is a "badger dog." However, it was the English who gave the dog this name, not the Germans. For reasons that I don't understand the Dachshund is *not* called a Dachshund in Germany. It's called a *Dackel*. Or a *Teckel* (an old German word for *Dackel* or Dachshund). This is just another one of those little linguistic mysteries that keep life interesting.

A German Gem

Today the Dachshund has the honor of being the national dog of Germany.

According to John Hutchinson Cook, affectionately known as "Mr. Dachshund" by the cognoscenti, Dachshunds might first have come to Germany/Austria (it was hard to tell them apart in 1477 when all this was taking place) when Maximilian (one of those Hapsburgs, complete with the famous Hapsburg lip) arrived in Burgundy to wed Mary, daughter of Charles the Bold, the last reigning Duke of Burgundy. In fact, after the marriage, there was no more Burgundy. (In case you were wondering, Charles the Bold got his name when he had Louis XI arrested—a nervy thing to do.) Apparently, C the B gave some Dachshunds to Maximilian as a wedding present. Mr. Dachshund argues that these dogs were the ancestors of the Doxies of today, and I suppose it's as good a guess as any. Others suggest that French basset hounds were crossed with German *Teckels*. If the resulting puppies had long legs, they were called *Dachsbracke*, while if they had short legs they were known as Dachshunds. All of this is so confused and murky that it seems rather a waste of effort to go into it too much further.

At any rate, the early Dachshunds were on the average larger than those we see today, many of them weighing thirty-five pounds. (If your Dachshund weighs that much, he is probably not in fighting trim.)

Badgers were not the only game of the early large Dachshunds. German hunters put them together in packs to hunt (unbelievably) wild boar. They used smaller varieties to track foxes and wounded deer, and very small ones to dig out hares and rabbits from their dens. Even today, miniature Dachshunds are no mere lapdogs, but excellent competitors in the field.

The earliest Dachshunds were the Smooth-coated variety. Their ancestors may have included the St. Hubert's Hound, forebear of Bloodhounds and Bassets. The Longhaired sort may have developed from crosses with spaniels or a German gundog known as the *Stoberhund* (from the German word meaning to "poke around" in stuff). Longhaired Dachshunds were first bred in 1820, but did not appear in shows until 1882.

Wirehaired Doxies officially appeared around the end of the nineteenth century, a result of crossing Smooth dogs with the German Wirehaired Pinscher and the Dandie Dinmont Terrier. A French hound-pointer known as *Braque* may also be implicated. ("Braque" is a colloquial French word for "crazy." Whether this has any connection with pointers or not is unclear, at least to me.) However, some maintain that Wirehaired dogs were developed much earlier, possibly in 1812.

America Adopts The Miniature

The first Miniature Dachshunds (all nine of them) were shown in this country at the Dachshund Club of America Specialty Show in 1934. The variety had only been in the country about four years. The Wirehaired Miniature was at first the most successful—at least at winning ribbons—but now all coats of Miniatures are showing well. This size became popular with the American public very soon after World War II.

Later breeders crossed their dogs with the Miniature Pinscher (for Smooths), Papillons (for Longhaired Dachshunds) and Miniature Schnauzers (for Wirehaired Dachshunds). These crosses were not made for fun, but to fine tune the hunting capabilities of the breed, each type being developed for slightly different purposes and terrain. Miniature Dachshunds can trace their heritage back to Rat Terriers and Chihuahuas. As a result, not only do the different kinds of Dachshunds differ in looks, but most Dachshund experts will tell you that each type has its own distinct personality. Nowadays, of course, this kind of out-crossing is forbidden. Breeds are expected to maintain their own distinct bloodlines (possibly to their detriment). Since most Dachshunds are no longer functional hunting dogs, but pampered pets, looks have become more important than working qualities.

The Dachshund Evolves

Some of the breeding changes made in the 1930s and '40s in America were anatomical improvements—such as the level topline and straighter legs. Other changes were not so felicitous. For example, some show breeders, both in the United States and Germany, became enchanted with the idea of a deeper chest for Doxies. This "improvement" not only made the dog unsuitable for working in the field, but it may well have predisposed this breed to bloat. In fact, of all small breeds, only Doxies are subject to this dread condition.

Dachshund Clubs

Interestingly, the honors of developing the first Doxie club belong to the British, who established their organization in 1881. In Britain, the Dachshund was favored as a pet and show dog, rather than as a hunter, thus the emphasis in looks over character. Doxies received a great boost in popularity due to the influence of Queen Victoria, who owned one named Dash. It was given to her by her German husband Prince Albert, and rumor has that the royal couple hunted with Dash in Windsor Forest.

The German Dachshund Club (the *Deutscher Teckelklub*) was established in 1888. Early on, the three varieties of Dachshund were listed: the Smooth (*Kurzhaar*), the Longhaired (*Langhaar*), and the Wirehaired (*Rauhaar*). In Germany itself, a split developed between those breeders who were primarily interested in showing dogs, and those who wished to maintain the breed as a working dog. These latter folks deplored the fact that show breeders seemed intent on creating a breed with an exaggerated body type. As a result, the Federation of German Working Dachshund Clubs was established to preserve the dog's ancient heritage. This organization set up tests that dogs had to pass before being admitted to the registry. Still later, in 1909, the Association of German Working Dachshund Clubs was created to bring together all the different Dachshund organizations. This group wrote the standard for the breed, one that is accepted today not only in Germany, but also in England.

The Dachshund in the United States

Dachshunds were brought to this country with the wave of German immigrants who arrived in the nineteenth century. The popularity of the breed was high during the latter part of that period, with the American Kennel Club (AKC) recognizing the breed in 1885. The Dachshund Club of America (DCA) was organized in 1895. In 1914, Dachshunds were well represented at the fabled Westminster Kennel Club Show. (None of them won Best in Show, though—the honors went to an Old English Sheepdog. This is not surprising. There is a significant prejudice against hounds at Westminster, and very few have gone on to win Best in Show there. No Dachshund ever has.)

The Pitfalls of Popularity

When demand for a breed becomes too great, legitimate breeders can't meet it—there just aren't enough good breeders producing good dogs. This opens the way for puppy mills and careless backyard breeders who make poor choices about breeding stock. The result can be dogs who lack good health, conformation, and temperament.

However, the number of Dachshunds sank scandalously low during and after the First World War, as the dog fell victim to anti-German sentiment, even though Dachshunds had nothing to do with shooting Archduke Ferdinand (or with anything else, at least so far as I can determine.) In a frenzy of chauvinism and jingoism some ignorant Americans actually killed Dachshunds—one breeder shot his entire kennel—simply because the hated

Three Longhaired Dachshunds enjoy the outdoors.   *Photo courtesy of Pamela Joslin*

Kaiser Wilhelm was fond of the breed. By 1923, only twenty-three dogs were registered in the entire country.

Beginning in 1930, however, the popularity of the breed rebounded. With the advent of World War II, Dachshund aficionados feared that again the breed's numbers would plummet. However, the Dachshund Club of America did a better job of public relations during World War II, convincing the American people that Doxies were not Nazis, but only harmless wienerhounds, and Dachshund numbers remained pretty constant. (This was despite the fact that Adolf Hitler owned a Dachshund. Apparently the American people were finally able to figure out that this wasn't the dog's fault.)

The Dachshund is now one of the most beloved dog breeds in the country. Doxies were rated fourth in AKC registrations in the year 2001.

Chapter 2
The Doxie Defined

The official standard for the Dachshund was developed by the Dachshund Club of America, and then presented to the American Kennel Club, a kind of "club of clubs." (Only breed clubs are "members" of the AKC. Individual human beings can't join. But you personally can become a member of the DCA, which itself is part of the AKC.) The official standard was developed to describe the "perfect" Dachshund, and of course there is no such animal. Even a Westminster winner has faults. I include the standard here for two purposes. First, if you haven't acquired a Dachshund yet and are looking for a show dog, the standard tells you what qualities to look for. Of course, if you are buying a puppy, there's a lot of guesswork involved, even by an experienced person. Second, if you already own a Dachshund, it's kind of fun to see how he "stacks up."

The Official Standard of the Dachshund

One of the good things about the Dachshund standard, as opposed to some others, is that it explains why some of its elements are included. Some parts of the standard are "cosmetic" only; it doesn't really matter for form or function if a dog's nose is black or brown. Other elements are part of what makes a Dachshund a Dachshund and not an Afghan or a Bichon Frise. And still other parts of the standard are clearly included to describe the characteristics of a healthy, sound dog, such as the standard's explanation of a well-formed "bite."

The specifics outlined in the standard are important to show folk and breeders. But don't worry if your pet Dachshund doesn't meet its strict requirements in every (or even any) particular. You still have the best dog in the world.

If you would like a pictorial standard, you can contact the Dachshund Club of America at their Web site; they can send you one for a nominal fee. Many of the descriptions appear vague and subject to opinion, and in fact, that's what judging dog shows is all about. What, for example, are "medium-size" eyes? The exact terminology of the standard is in italics. My comments are in regular type.

The Standard in Detail

General Appearance—*Low to ground, long in body, and short of leg with robust muscular development; the skin is elastic and pliable without excessive wrinkling. Appearing neither crippled, awkward, nor cramped in his capacity for movement, the Dachshund is well-balanced with bold and confident head carriage and intelligent, alert facial expression. His hunting spirit, good nose, loud tongue, and distinctive build make him well-suited for below-ground work and for beating the bush. His keen nose gives him an advantage over most other breeds for trailing.* This part of the standard sets forth the basic premise of the Dachshund: He is a hunting dog, and all his attributes should reflect that purpose. *NOTE: Inasmuch as the Dachshund is a hunting dog, scars from honorable wounds shall not be considered a fault.* I'm not sure how a judge can tell if a wound was received honorably, but that's what it says.

Size, Proportion, Substance—*Bred and shown in two sizes, standard and miniature, miniatures are not a separate classification but compete in a class division for "eleven pounds and under at twelve months of age and older."* Weight of the standard size is usually between sixteen and thirty-two pounds. Notice that the only difference between the two varieties is size; otherwise they conform to the same standard.

Head—*Viewed from above or from the side, the head tapers uniformly to the tip of the nose. The eyes are of medium size, almond-shaped and dark-rimmed, with an energetic, pleasant expression; not piercing;*

very dark in color. It's desirable if the eyes have a dark rim—as though the dog is wearing eyeliner. Contrary to conventional wisdom, by the way, Dachshunds—indeed all dogs—can see colors, but not as many or as vividly as we do. Yellow and blue are the easiest colors for them to distinguish. Dachshunds can see a moving target much better than people can, but they don't see very well close up. This may be the only reason why Doxies can't read. *The bridge bones over the eyes are strongly prominent. Wall eyes, except in the case of dappled dogs, are a serious fault.* (A wall eye is an eye with a whitish iris.) *The ears are set near the top of the head, not too far forward, of moderate length, rounded, and not narrow, pointed, or folded. Their carriage, when animated, is with the forward edge just touching the cheek so that the ears frame the face.* Dogs can hear about four times as well as people do. In fact their hearing range spans from about twenty hertz to over fifty thousand hertz, much wider than that of humans. They are especially good at picking up high notes (hence the "dog whistle") and faint sounds. *The skull is slightly arched, neither too broad nor too narrow, and slopes gradually with little perceptible stop into the finely-formed, slightly arched muzzle.* The "stop" is the area between the dog's eyes where the nose meets the cranium. *Black is the preferred color of the nose.* This is an aesthetic preference only. Dachshunds with light-colored noses can smell perfectly well, which is the important thing. *Lips are tightly stretched, well covering the lower jaw. Nostrils well open.* This is, of course, to help the Doxies scent better. Dogs have many, many more scent receptors in their noses than we do. Dachshunds, being scent hounds, are unusually good at discriminating between various scents, filtering in what interests them, and filtering out what they find boring. *Jaws opening wide and hinged well back of the eyes, with strongly developed bones and teeth.* Inside the jaws is the tongue. The standard doesn't say anything about the tongue, but it's a good thing your Doxie has one. It's essential to the digestive and heat regulatory system. Curiously, even though a dog's tongue is much bigger than ours, it has fewer taste buds, and those it does have are further back. There are even a few in the throat! This explains why Dachshunds may "wolf" their food. That's how they taste it. *Teeth—Powerful canine teeth; teeth fit closely together in a scissors bite. An even bite is a minor fault. Any other deviation is a serious fault.* This is important. In a correct scissors bite, the upper teeth slightly overlap the lowers ones. This formation enables the dog to chew properly, and while this is not as critical for canines as it is for us, teeth that don't meet properly can be worn down.

Neck—*Long, muscular, clean-cut, without dewlap, slightly arched in the nape, flowing gracefully into the shoulders.* A long neck imparts grace and elegance to the whole dog.

Trunk—*The trunk is long and fully muscled. When viewed in profile, the back lies in the straightest possible line between the withers and the short, very slightly arched loin. A body that hangs loosely between the shoulders is a serious fault.* Because Dachshunds can have problems with their backs, this is one feature of the anatomy that should be given careful attention. Whatever his back looks like, however, keep your Dachshund at a proper weight so as not to overstress it. *Abdomen—Slightly drawn up.*

Forequarters—*For effective underground work, the front must be strong, deep, long and cleanly muscled. Forequarters in detail: Chest— The breast-bone is strongly prominent in front so that on either side a depression or dimple appears. When viewed from the front, the thorax appears oval and extends downward to the mid-point of the forearm. The enclosing structure of the well-sprung ribs appears full and oval to allow, by its ample capacity, complete development of heart and lungs. The keel merges gradually into the line of the abdomen and extends well beyond the front legs. Viewed in profile, the lowest point of the breast line is covered by the front leg. Shoulder Blades—Long, broad, well-laid back and firmly placed upon the fully developed thorax, closely fitted at the withers, furnished with hard yet pliable muscles. Upper Arm—Ideally the same length as the shoulder blade and at right angles to the latter, strong of bone and hard of muscle, lying close to the ribs, with elbows close to the body, yet capable of free movement. Forearm—Short; supplied with hard yet pliable muscles on the front and outside, with tightly stretched tendons on the inside at the back, slightly curved inward. The joints between the forearms and the feet (wrists) are closer together than the shoulder joints, so that the front does not appear absolutely straight. Knuckling over is a disqualifying fault. Feet—Front paws are full, tight, compact, with well-arched toes and tough, thick pads. They may be equally inclined a trifle outward. There are five toes, four in use, close together with a pronounced arch and strong, short nails. Front dewclaws may be removed.*

Hindquarters—*Strong and clean muscled. The pelvis, the thigh, the second thigh, and the metatarsus are ideally the same length and* *form a series of right angles. From the rear, the thighs are strong and powerful. The legs turn neither in nor out. Metatarsus—Short and strong, perpendicular to the second thigh bone. When viewed from behind, they are upright and parallel. Feet/Hind Paws—Smaller than the front paws, with four compactly closed and arched toes with tough, thick pads. The entire foot points straight ahead and is balanced equally on the ball and not merely on the toes. Rear dewclaws should be removed. Croup—Long, rounded and full, sinking slightly toward the tail. Tail—Set in continuation of the spine, extending without kinks, twists, or pronounced curvature, and not carried too gaily.*

    Gait—*Fluid and smooth. Forelegs reach well forward, without much lift, in unison with the driving action of hind legs. The correct shoulder assembly and well-fitted elbows allow the long, free stride in front. Viewed from the front, the legs do not move in exact parallel planes, but incline slightly inward to compensate for shortness of leg and width of chest. Hind legs drive on a line with the forelegs, with hocks (metatarsus) turning neither in nor out. The propulsion of the hind leg depends on the dog's ability to carry the hind leg to complete extension. Viewed in profile, the forward reach of the hind leg equals the rear extension. The thrust of correct movement is seen when the rear pads are clearly exposed during rear extension. Feet must travel parallel to the line of motion with no tendency to swing out, cross over, or interfere with each other. Short, choppy movement, rolling or high-stepping gait, close or overly wide coming or going are incorrect.* The Dachshund must have agility, freedom of movement, and endurance to do the work for which he was developed. The work for which he was developed does not include a lot of jumping and twisting, something about which I will have more to say later.

    Temperament—*The Dachshund is clever, lively, and courageous to the point of rashness, persevering in above and below ground work, with all the senses well-developed. Any display of shyness is a serious fault.* Together with health, temperament is the most critical element of the Dachshund. A shy or aggressive animal is a discredit to this bold and charming breed.

    Special Characteristics of the Three Coat Varieties—*The Dachshund is bred with three varieties of coat: (1) Smooth; (2) Wirehaired; (3) Longhaired and is shown in two sizes, standard and miniature. All three varieties and both sizes must conform to the characteristics already specified. The following features are applicable for each variety.* I say more about these in the next chapter, as well.

Smooth Dachshund—Coat—Short, smooth, and shining. Should be neither too long nor too thick. Ears not leathery. Tail—Gradually tapered to a point, well but not too richly haired. Long sleek bristles on the underside are considered a patch of strong-growing hair, not a fault. A brush tail is a fault, as is also a partly or wholly hairless tail. Color of Hair—Although base color is immaterial, certain patterns and basic colors predominate. One-colored Dachshunds include red (with or without a shading of interspersed dark hairs or sable) and cream. A small amount of white on the chest is acceptable, but not desirable. It has been estimated that Dachshunds can be found in 176 colors and patterns. The new "piebald" color seems to go against the undesirable "small amount of white on the chest," but the color of a dog's hair doesn't seem to matter much to him. *Nose and nails—black.* Obviously nose and nail colors are purely cosmetic. It is true, however, that black nails seem to be stronger and less likely to split than white ones. The great disadvantage of black nails is that it's impossible to see the quick when trimming them.

Two-colored Dachshunds include black, chocolate, wild boar, gray (blue), and fawn (Isabella), each with tan markings over the eyes; on the sides of the jaw and underlip; on the inner edge of the ear, front, breast, inside and behind the front legs; on the paws and around the anus; and from there to about one-third to one-half of the length of the tail on the underside. Undue prominence or extreme lightness of tan markings is undesirable. A small amount of white on the chest is acceptable but not desirable. Nose and nails—In the case of black dogs, black; for chocolate and all other colors, dark brown, but self-colored is acceptable. Dappled dachshunds—The "single" dapple pattern is expressed as lighter-colored areas contrasting with the darker base color, which may be any acceptable color. Neither the light nor the dark color should predominate. Nose and nails are the same as for one and two-colored Dachshunds. Partial or wholly blue (wall) eyes are as acceptable as dark eyes. A large area of white on the chest of a dapple is permissible. A "double" dapple is one in which varying amounts of white coloring occur over the body in addition to the dapple pattern. Nose and nails— As for one and two-color Dachshunds; partial or wholly self-colored is permissible. Brindle is a pattern (as opposed to a color) in which black or dark stripes occur over the entire body although in some specimens the pattern may be visible only in the tan points.

Wirehaired Dachshunds—Coat—With the exception of jaw, eyebrows, and ears, the whole body is covered with a uniform tight, short, thick, rough, hard, outer coat but with finer, somewhat softer, shorter hairs (undercoat) everywhere distributed between the coarser hairs. The absence of an undercoat is a fault. The distinctive facial furnishings include a beard and eyebrows. On the ears the hair is shorter than on the body, almost smooth. The general arrangement of the hair is such that the Wirehaired Dachshund, when viewed from a distance, resembles the Smooth. Any sort of soft hair in the outercoat, wherever found on the body, especially on the top of the head, is a fault. The same is true of long, curly, or wavy hair, or hair that sticks out irregularly in all directions. Tail—Robust, thickly haired, gradually tapering to a point. A flag tail is a fault. Color of Hair—While the most common colors are wild boar, black and tan, and various shades of red, all colors are admissible. A small amount of white on the chest, although acceptable, is not desirable. Nose and nails—Same as for the smooth variety.

Longhaired Dachshund—Coat—The sleek, glistening, often slightly wavy hair is longer under the neck and on the forechest, the underside of the body, the ears, and behind the legs. The coat gives the dog an elegant appearance. Short hair on the ear is not desirable. Too profuse a coat which masks type, equally long hair over the whole body, a curly coat, or a pronounced parting on the back are faults. Tail—Carried gracefully in prolongation of the spine; the hair attains its greatest length here and forms a veritable flag. Color of hair—Same as for the Smooth Dachshund. Nose and nails—Same as for the Smooth.

The foregoing description is that of the ideal Dachshund. Any deviation from the above described dog must be penalized to the extent of the deviation, keeping in mind the importance of the contribution of the various features toward the basic original purpose of the breed.

DISQUALIFICATION
Knuckling over of front legs.
Approved April 7, 1992
Effective May 27, 1992

Lizzie, a smooth, miniature chocolate/tan dapple   *Photo courtesy of Daisy Buchignani*
Owners: Frank & Renee Renwick

But What is a Dachshund Like, Really?

The official standard can scratch the surface of Dachshund-ness, but only just. For the true Dachshund is so much more. To me, the defining characteristic of the breed is his adaptability. For most breeds of dog, you have to adapt to them. But a Dachshund becomes so much a part of your family that his intelligent and versatile nature can tolerate anything (other than mistreatment).

If you live in the country, you have the ideal partner for rambling. If you're a city dweller, the chic Doxie will be your ideal companion. And suburbanites find their picketed backyard just the perfect size for Dachshund adventures.

Dachshunds are long-lived dogs, many reaching their mid and late teens. Even more delightful is the fact that they stay active. While many other breeds are sedate and laid back by the age of five or six, a Doxie is still whizzing around the house like a puppy. If you like an active dog, this is the breed for you!

A Dachshund Walks into a Bar

One place to look for information about this breed is the Dachshund Club of Germany (Deutscher Teckelklub or DTK): www.teckelklub.de The site informs us that the DTK is a member of both the Federation Cynologique International and the Jagdgebrauchshundverbandes, which is good to know. Since my own German is truly, truly awful, I clicked on the English translation version of the text. Here I came across the following sentence, which was too charming to omit: "Keeping of the Dachshound [sic] is possible without problems, since they need very little room and no dog saloons."

Stanley found the bone!   *Photo courtesy of V. Jean Trefes*

This then is the Dachshund:

D	Debonair
A	Alert
C	Courageous
H	Habit-Forming
S	Sensitive
H	Hilarious
U	Ultra-cool
N	Noble
D	Devoted

If you allow a Dachshund into your life—you may take on some of these qualities yourself.

Ch. Von Maser's Caramel with Almonds, miniature wheaton wirehair

Photo courtesy of Joella Maser

Chapter 3
The Diversity of Dachshunds

The diversity found in Dachshunds—two size classifications, three coat types, countless colors and patterns, and an infinite variety of personalities—is one of the most charming qualities of the breed. It's great fun to take a stroll along the Dachshund smorgasbord, although we will not, of course, actually *eat* any Dachshunds, no matter how much they look like wieners.

The Dachshund Character

The Dachshund not only *is* a character, he also has one. Every Doxie has a bold and engaging personality. The Dachshund combines self-sufficiency with a sociability that makes him a star wherever he goes. All Doxies are active and sprightly, and can adapt to city, suburban, or country life with ease. All Doxies are watchful, intensely loyal, and brave. (In fact, the breed was developed for courage, even to the point of recklessness.) No Dachshund will suffer fools gladly—and all require kind, consistent, and fair treatment.

Brave enough to badger a badger, bright enough to baffle a burglar, and bold enough to beat up a bully—the Dachshund is no ordinary dog.

Miniature Longhaired Dachshunds   *Photo courtesy of Pamela Joslin*

Size

Each variety of Dachshunds is found in both standard and miniature sizes, although, as we shall see, there are certain confusing elements about this. For example, the miniature Dachshund should weigh eleven pounds or under at one year of age, while the standard should weigh between sixteen and thirty-two pounds.

Of course, that leaves us with a number of uncategorized animals weighing in between eleven and sixteen pounds—the so-called tweenie wieners. Some consider these "tweenies" to be the result of careless breeding, perhaps even a sign that the dogs came from a puppy mill, but that is not necessarily the case. More charitably, people refer to these "tweenies" as small standards or "oversized miniatures." I rather like the term tweenie myself.

There is some male/female dimorphism within the regulation size range for the standard dog. The standard male tends to weigh closer to thirty pounds, while the female tends to be closer to twenty pounds. Some people think that the currently allowable top range of the standard is really too big for a classic Dachshund, while others have no problems with Doxies that weigh as much as forty pounds. (This is assuming that the dog is not overweight, of course.) At the other end of the scale, many breeders also believe that male standard Dachshunds should weight at least twenty-two pounds, and will not show a standard weighing under that. In general, Longhairs attain the greatest size, and Smooths tend to be smallest.

The Dainty Dachshunds of Deutschland

The Germans divide their Dachshunds into three groups, depending on chest circumference. The smallest is the *kaninchen teckel* (rabbit dog), which can squeeze into small burrows after rabbits. The *kaninchen teckel* weighs under 7.7 pounds and has a chest circumference of twelve inches or fewer. The midsize is the *zwerg teckel* with an upper weight limit of 8.8 pounds and a chest circumference under fourteen inches. The heavy *teckel* has an upper weight of 19.8 pounds. So we see that the Europeans prefer a Dachshund on the small side, feeling that only the slighter dogs can properly perform their original duties. The larger Dachshunds often found in America must have extremely good conformation, including an oval chest and tight shoulders, to perform adequately in Earthdog trials.

Although all Dachshunds have a propensity to bark, the habit seems strongest in miniatures. In addition, miniatures make a high-pitched sound that can be well-nigh intolerable to the unaccustomed ear. While very tiny Dachshunds are cute, they can be difficult to breed. There are also prone to certain anatomical difficulties, such as patellar luxation, that plague all small dog breeds.

A New Breed

One group, the National Miniature Dachshund Association, formed in 1951, has petitioned to separate the two sizes into two different breeds, so far without success.

The Dachshund's Coat

The Dachshund is an amazing dog when it comes to the coat. The combinations of coat type, colors and patterns are almost endless.

Coat Type and Disposition

Coat type is an important way to classify Dachshunds, and not just for appearance. The various coat types resulted from historical out-crosses with other breeds. These crosses gave each differently coated variety of Dachshunds its own special outlook on life.

For example, the Smooth Dachshund is perhaps the most willful of the bunch—even stubborn. He loves his own way. The Longhaired Dachshund is known for his mellow demeanor, but ironically, he often makes the best hunter of the three types. This propensity may reflect his spaniel ancestry. Lastly, the Wirehair is the clown of the group, and many people think he has a terrier's bold personality. His almost shed-free coat makes him a relatively good choice for people with allergies to dogs.

Kaymors Snoopin Around "Snoopy"   *Photo courtesy of Pamela Joslin*

Color

Most people are familiar with solid red, and black and tan Dachshunds, which are the most common Dachshund colors. Because show judges have shown a preference for these prevalent colors, these dogs are most likely to be bred. But Dachshunds appear in an amazing 176 colors and combinations of colors and patterns, and other colors and patterns have become increasingly popular. Caution: there are some unscrupulous breeders who tout these colors as "rare" and charge much more for them. They are not rare. They simply have not historically been desired, and so have not been bred for.

The Cause of Color

The origin of a dog's color is actually a somewhat complicated subject. For one thing, no single gene is responsible for causing a dog to be any particular color. Researchers have identified at least ten genes for dog hair color patterns, as well as well as color type, distribution, and intensity.

Another word for a solid color in Dachshunds is "self." But a solid or self-colored Dachshund doesn't necessarily mean what you think it might. True, self-colored Dachshunds may be all red, but it may also refer to an animal with a solid dark coat (say, black) and lighter (tan) markings. A Dachshund can have only one self-color.

Of course you can have five red Dachshunds all of different colors, since "red" does not accurately describe a certain wavelength. Red can be deep red, pale red, or russet. Some "red" Doxies have a sprinkling of black hairs.

The most common two-toned Dachshund is the classic black and tan (the tan should be neither unduly prominent nor too light, according to the standard). Other two-toners are chocolate and tan, and some have a base color of gray—which is called "blue" in Dachshund circles. Still others have a fawn color as their base, a color that Doxie people also call "Isabella," for reasons that escape me. (In case you're wondering, nearly all breeds have generated their own unique way of referring to coat colors.

Dachshund people are no crazier than any others.) There's also a color known as "wild boar," a mixture of light and dark hairs throughout. This is indeed the color of wild boars, and it is found most often in Wirehaired Dachshunds. A less frequently seen color is cream, but it is becoming rather sought after.

Faith   *Photo courtesy of Daisy & Charles Buchignani*
                                  Owners: Sandi & Hector Loredo

Patterns

In addition to solidly colored and traditional two-toned dogs, Dachshunds can boast a variety of patterns. Such patterns include dapple (and double dapple), brindle, sable, and piebald. Any pattern can be superimposed over any solid (self) color. So you can have a black and tan dapple. Or a red brindle. And so on. When identifying a Dachshund, the color is noted first, followed by the pattern. Hence "red dapple," would be correct, but "brindle blue" (although it sounds nice) would not.

Dapple dogs have patches of color all over, mingled with patches of the self color. In addition, there might be a large white area on the chest, which is permissible under the breed standard for this pattern. A black and tan dapple will have silver hairs threaded among the black of the body. If the dappling extends

Dave, a smooth-haired miniature, red double dapple
Photo courtesy of Daisy & Charles Buchignani

across the face, you might end up with a blue or bi-eyed dog, which is not desirable under the breed standard. The standard calls for "very dark" eyes. Alternately, the eyes might be speckled with blue (but that's not good either, at least as far as the show ring goes). Chocolate and tan dapples may have yellowish hair amid the chocolate.

Dapple puppies must have a least one dapple parent, but even one tiny little freckle is enough to qualify as a dapple. So if you own a dapple puppy, you know that mom or dad has at least one spot somewhere, even if you never noticed it. (It may even have faded away as the dog matured!) That's why the AKC requires you to register such a dog as a dapple, even if it is *nearly* self-colored.

Two dapple dogs may produce *double dapple* offspring. Double dapple dogs have lots of white patches as well as colored ones. Neither the light nor the dark color predominates, but are seen in addition to the self pattern. A double dapple may have white blazes, blue eyes, and white-tipped tails. It may look appealing, but it's also genetically dangerous. Double dapples carry a white (Merle) gene, which has a disconcerting habit of causing deafness, partial deafness, reduced eye size, or even missing eyes! I don't think this is something to be encouraged.

Another Color Curiosity

Sometimes black and tan dapple dogs are mislabeled "silver dapples." This is incorrect. Silver is not an accepted color name in Dachshunds. There's no special reason for this, but it isn't.

A *brindle* Dachshund has zebra-like stripes over the self color. Thus, a red brindle will have black stripes all over the body. So will a black and tan brindle, except you won't see the black stripes over the black part of his body, only over the tan. A brindle Dachshund must have a least one brindle parent.

A *sable* Dachshund has dark-tipped hairs. That means that each single hair (except those on the face and feet) has a black or very dark tip. Accordingly, a red sable looks a lot like a black and tan two-tone—you have to ruffle the fur backward to see the red underlay. A sable dog must have a sable parent.

A fairly new color is *piebald,* which refers to a dog who is primarily white with large splotches of one or two colors. Some piebalds are nearly all white, with color patches on the head and tail. Others have what is known (for some reason) as "Irish spotting." Irish spotting refers to a white chest, white collar, white belly, and white feet. There is no variation in the solid-colored spots as in a dapple Dachshund. True piebalds never have blue eyes, and always have a white-tipped tail. Currently this pattern is considered marginal enough not to appear in the breed standard (or the show ring), but there is no doubt that a piebald can be a strikingly handsome animal! Both parents must be piebald, or at least carry the piebald gene to produce a piebald puppy.

The Dachshund Dictionary

Dachshund nomenclature forbids calling black and tan piebalds "tricolors," even though that's what they look like.

Deciphering Dachshunds

Despite differences in size, coat type, and color, all Doxies speak basically the same language. Once you learn to decode it, you'll go a long way toward forming a permanent and understanding partnership with your best friend. Since we expect dogs to understand some of our language, it's only fair to learn some of theirs!

Real communication is possible only if we learn to listen (and look) as well as talk. A Dachshund has plenty to say and he is completely honest. Communication failures occur when we do not pay close attention to what our dog is trying to tell us. Although it's nice for both our dog and us if we can understand him, it's equally important to the Dachshund to convey his feelings to other dogs, and we humans need to understand the basics of dog-to-dog communication as well.

Body Language

Dachshunds vocalize but they rely more heavily on their expressive bodies than on their voices to communicate. Here's a phrase guide to dog talk. I should note, however, that the following "rules" are generalities only. Every dog is an individual, and although most dogs indicate displeasure by growling, some dogs use growling to indicate fear or even deep joy:

Standing "tall":	Dachshunds who stand tall and proud are exhibiting confidence. Being Dachshunds, of course, standing tall is a relative thing.
Standing tiptoe:	Confidence has edged over into dominance and potential aggression.
Rolling over:	Rolling over is submissive behavior. By being "vulnerable" dogs are asking you (even if only in play) to have mercy on them. When you cooperate by giving your Dachshund a good belly rub or scratch, you are rewarding him for his submission.
Leaning against you:	Leaning into his owner is a way a dog shows proprietary affection.

Pawing: Dachshunds often paw when they want attention. If this is annoying to you, don't encourage the behavior by responding with attention. Just get up and walk away.

Bowing: Bowing is play-soliciting behavior; your dog is saying that he wants to romp.

Raised hackles: Fear or hostility is associated with raised hackles.

"Humping" human legs: He's trying to assert his authority over you.

Scratching: Not all scratching means fleas or allergies. Dogs may scratch when they are anxious, much as people bite their fingernails.

Shoving and cramming: It's tempting to think that your precious Doxie just wants to be as close to you as possible, but it's just as likely he is trying to make *you* move by claiming your space. In the dominance game, this is one of the oldest plays in the world. Don't allow this to happen. Even if your Dachshund is the sweetest dog in the entire world, it's not pleasant to be pushed off the couch, crowded in the hall, and generally be made to feel as if you are in the way every minute. Couch-crowding is the most common technique dogs use to assert their bossiness. It is simply amazing how much space the smallest Dachshund can take up, once he sets his mind to it. Some dogs actually lean away from you and press against you with their feet, making it very clear that you are taking up entirely too much room. One way to prevent this is to make half the couch simply unavailable to the dog. Pile up a bunch of books or some other uninviting items on the vacant side of the couch. Praise and pet your dog when he sits quietly (undemandingly) at your feet instead of pushing you over the edge.

Tail Talk

A dog's tail is his most important indicator of his emotions. Dachshunds belong to one of the breeds in this country that do not have their tails docked. (This unfortunate custom is not only needlessly painful to a puppy, but deprives him of an important method of canine expression.) The Dachshund tail is a veritable dictionary of words. Every aspect of the tail conveys special information: how it's carried, how much and how fast it's wagging, even its general shape. In fact, studies have shown that dogs with intact tails are much less prone to getting into trouble; they can communicate their needs.

High tail:	In most dog dialects, a high tail is a sign that the dog is posing a threat. But he might just feel great.
Slow, rhythmic wag:	Possibly a sign that your dog is wary, or perhaps even hostile.
Faster wag, tail held low:	This combination usually means happiness, playfulness, especially combined with "bowing."
Tucked tail:	A "tail between the legs" suggests fear or submissiveness.
Tail chasing:	Chasing one's tail is a sign of excitement, and many dogs continue this behavior when they notice that their human audience appreciates it. If that happens, tail chasing can turn into an obsessive convulsive disorder. To prevent this from occurring, ignore your dog when he exhibits this behavior. The long-bodied Dachshund is perhaps less apt to chase his tail than are other breeds.

Link, a standard red Longhair

Photo courtesy of Daisy Buchignani
Owner: Jean Trowe

Head Talk

Dogs approach us and each other head first, and so a lot of important signals are concentrated there. Dogs who have facial hair that largely covers their eyes or ears may be at a disadvantage when it comes to effective communication. Dachshunds with multi-colored faces have even easier to "read" expressions than those with solid-colored heads. In fact, this is an important factor in pack-oriented dogs like hounds. Loner breeds like Chow Chows are more often a solid color, although admittedly, a lot of this has to do with breeders' preference.

Head cocked: Curious and listening.

Lowered head: Bored, sad, or anxious.

High head: Alert, on the watch.

Mouth Meaning

Face licking: Submissive dogs lick the faces of "superior" dogs to appeal to their good nature. Puppies also lick their mother's faces—perhaps to get the last bit of food. Dogs lick their owners to greet them, to show affection, and unless you are careful to wipe your chin neatly, also to get the last bit of food.

Private part licking: It looks and sounds disgusting, but it's the only way your dog knows how to give himself a bath. The private areas have less hair than other regions of the dog, and are thus prone to more skin irritations. He also licks his privates to remove excess fluid from the anal sacs.

Yawning: Yawning might mean your dog is tired, but it's also an indicator of stress and nerves. Dachshunds will often yawn mightily in their dog boxes before being released for a run after rabbits.

Opening and relaxing mouth: Normally this means your dog is happy and relaxed.

Panting: Panting might indicate eagerness or excitement, but it also might just mean that your Dachshund is hot.

Closing mouth: Anger, hostility, or depression(accompanied by staring).

Expressive Eyes

Dogs have much better eyesight than is commonly believed, but it's different from human vision. They can detect movement ten times better than we can, but they have a poor ability to distinguish shapes. Their vision at night is better than ours, but their color vision is poor. A dog's vision doesn't mature until he is about four months old; before then things seem very fuzzy to him, and he may have trouble recognizing his owners visually. Here's how a dog uses his eyes as lingo:

Staring:	Staring is a direct challenge in dog-speak. It could be directed at another dog or at a person.
Side-stare, or looking over his shoulder:	An indirect look is often eliciting play. Your dog is being "coy."
Wide eyes:	Surprise!
Averted eyes:	When a dog looks away, he is showing surrender or submission.
Half-closed eyes:	Sheer bliss.

The eyes have it here.   *Photo courtesy of Karen Wheeler Gray*

What the Nose Shows

Nose wrinkling:	Wrinkling his nose is a dog's prelude to a snarl or direct attack.
Sniffing around:	With their super-sensitive noses, dogs can collect all kinds of valuable information. When they sniff the urine or anal sac region of other dogs, they learn about that dog's sexual status, social position, age, and even health. Other parts of the body contain some

of the same information, but it's more intense in the anal region. Don't discourage your pet from using this time-honored greeting with other dogs: it's part of the normal socialization process.

Sniffing inappropriately: Dogs sniff at people in ways we find uncomfortable or embarrassing. A Dachshund isn't tall enough to stick his nose in an adult's crotch if the person is standing, so he simply waits for the person to sit down. Then he goes for him. The Dachshund doesn't know he's being rude; in fact, he probably wonders why the person doesn't return the compliment! Try to re-direct your dog's attention with a treat. He'll soon learn there's a bigger payoff in watching stranger's hands than in sniffing their butts. I suppose you could ask all your guests to spray their crotches with a dog-repellent spray, but they'd have to be awfully good friends to go along with that plan.

The Dachshund's Amazing Sense of Smell

Dogs possess a vomeronasal organ, a paired structure lying in the nasal septum that detects pheromones. Each vomeronasal organ opens into the incisive duct, the passage that connects the oral and nasal passages. It helps dogs recognize their relatives and directs their sexual behavior. Many times you'll see your Dachshund curl his upper lip as he gets a good whiff of whatever he's smelling. This is called the Flehman response and facilitates access to the incisive duct. The vomernasal organ sends a message to the hypothalamus, which controls sex and appetite, and lets it know what's going on.

"I'm Happy" say the ears on Exquisite, a standard red longhair owned by Jean Trowe
Photo courtesy of Daisy Buchignani

Emotional Ears

The Dachshund's long, floppy ears give evidence of submission and docility. All scent hounds (with the notable exception of the Norwegian Elkhound), have floppy ears. Although Dachshund ears are not as mobile as that of most other breeds, careful owners can still learn a few things from them.

Ears relaxed, tips swung forward: Your Dachshund is content and comfortable, with nothing that especially grabs his attention.

Raised ears: Something is happening!

Laid back ears: Laying the ears back against the head shows fear or hostility.

"Confused" ears: One up and one back or down. Your dog is of two minds about a situation and is indecisive about how to respond.

Bathroom Business

Leg raising: Mature male dogs raise their legs against a vertical object (such as a tree or a fire hydrant) when they urinate. The rationale behind the behavior is this: the higher I urinate, the bigger other dogs will think I am, and the more impressed they will be when they come by this spot. When a new dog wanders by to sniff the spot, the scent goes straight to his powerful nose. (Dachshunds just can't win at this game against other breeds, but it's not for lack of trying.)

"Covering:" Sometimes you may notice your Dachshund (especially males) kick up the dirt around a spot where he has recently defecated. No, he's not trying to imitate the family cat. He's merely spreading his scent around a wider area. (He has some important sweat glands in his feet.) It is mostly dominant dogs who will do this, since timid dogs aren't eager to let anyone know they're around.

Inappropriate urination: Dogs are strange. Sometimes they urinate when they wish to assert their dominance. On the other hand, dogs also urinate when they're overexcited, when they're afraid (as the streaks of urine adorning the floor of any vet's office will attest) or to show they are definitely not dominant. Submissive or fear peeing disappears as a dog grows more comfortable in his environment. If your dog is subject to submissive urination, try not to make a big deal of it. Don't stare fixedly at your Dachshund—in Dachshund-talk this is a hostile, frightening action. It's best to turn your head slightly to one side and gaze off a little into the distance. Speak gently to your dog. Give him plenty of space and time. If he pees on the floor, wait a bit and then wipe it up without comment. (Don't do it right away; the dog might conceivably think you are rewarding his behavior.) In fact, the less attention you pay to your submissive Doxie, the better. Gradually he will get the idea that you don't have it in for him, after all. Patience is the key to ending this conduct. If a previously housetrained dog begins to urinate on the floor, he may have a urinary tract infection; take him to the vet. Dogs even urinate when they actually have to pee. One thing dogs do not do is to urinate to show that they are angry with you or to get "revenge." Dogs don't think like that. Although I have to say that I have seen male dogs poop in front of each other as a sign of disdain.

Marking: Urinating on a spot is a dog's way of saying "Kilroy was here." This is one reason why a walk with a male dog can take forever. One of the great mysteries of the canine world is that males are always able and willing to produce urine—over and over again. You can eliminate or reduce most marking by having your male dog neutered. But if many Dachshunds share a house, marking behavior may occur while the canine hierarchy is being sorted out.

Chapter 4
Doxies In Demand

Dachshunds are one of the truly great dog breeds—but they aren't for everyone. No breed is. So before you decide that a Dachshund is for you and yours, carefully assess all the characteristics of the breed. Take your time, and resist impulse buying. The best way to do this is not to bring your checkbook while you're out looking. It's practically impossible to resist a puppy, and while every older dog who needs a home may tug at your heartstrings, this is a decision that needs to be made with your head first and your heart second. Dachshunds are long-lived dogs, and your decision will determine to some extent the next fifteen or sixteen years of your life.

Is the Dachshund the Dog for You?

Be honest with yourself about your desires (and capabilities) as a dog owner, the circumstances of your household and the needs of a Dachshund. Think about the following considerations.

The Members of Your Family—Human and Otherwise
A Dachshund may not be the ideal dog for a family with toddlers or unruly children. Dachshunds are sensitive souls, and don't appreciate being tripped over, sat on, tugged at, or ridden. Not that your children would do anything like that, of course, even if you weren't looking. Still, young children have been

Dreamy and Faith   *Photo courtesy of Daisy & Charles Buchignani*

known to mistake the family dog for a stuffed animal or a pony, and while some breeds are exceptionally tolerant of this behavior, Doxies most assuredly are not. Situations like this are the breeding ground for a bite-incident. However, if your children are older and well behaved, you won't find a more loyal family pet. (As a side benefit, studies show that children who are exposed early to pets have a lower risk of developing asthma and pet allergies. They are also less aggressive, better adjusted, less liable to depression, and get better grades in school. Most presidents of the United States have also owned dogs, so I assume that getting a family dog will give your child a head start in the race for president.)

If you are a senior citizen or live with one, older, more sedate Dachshunds make excellent pets, providing both companionship and a reason for exercise.

Most Dachshunds get along very well with other dogs, as long as you introduce them carefully to each other, and allow each his or her "space." Some squabbling might occur at first, but after about two weeks they should have settled between them which dog is to be "alpha" dog, a decision you cannot influence. As a general rule, dogs of opposite sexes get along better than same-sex pairs.

About one-quarter of people who own pets have both cats and dogs. Dachshunds do require inter-species socialization to be at their best with cats. Interestingly, people who own two or more cats can add a dog more successfully to their homes than those who own only one. A single cat may compete with the dog for dominance. However, most Doxies manage to do very well with felines, so long as they are introduced slowly.

The same cannot be said, however, for rabbits and rodents such as mice. Your Doxie sees these creatures as small game. If you do keep these pets, never allow them to run free around a Dachshund. He will eat them. Honestly!

City Life

Dachshunds make excellent city dogs, and do well in apartments if they don't have too many stairs to climb. However, if you have persnickety neighbors and thin walls, be advised that Dachshunds tend to bark.

Temperament–The Dog's and Yours

A Dachshund owner really needs to be stalwart. Dachshunds enjoy their meals—and their between-meals as well. If you allow them to, Dachshunds would look more like blimps than dogs. You must have a strong character to resist those oh-so-appealing eyes. Do you?

As members of the hound group, Dachshunds are celebrated for their determination and excoriated for their stubbornness. Of course, it's the same trait. All this was very useful when Dachshunds actually did the work for which they were bred, of course, but now it's a different story. While Dachshunds are fiercely loyal, they also have their own ideas about how things should be done. When a dog is persistent in doing what we want, we credit him with perseverance. When he does what he likes against our wishes, we label him hard-headed.

Diggers by nature...   *Photo courtesy of Edith Colaneri*

Dachshund Downsides

Dachshunds are barkers. Again this served them well in the olden days—when their vocalizations were used to call hunters to the task at hand. Now it can be annoying, and although Dachshunds can be trained not to bark, they all have a propensity to vocalize.

Dachshunds (like all scent hounds) are wanderers. Unless properly fenced, they will wander off in search of adventure. You must be willing to fence your yard or walk your Dachshund regularly, if you want this breed.

Gardeners beware. Dachshunds are diggers by nature and if a perfectly kept lawn is important to you, you may have to reconsider getting a Dachshund. You can manage a digging problem, but it takes effort and some imagination on your part.

Dollars for Dachshunds

Keeping a Dachshund isn't cheap. Although Dachshunds are not more expensive than any other breed, they cost a lot—and I don't mean the initial purchase. In fact, you may be able to get a really nice Dachshund for free from your brother-in-law or the local pound. Dachshunds are expensive to maintain, just like every other dog. This expense will come primarily in the form of vet bills. Dachshunds are not more sickly than other dogs, but all dogs need regular veterinary care, and this is just not cheap.

Other expenses include high-quality food, supplements, puppy kindergarten and obedience classes, professional grooming, toys, dog beds, crates, and other supplies.

All in all, you can expect to pay more than a thousand dollars a year for your dog in various dog-related costs. (I'm not including the Dachshund t-shirts, hats, pins, calendars, bracelets, umbrellas, and so on that you will want to buy for yourself. I own a pair of Dachs-sox that I wear as often as possible while writing this book. Of course, I have to wash them sometimes.) It is also wise to consider how you would financially manage if your dog is stricken with a life-threatening injury or illness, which could easily cost hundreds if not thousands of dollars.

Your Time

Choose a Dachshund only if you want a constant companion, for Dachshunds don't take kindly to being left out of things. They prefer to be the center of attention, but will settle for sharing the spotlight with you. What they don't care for is being ignored. In fact, Doxies refuse to be ignored and will take steps to make sure it doesn't happen. If you don't have time to spend playing with,

Keeping an eye on the neighbors.   *Photo courtesy of Karen Wheeler Gray*

Should I eat it?   *Photo courtesy of M. Brown*

walking, and generally hanging out with your Dachshund, don't get one. Puppies especially need a lot of one-on-one contact to grow up healthy and mentally balanced. If you really don't have the time to socialize a puppy, choose a well-adjusted older dog who needs a home.

Choosing Your Dachshund

Okay, you want a Dachshund (I don't blame you) and your home is just right to welcome one. Now comes the agonizingly fun part—getting the dog.

Getting a puppy is so exciting! However, before you decide on a puppy, don't underestimate the work and expense involved in puppy ownership. Puppies never seem to housetrain quite as fast as you want. They go through a chewing phase, a fearful phase, a nipping phase, and they have to be watched constantly. Many people decide to get a puppy so that it will "grow up with the kids." This is a mistake. Dachshund puppies are not well suited as companions to toddlers or young children, and by the time your toddler has lost his first baby tooth, the Doxie will be an adult anyway.

If you are considering showing your Dachshund, you're better off choosing a young adult or older puppy rather than a newly weaned one. Buying a show puppy is a gamble that can be lost even by an experienced show person with a keen eye. Many breeders hold back on their likely show prospects until they see how the dog develops, and to find just the right "show home." If you get an older dog, you already know what he looks like, and you'll also have a better gauge of his activity level.

Get to Know the Breed

If you haven't seen a lot of Dachshunds in one place, call your local Dachshund Club (the one nearest you can be found on the DCA Web site: www.dachshund-DCA.org. Ask when the next specialty or "major" is and explain that you want to look at the breed. Ask about joining the club, as well. Experienced owners dedicated to the breed can provide a wealth of critical information for you.

For many experienced dog owners, the joys of puppyhood are heavily outweighed by the purer pleasures of opening your heart and home to an older dog who desperately needs a home.

Getting A Puppy

If your heart is set on a puppy—here's how to go about making a good choice. First, find the breeder, then find the dog. While everyone needs to get started sometime, if *you* are new to Dachshunds, go to a recommended breeder who has been working with the breed for at least several years.

A responsible breeder is not a professional. She doesn't breed dogs to supplement the family income. On the contrary, a responsible breeder is an *amateur*, which literally means someone who breeds *for love* of the breed. A responsible breeder is also knowledgeable about dogs in general and Doxies in particular. While many responsible breeders do work with two breeds (in fact, I think every dog breeder should know at least one other breed well), beware of individuals who breed a number of different breeds. The more breeds a breeder deals in, the more likely it is that you are dealing with a puppy mill.

Tina with pups   *Photo courtesy of Karen Wheeler Gray*

How do you spot a good breeder? A good breeder will not sell puppies before they are eight weeks old. Most breeders wait until the dog is between nine and twelve weeks of age, although many will allow you look at the puppies before that. Dogs taken away from their litter too early will bond with their human owner very strongly, but will not take to other dogs or to other people well. Puppies need time with their littermates to learn canine socialization skills. I cannot overemphasize the importance of this socialization process to your dog's well being.

A good breeder is not dying to sell you a puppy. She has plenty of people lined up and can afford to be choosy. Her primary interest is the puppy's welfare—not your desire for a dog. If the first question out of her mouth is "Visa or MasterCard?", walk the other way. A breeder who is not particular about homes for her puppies was probably not very particular about breeding them, either.

A good breeder belongs to the Dachshund Club of America and probably to your local Dachshund and all-breed Kennel Clubs as well. This is a sign that she is always learning more, and is working with others to constantly improve the breed.

A good breeder will ask you plenty of questions. She'll want to know how many children you have, and their ages. She will want to know how long the dog will be at home alone, and how you plan to entertain him during that time. She'll ask you questions about your yard, your house and your fence and may ask to visit your home. She might want to know who your veterinarian is, and may want to speak with him. She may even ask you about your finances. Is she being nosy and intrusive? No. She's making sure her puppy goes to the perfect home. Don't get ruffled. Be glad that the breeder cares this much about the dog.

A good breeder interacts well with the puppies and adult dogs. The dogs seem happy and comfortable around her. If the puppies are at least six weeks old, the mother dog (dam) should be friendly toward you as well. Note that mother dogs can be protective of small puppies, and may not welcome your visit when the puppies are quite young.

When you visit the facilities of a good breeder, you'll see that the puppies are raised in the home—not in an outside kennel. There is no excuse whatever for this breed to be housed outside. In my opinion, it is difficult to socialize puppies raised outdoors unless you live outdoors with them—or a least spend most of your time out there. It's easier to bring the dogs inside. The area the puppies are kept in should be clean. The yard should be well picked up and free of dog feces. Never get a puppy from dirty or unsanitary surroundings.

Cedarbends Anna Fantasia, CD, CGC, TDI with pups

Photo courtesy of Catherine Johnson

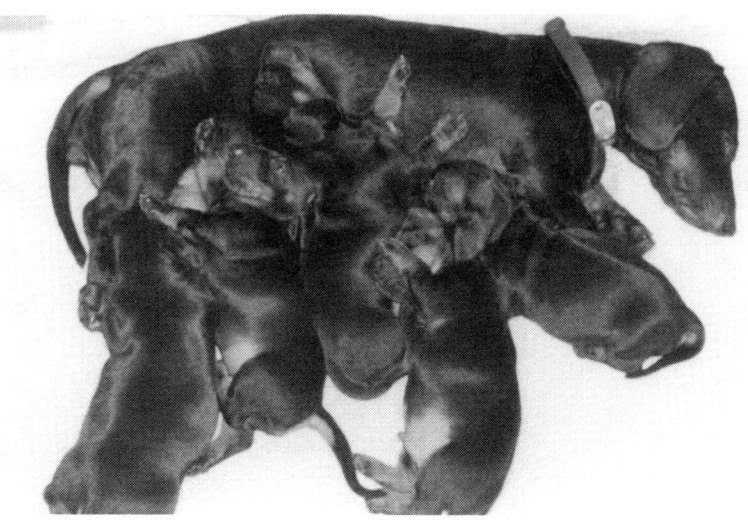

A good breeder is actively engaged in showing her dogs in conformation, field trials, Earthdog events, or obedience. She should be able to prove it with photos, ribbons, and paper documentation.

A good breeder has done genetic testing on her dogs, and will show you the paperwork to prove it. She will have a breeding program. She knows what she is doing and has set certain goals for herself. For a quick and easy check on the knowledgeableness of the breeder, ask her what her breeding goal is. A good breeder will tell you more than you ever wanted to know. A bad one will stare at you blankly.

But where is one to find this breeder? Join your local Dachshund or kennel club and *ask*. The Dachshund lovers in your area know who is a good breeder and who isn't, and they will be happy to steer you in the right direction. Believe me, the best advertising is word-of-mouth by people in the know. Be prepared to wait—most responsible breeders don't breed very often, and they may have waiting lists. If you can't wait, call your nearest Dachshund rescue organization, and fill the life of an older dog with joy.

Can we dig our way out?   *Photo courtesy of Karen Wheeler Gray*

Sources to Avoid

Pet stores: Pet stores sell dogs from puppy mills. No responsible breeder would *ever* sell a puppy to a pet store. That's the truth. Don't patronize stores that sell puppies. If you do find yourself face to face with an irresistible pet store puppy, you will be paying an inflated price for a less-than-well-bred dog. If you take the dog anyway, you will be saving that individual dog, but supporting the puppy mill business. This doesn't make you "wrong" to select such a puppy. The puppy will be grateful to be released from his prison, but you must make up for it by promising to fight puppy mills legally with all your heart and soul.

Newspapers ads: Most people who advertise in the paper are what we call "backyard" breeders. They happen to own two dogs of the opposite sex and decide they'd make cute puppies. It is very unlikely that the parents will have had genetic tests done or that the owners researched the pedigree. What I say about newspaper ads also hold true for ads in dog magazines, even good ones. You may find good breeders by the route—but it's questionable.

Dog shows: What!?! Everybody tells you to go to dog shows to find a good breeder. You can find *great* breeders at a dog show, and you can also find busy, harassed, frustrated people who don't feel like talking to you. You can also find your share of bad breeders at dog shows. I've seen them.

The Internet: Maybe and maybe not. Many fine breeders are listed on the Web through breed club Web sites. This is a good way to locate breeders near you. However, breeders who use the Internet to advertise cute puppies for sale are suspect in my view.

Picking Your Puppy

Look for a puppy with bright eyes, clean ears, and a discharge-free nose. A pot-bellied puppy may have worms. When you pick one up, he should feel heavier than he looks. Puppies should be lively, playful, and inquisitive. They won't cower in a corner, or try to run away.

Ask the breeder which pups seem to be submissive, and which are the alpha pups. A good breeder will probably have had the litter evaluated and temperament-tested. Basic types of canine temperament are: responsive, sedate, nervous, shy, or aggressive. These temperament types are not the product of training but of genetics. They cannot be altered, although they can to some extent be controlled. Obviously, you do not want a dog falling into any of the latter three classes. Dogs in those categories make difficult pets and best suited to experienced dog handlers who know how to deal with their behavior. If you have a busy, active household, consider getting a responsive dog, who is happy, good-natured, and extroverted. A sedate dog, however, is just the ticket for a couch-potato family or older person.

Prices will usually vary according to quality and coat color. "Show quality" Dachshunds will generally cost more than those who are not—a thousand dollars and up in some locations. Some breeders charge the same amount for each puppy in the litter. There's no wrong or right about this—it's just an individual preference. Certain colors are popular, and may command higher prices, but beware. The conservative show circuit still favors black and tan and solid colors. Don't get talked into a "rare" color hoping it will further your chances in the show ring.

Paperwork

Your purebred puppy should be registered with the American Kennel Club. This is a minimum requirement that ensures your dog's pedigree. Having your dog registered with the AKC allows him to participate in many canine events from agility to obedience, although it's fair to say that other organizations sponsor some of these same events without requiring AKC registry. Be aware that registration with the AKC does *not* ensure the dog's quality. (I have seen some really ugly Dachshunds registered with the AKC.)

Hilda and puppies

Photo courtesy of Karen White Maddox and A.J. White

When you buy your puppy you should also get a copy of his pedigree, going back at least three generations. A pedigree is your dog's family history. The pedigree will confirm that your dog is indeed a Dachshund, and will also list his variety, gender, breeder, date of birth, and color. Your dog's individual registration number or his litter registration number will be listed. Your dog's sire (father) will appear at the top and his dam at the bottom of the pedigree. You can order (for a fee) a copy of your dog's pedigree for as many generations back as you want. All the titles and awards for the forebears are automatically included. Dogs who have completed their championship will have their names written in red ink. The pedigree will also list certification numbers issued by certain bodies, such as the Orthopedic Foundation for Animals or the Canine Eye Registry Foundation. If a DNA profile has been done, the number will be shown.

Don't be fooled by the words "champion bloodlines," that some "breeders" use to impress the hapless buyer. Most AKC dogs are from champion bloodlines if you only go back far enough. The sire or dam of your puppies (preferably both) should be champions, and there should be several champions in the previous few generations as well. That's what "champion bloodline" should mean. A champion is a dog who has won a title in AKC conformation shows; it is evidence that the dog is an excellent example of the breed who has competed and won against others.

When you buy your puppy, you'll get a registration form (blue slip) that you can submit to the AKC with a fee. You will also get to name your puppy, although many breeders have a "kennel" name they will require you to use as a "prefix." Of course, you can call your dog anything you like around the house!

In addition to the AKC registration, a good breeder will ask you to sign a sales contract that outlines the responsibility of both buyer and seller. The contract should be extremely clear and specific—be sure you understand every word of it. The contract should contain health warranties and information regarding vaccines. Some contracts agree to exchange a sick puppy for a healthy one, or agree that the breeder will pay reasonable vet fees if the dog turns out to be sick. It may state whether the puppy is expected to be shown. The contract should state whether the breeder will take back the dog in case things don't work out. The best contracts have a "right of first refusal" clause, stating that if the buyer needs to give up the dog for any reason, he must offer it back to the breeder before placing the dog elsewhere.

First Things First

Review the breeder's contract before you ever look at the puppies. Once you see them, your heart is lost already.

Sometimes a breeder will offer a "limited registration" agreement, providing that if your dog is bred, the puppies cannot be registered. A breeder will do this when she is selling a puppy she does not believe is "show quality." If the dog turns out to be show quality after all, you can ask the breeder to change the limited registration if you plan to become a serious breeder yourself! (I never advise this. Too much work.)

Molly, a shorthair   *Photo courtesy of Dave Wolfe*

If a Breeder Turns You Down

Because reputable breeders usually have more potential cus-
tomers than they have puppies, they can afford to be choosy. If a
breeder does decline your offer, instead of getting angry or
stomping off to the nearest pet store, ask her what you might do
to qualify. The answer might be as simple as "wait until your children are older." Perhaps the breeder requires all buyers to have a
fenced yard, that they crate-train their puppy, or take their dog to
obedience classes. Maybe she feels you are gone for too much of
the day, or she is unsure about your commitment to neuter or
spay your dog. In some cases, you might be able to meet her
requirements with some adjustments to your schedule. I don't
suggest putting your kids up for adoption, but some people are
willing to do almost anything for a Dachshund.

The Joys of Older Dog Ownership

Please consider adopting a senior dog. Most of these dogs are great pets, and they wouldn't have gotten to their stage in life without being good tempered and in good health. Dachshunds are a long-lived breed, and even Dachshunds who have attained the age of ten or so have many, many good years left. Let one share your life.

Reputable Rescues

If you are considering adopting an older dog, choose a responsible rescue organization or shelter first, then find the dog. Many Dachshunds end up in shelters or rescue groups through no fault of their own. These "disposable" dogs are "dumped" in rescue for a variety of reasons—too old, too big, too small, needs too much attention, doesn't match the couch—we've seen everything. A good rescue has high standards for its potential adopters. Rescue dogs have already been through at least one home (sometimes a bad one) and a reputable rescue wants to make sure that their dogs will go to their "forever home" at last. Getting a rescue dog is not without peril, of course. Many of these dogs have been neglected or abused and need special attention and extra love. But a good rescue evaluates its dogs thoroughly and provides support to its new owners. If worst comes to worst, it will also take back the dog.

Don't come to rescue expecting a bargain, though. Rescue is an expensive business. (In the rescue I work with, we spent more that $35,000 on vet bills alone in one year.) Usually adoption fees make up only part of the operating costs. Don't feel as if you are "paying for a dog." Instead think of it as supporting rescue activities and helping to save dogs from death.

Your Rights as an Owner

As a potential Dachshund owner, you have some rights that rescue groups and breeders should both honor.

Selection: Although you may not be able to get your first choice, you should have some control over the dog you buy or adopt. Never allow anyone to foist a dog off on you that you truly do not love. That is not fair to either the dog or yourself. While there may be valid reasons why a breeder or rescue may decide a certain dog is not for you, you should certainly have some choice in the matter.

Information: You have a right to be as fully informed as possible about your dog's health and history. Rescue staff may not know much about the background of many of the dogs they serve, but they should provide you with everything they do know. Breeders have the responsibility of explaining any health or other problems that may be in the line they breed. If a breeder is not forthcoming with this information—if you have to ask for it—she may be trying to hide something.

Basic preventive care: Your new dog should have had a veterinary examination, appropriate vaccinations, and all other routine care. Rescue dogs should be spayed or neutered. Most dogs should have had a heartworm check and be on heartworm prevention. They should be on flea or tick prevention as well. Some puppies, of course, are too young for many of these medications, but the breeder should be able to provide paperwork to show a veterinarian has seen the puppies.

References: Both rescues and breeders should be able to provide references. It is your job to follow up and call the references.

Rapid review: No rescue group or breeder should keep you hanging. They should move with all "deliberate speed" to process your application.

Doubling Your Dogs—When One Is Not Enough

It's almost always better to select a dog of the opposite sex for your second Dachshund. Spayed females fight the most, but two intact males can seriously damage each other. If you decide to get a dog other than a Dachshund, be aware that a large dog of another breed can seem a threat to a Dachshund. This addition to the household could make your Dachshund aggressive, even if the other dog is tolerant and friendly.

Madison and Morgan, twice the love   *Photo courtesy of Eileen Scacetti*

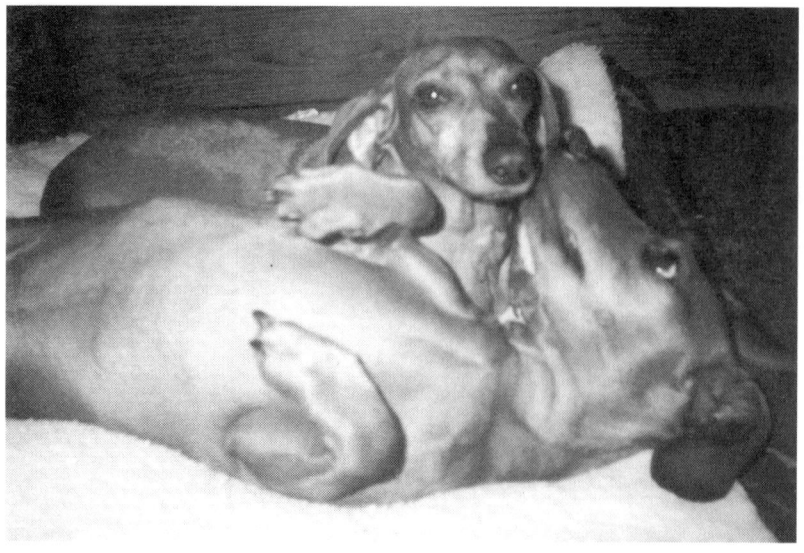

Chapter 5

The Dachshund's Domain

Bringing your new Dachshund home is always exciting. Although you will usually have your Doxie safely in a crate or seatbelt during transport, on his very first ride home, you can get someone else to drive, while you cuddle up in the back seat with your precious new pet. Because he is liable to be nervous or even frightened—being away from his mom, siblings, and the only home he has ever known, this is the time to hold him close and speak lovingly to him. In no time at all, he'll probably be asleep!

When you arrive home, allow the little guy to walk about the yard. With any luck he'll relieve himself immediately, and you can praise him. This is about as much housetraining as you can expect right away—the important thing now is get him to bond to you.

Choosing a Veterinarian

Bring your puppy in for a health check right away—ideally, you will be able to have your vet examine your puppy before you bring him home. If you don't already have a vet, you need to establish a relationship with one. You and your vet will be partners for the life of your Dachshund. How long that life is depends in part on how well you choose your vet. Here are some criteria for the best vet for you.

Proximity: Choose a vet who works close by. This can literally make the difference between life and death for your dog.

Expertise: Choose a vet who is experienced in working with Dachshunds. This breed has special anatomical structure issues that need to be managed by an expert.

Empathy: You want a veterinarian who cares about both you and your dog. Your vet should listen to your concerns, and speak to you as an intelligent person. He should demonstrate by his actions that he really loves your dog.

Cleanliness: A good facility looks clean and smells clean. Your new vet should be happy to give you a tour.

Professional: The staff should be friendly and competent.

When you come inside, let the puppy have some water, although he might be too nervous to eat. Sit on the floor with him and allow him to investigate his new surroundings, including you. If you have children, let everyone get acquainted (without too much noise or boisterous action). Children too young to hold a baby should not be allowed to pick up a puppy; there is too much danger of the child dropping the dog. This could not only hurt the puppy, but could also make him fearful of children or of being carried. Play it safe and keep the dog on the floor unless the children are entirely trustworthy to carry him. Limit the interaction—a little petting and snuggling from kids will go far on a puppy's first day.

Canines and Kids

Research has shown that children from dog-owning families are more empathetic and nurturing than those raised in dogless homes. However, you should never get a dog "for the kids" unless you yourself are committed to caring for him. No matter how much children promise to look after the family pet—they'll forget. And while Dachshunds are intensely loyal to children who love them and treat them well, they will not put up with being bullied or hassled by the other kids in the neighborhood.

Puppy Proofing

If you have a puppy, it's your job to keep him safe. Dogs don't know anything about the dangers of electrical wires, plastic bags, toxic plants and chemicals, and steep stairs. To puppy proof your house, crawl around on all fours to get a dog's eye's view of the place. (For a Dachshund puppy, this means getting down really low.)

Puppies love to chew on electrical cords (which is bad for both the dog and the wire). Tack electrical cords close to walls where they won't be conspicuous. Extension cords that trail across the center of the floor are especially tempting. Safe Living/Smart Products makes a pet-safe extension cord called the Smart Cord, that sells for $14.95. It contains an advanced internal monitoring system that stops electrical flow in 25/1000 of a second. Even if your Dachshund's teeth sink into it, he won't get shocked. The Smart Cord also provides built-in fire protection.

Put the kitty litter box out of your puppy's reach. For some reason, every dog in the world likes cat poop. Stow away stray pieces of fabric such as washcloths, dishtowels, and small items

Playful puppies   *Photo courtesy of Karen Wheeler Gray*

of clothing that could choke your pup. Remove poisonous plants from the home.

And always supervise your puppy. Never give a rambunctious young puppy free rein of the house until you know it is safe to do so. (That's usually quite a while after you've had him.) Don't forget the outside of your home, either.

Smart Shopping

Browse through your local department or hardware store before you bring your puppy home. Many items marked as baby-proofers work equally well for dogs.

One of the most common dangers to puppies is children. Even the best-behaved child can step on or fall on a dog. Less well-behaved kids pull tails, scream, and chase the dog. This behavior is especially dangerous with puppies, who are not only more fragile than adult dogs, but whose opinion of people, especially little people, is just forming. It's up to you to socialize both your child and your dog, so be sure to supervise them when they are together, and keep each member of the play team safe and happy. Make sure your puppy has a safe refuge (like his crate) to go to when he is tired of playing, and make sure your child knows the wisdom of "let sleeping dogs lie." Your dog's crate or bed should be off-limits to kids.

Puppies chew everything in sight, but they have their favorites (in fact, older dogs seem to have the same preferences). Note that dogs like the following things best:

▼ Expensive items
▼ One-of-a-kind sentimental items
▼ Brand-new items
▼ Dangerous items

I'm just joking of course, but in all honesty, you cannot expect a dog to know what to chew and what not to chew. To teach him, you need to lock up, put away, or soak with bitter spray every unsuitable thing that tempts him, while providing him with a variety of safe-to-chew items. Of course, supervising your puppy at all times will help to minimize damages.

Active Supervision

Correct supervision is active—it does not entail sitting around watching TV and yelling "no!" at the dog every time he tries to investigate something. It means playing and interacting with him, and gently distracting him from forbidden objects. (After the play session, think about how you can separate the dog from the desired object. If it's too big to move, you'll just have to keep the dog out of that room when you're not home.)

Dachshund Essentials

The following items are essential to keep your Dachshund safe and happy.

Doxie Dishes

Because your Dachshund will need a supply of clean, fresh water at all times, as well as to be fed on a regular basis, the dog will need his own set of dishes. I prefer to use stainless steel to feed my own dogs—they are cheap, tough, and easy to clean.

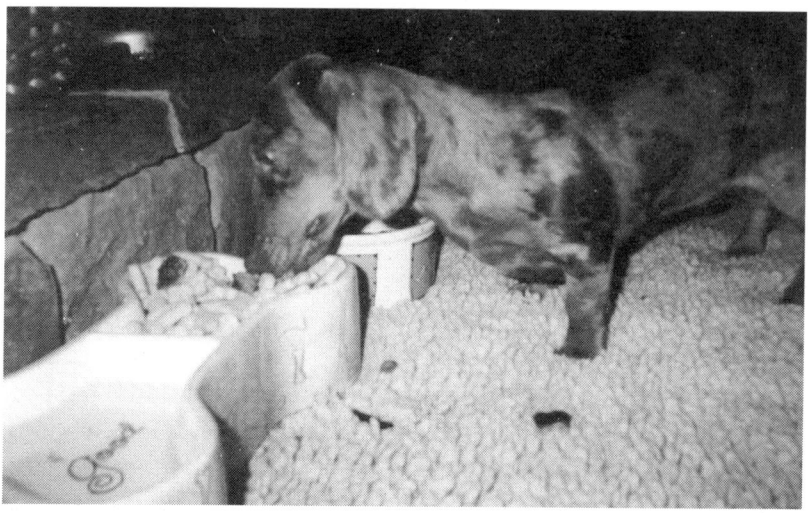

Faith, a smooth, miniature chocolate/tan dapple

Photo courtesy of Daisy & Charles Buchignani
Owners: Sandi & Hector Loredo

Ceramic dishes are prettier, though, and are also suitable. Both come in weighted varieties that resist being tipped over by a playful puppy. A new item in the world of dog dishes is the AgION-impregnated water bowl. These bowls kill algae and bacteria on contact.

I don't recommend plastic, for two related reasons. First of all, Dachshunds can and will chew through cheap plastic, and second, plastic can develop cracks and gaps that harbor dangerous bacteria. Whatever style you choose, you should wash them frequently in hot soapy water—just as you would your own crockery. Dachshunds deserve no less!

The Crate: Your Dachshund's Den

Next to eating, sleeping is number one on the agenda of most dogs, and a crate is a safe, comfortable place for that activity. Although crates may look like a cage, a properly trained Dachshund has no such prejudice. He thinks of the crate as a safe haven—a den of his own. (To help ensure that your dog retains a positive attitude toward his crate, never scold your dog while you are placing him in it.) A crate is not a place of banishment or a baby sitter, though, and dogs should not be locked in their crates for more than two hours at a time (except at night when they should be sleeping). This doesn't mean your dog *has* to sleep in a crate, of course. Mine never do. But he should be taught to accept a comfortable crate when asked. This is important for traveling, or when the dog is sick and needs to have his activity restricted, or when you want to keep him away from Cousin Ethel's bratty kids. A crate is also a great housetraining tool.

Crates come in three basic styles: wire mesh, sturdy fiberglass or plastic, and fold-up nylon mesh. Each has its distinct advantages, and many dog owners eventually end up with one of each. Your Doxie's crate should be not only high enough for him to stand up in (an easy requirement), but big enough for him to turn around in easily and to stretch out in completely.

The wire crate offers the best ventilation and view. Once inside your dog can look around and see what's happening. This type of crate is wonderful in summertime, taking advantage of the breeze. On the other hand, it offers no protection from the sun (unless you drape it with a towel) or cold wind.

The fiberglass or plastic crate is very tough and good for traveling and sleeping. It provides the most den-like atmosphere, and many dogs feel especially secure in one.

The new fold-up nylon mesh crates are indispensable for traveling and quick setup. They can go anywhere! Their main disadvantage is that a dog not used to crates can tear them with their claws.

The Apple Jack Gang!    *Photo courtesy of Karen White Maddox and A.J. White*

Whatever crate you and your dog choose, be sure to provide a soft, cushy, washable mat for your dog's sleeping comfort. (When you are housetraining, however, you may want to omit the mat—dogs are often driven to urinate on soft, absorbable surfaces, for obvious reasons.)

One handy piece of gear for any busy Dachshund owner is the Tutto Pet on Wheels. This crate-on-the-go is similar to a luggage carrier, but it is has mesh on three sides and is made for small pets. It even has flop-down flaps in case your dog requires some privacy. This carrier folds flat for storage and retails for about $160.

Baby Gates

Baby or specially designed dog gates are essential for limiting your Dachshund's access to rooms that are off limits. They generally run about $25 each. If your puppy is a major chewer, don't get a wooden gate.

Exercise Pens

An exercise pen, or "x-pen," is a portable puppy playpen. It serves as a compromise between the isolation of the crate and the free range of the kitchen or living room. During times when you want your puppy around you, but not out of sight, the x-pen is a great way to oversee him. It allows you to watch each other while you are cooking dinner or cleaning the refrigerator. Keep an eye out for those telltale squirming signs, and you can use the x-pen as a housebreaking tool as well as a containment device.

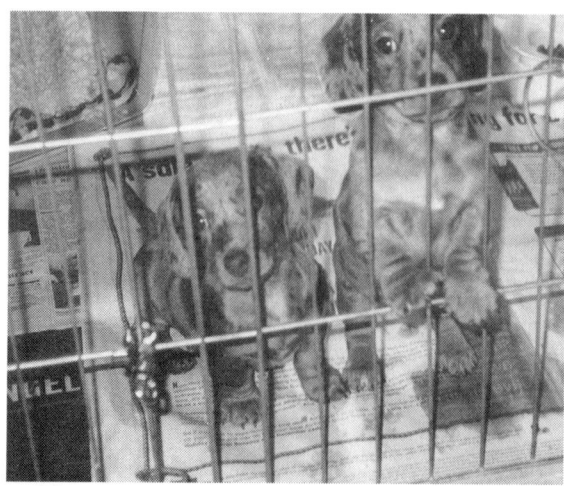

Exercise Pens

Lizzi and Dodgie

Photo courtesy of Daisy & Charles Buchignani

Doxie Neckwear and Leads

Your dog should wear a buckle collar and identification tag at all times. Never mind anything you may have heard about dogs choking on their collars, catching their collars on branches or furniture, or being stolen by having their collar grabbed. Collars are lifesavers—literally. In case of emergency, your Doxie can be held and safely restrained by his collar. Most important, a collar carries that indispensable ID tag. Lost dogs without visible identification are not likely to be returned to their owners. And that is a statistical fact. Adjust the collar so that you can insert four fingers under it, and if you have a puppy, check the fit of the collar frequently. The principle here is simple: you want a collar that won't slip off, but that won't obstruct breathing, either. A too-loose collar can result in your dog's getting a foot or leg stuck in it. If you have a puppy, it's important to check the collar every week to make sure it isn't getting too tight.

Dachshund ID

In addition to always keeping a legible ID tag on your Dachshund, I also recommend that you get your dog microchipped. The microchip is a pellet the size of a rice grain that your veterinarian can slip under the skin between the shoulder blades. The chip can be "read" by equipment at humane societies, animal shelters, and many vet clinics. The American Kennel Club keeps a database of microchipped dogs.

You truly have a plethora of collar choices awaiting you. Sturdy rolled leather collars have no frayed edges, and lightweight elastic or nylon collars are nice for puppies.

Never put a choke chain or prong collar on a Dachshund. They are unnecessary, ugly, and injurious to your dog, no matter what their manufacturers—or dog trainers who use punishment and force—may claim. In addition, it is all too easy for a choke chain to get entangled with other objects. If you absolutely must have a choke collar, get one made of nylon and not a chain. However, a simple buckle collar is all a correctly trained dog ever needs, especially a small dog like a Doxie.

Breakaway Collars

For those extremely wary about the dangers of a collar getting caught, you might consider the breakaway collar made by Chinook and Company in partnership with Premier Pet Products. The collar comes with a plastic clasp, which, when pulled hard enough releases, allowing the dog to escape from a dangerous situation.

Some people are lucky enough to own two Dachshunds. These fortunate folks should consider buying a coupler, a short lead with two straps that can be attached to a regular leash. Couplers are especially wonderful if you have two dogs who prefer (invariably) to walk in opposite directions. With two leashes you're in danger of being torn slowly apart by your unconcerned pets. With a coupler, the dogs will have to work it out between themselves. You're home free.

A lead can be any style and length you choose, but avoid chain leashes. They look ridiculous, break without warning, and are noisy. Dachshunds look especially chic with leather or elegant nylon leashes; one of no more than a half-inch in width is fine. Examine leashes carefully to make sure they have a secure snap and that they haven't worn out in places. At least one lead should be the standard six-foot kind, but you may also want to try a Flexi-lead, which allows your dog more room to roam on walks.

Doxie Davenports

Gone are the days when you could throw an old towel on the floor and forget about it. As you might expect, dog bed manufacturers are all too eager to help you with your pet furniture needs. You can opt for a simple stuffed pillow bed (in a variety of sizes, shapes, and colors) to a more elaborate "orthopedic bed" for aging or arthritic animals. Some have several layers of orthopedic foam. You can get your dog a miniature couch of his own, or a dog bed that looks deceptively like a couch. (One company, the Barking Cat, makes a "mission dog bed." It is very handsome, but the small model costs $625 and the large one is $725.) A particular favorite in my house is a steel-framed raised bed that

Faith and Dreamy snug in bed   *Photo courtesy of Daisy & Charles Buchignani*

stands slightly off the floor (and it is exceptionally easy to clean). My dogs seem to prefer it unadorned in the summer (cooling air can get underneath). In the winter I throw a thin dog bed on top for extra warmth. You can also buy cooling and warming pads to help your pet find comfort in during the changing seasons. I don't recommend a wicker bed; your dog will probably begin to eat it, especially since wicker provides a great hiding places for dog biscuit crumbs. They are also quite difficult to clean.

With all the great dog beds out there, I feel compelled to say that most dogs still prefer the couch—or your own bed. Whether you indulge them in their taste is up to you. However, because dogs equate height with power, those who are territorial or dominant should be required to sleep at ground level. If your Doxie is not the dominant type and he sleeps in the bed with you, be sure you lift him on and off it to protect his back.

The Bed's Room

Placement of the bed is important too—away from drafts and out of the direct line of traffic. On the other hand, don't put the bed in Outer Mongolia. The best spot is usually a quiet corner where the dog can keep his eye on the family activities, at least until he falls asleep.

Dachshund Diversions: Toys

Select toys that safe, interesting, washable, and durable. Of course, what fascinates one dog may leave another cold, but you generally can't go wrong with something that allows a dog to safely chew it, and perhaps makes some heart-rending noise during the process. Avoid anything with a battery—it never ceases to amaze me that they actually sell dog toys with batteries. Even a carefully supervised dog can swallow a battery quicker than you think—and then your dog is in serious trouble.

One perennially popular toy is the Kong, a practically indestructible, bouncing toy that has a hollow center. The toy is thrilling on its own, but it can also be filled with delicious snacks like peanut butter or cheese that keep a dog interested for hours. Similar toys hide dog biscuits or other treats inside.

Favorite dog toys often contain squeakers. In fact, the squeaker is often the whole point of the toy—the Dachshund is determined to get that thing and kill it. However, the opposite event may occur, if the dog swallows it. So, while squeaker-containing toys are fun for your dog, supervised play is safest.

It's a good idea to offer only a few toys at once. Too many toys to choose from might overwhelm your dog, or you might just succeed in boring him. I've noticed the same phenomena in children. It's usually best if you can rotate toys. Give your dog a handful to play with, while keeping the rest in the closet (or on

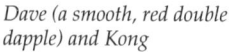

Dave (a smooth, red double dapple) and Kong

Photo courtesy of Daisy & Charles Buchignani

top of the refrigerator the way I do). Every once in a while you run into a dog, especially one from a shelter, who doesn't even know how to play. To encourage him to chew the toy rather than your furniture, rub the toy with a little peanut butter or soft cheese. The dog will soon begin to nibble on the toy for the flavor, then gradually progress to chewing the toy on its own merits. Praise your Dachshund when he selects the toy and chews it in preference to the couch.

Toy Tips

Unfortunately, there are a lot of toys that you should keep away from your dog. Never give a puppy a toy he can swallow. I don't like rawhides for this reason. Some dogs try to tear large pieces off, succeed in partially swallowing them, and then choke. The same thing can occur with pieces of rawhide that are too soft, or too small to begin with. Many rawhides also contain questionable ingredients, especially if they come from places like Thailand. I'd avoid the whole lot of them.

As your puppy grows, he can handle harder toys, but never give him anything harder than tooth enamel. This includes hard dry bones, and smoked cow hoofs. Both these items are leading causes of tooth breakage in dogs.

Avoid laser pointers as toys. Although the pointer offers a continual target, it never gives the dog the opportunity to seize the prey. This sets up a kind of frustration that can evolve into obsessive/compulsive behavior.

Grooming Supplies

No self respecting Dachshund wants to appear unkempt, so be sure you have the proper set of grooming tools for your dog's coat type. For Longhaired and Wirehaired Dachshunds, you need a slicker brush (a curved brush with many bent metal prongs, desirable for grooming the undercoat) and a pin brush, preferably with rubber tips. Smooth Dachshunds do best when brushed with a bristle brush, preferably of natural bristles. A rubber curry comb also comes in handy with shorthaired dogs when shedding season comes round. And all types need nail clippers, shampoo, and dental supplies.

Home Life

As a Dachshund owner, there are two basic requirements you must fulfill for your dog. First, you must keep him safe from household hazards and second, you must be good company. The best way to do both is to keep the dog with you at all times day and night, but this is obviously not practical. However, some people make the mistake of segregating their new dog completely from household activities by relegating him to the basement, laundry room, or even the garage. Please do not do this. Dogs are social creatures and pine away if ignored and left on their own.

Some people get into the vicious cycle of keeping their dog locked up because when he is not locked up, he becomes destructive. The longer the dog is locked away from the family, however, the more destructive he gets and may even start to tear apart "his" room or area. It's much better to provide your dog with the company and attention he craves.

Make your dog part of your family. Keep him with you while you are home, and let him sleep in your bedroom—either in your bed or safely in his own bed or crate at your side. When you must leave him, keep him in a safe, familiar room like the kitchen.

The First Few Days

The transition to a new home is very taxing on a puppy (and on adult dogs) so do what you can to take the edge off. Most responsible breeders will give you a supply of the food the puppy has become accustomed to. If you prefer another kind, it's all right to switch, but it's better to do so gradually. Feed him the old food for a day or so, while your dog settles in, then gradually starting mixing the new food with the old over three or four days until the switch is complete. If you plan to feed your dog a variety, let him get acquainted to the practice gradually to avoid any gastric upset and diarrhea.

Creating a Good Vibe

If you have a rescue Dachshund, try hand-feeding him or her for the first few days. This works wonders in forming a bond between you and your new dog.

Feed your puppy in a quiet corner, away from kitchen traffic and other pets if you have them. You, however, should stick around. You do not want to encourage food-guarding and your puppy should get used to your presence while he eats. Pet him a bit while he has his dinner so that he learns to accept some interruption. If your puppy gets used to surrendering whatever he has in his mouth to you, you'll have a safer pet. When you do take something from him, be sure to reward him with something even better. In this way, your dog will regard your presence near his food bowl with optimism rather than hostility. Sooner or later, some kid will run up and try to grab something out of his mouth; this is a time when a snap or bite is most likely to occur. Preventive training is the best defense.

Von Maser's California Crunch, a mini wirehair and Ch. Von Maser's Premier Edition, a mini smooth *Photo courtesy of Joella Maser*

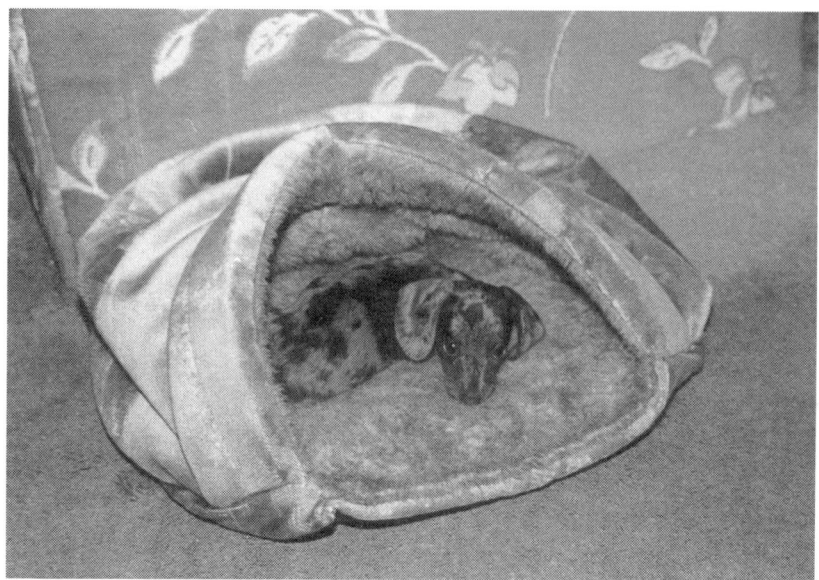

Peanut   *Photo courtesy of Daisy & Charles Buchignani*

The First Few Nights

The first night together is traditionally a horrible ordeal that owners and puppies must suffer through, but it does not have to be a dreadful experience. It's dreadful because people often insist on having their new puppy sleep in his own room, which is usually the kitchen, laundry room, or some other place of exile. No wonder the dog is miserable. He's been kidnapped from his mother and his littermates, and forced to live with a bunch of strangers. Then there's a lot of noise and confusion and he's put in a strange room, and left alone in the dark. Why shouldn't he cry? I cry just thinking about it.

The solution is so easy. Simply allow your new Dachshund to sleep in the bedroom with you, in his own bed by your side. There is no need to terrorize him by forcing him to sleep alone in a distant part of the house. It is neither necessary nor advisable. Furthermore, it will ease your housetraining chores considerably if you are close to your puppy. When you sense he is beginning to stir, you can jump right up and head outside with him into the bitter cold night.

Having your puppy sleep with you in your bedroom will not "spoil him." It will simply make him aware that you are his parent, and will be there to comfort him the way his own mother did before you. Some people allow their dogs to sleep in the bed with them, and if you are entertaining this idea, you can start him right off snuggled by your pillow. Snuggling up your puppy will make your dog more, not less secure. However, since I strongly advise that you crate train your puppy, you are best off letting him sleep by your side in his own crate. That way he won't (a) fall off the bed (b) wander around the house and get into trouble (c) call the Humane Society and claim he is being abused. Remember that a crate should never ever be used as a punishment. It should be a den and refuge.

If your puppy cries during the first nights in your house, talk to him quietly (tell him a few jokes) until he falls asleep. Make sure he is warm. He may wake up once or twice during the night, but this is normal. He'll soon sleep contentedly throughout the night.

Establishing Routines

One of the best ways to ensure success at bringing up a dog is to provide him with a routine. A routine not only makes housetraining easier, but it also gives your puppy a sense of security that can reduce the likelihood of separation anxiety, keep him more relaxed around the house, and give you a sense of control.

A beautiful longhair *Photo courtesy of Pamela Joslin*

A dog who never knows when he's going to be fed next will be constantly whining for dinner. A dog who never knows when walk-time is will demand to go out all the time. A dog who is uncertain when he gets to play with you will be forever dragging his toys up to you for a game. This doesn't mean that you can't ever forget the routine or give him extra attention. It does mean that he should expect certain things at certain times. Although it may seem like a chore to develop a fixed routine for your puppy, in the long run it will make life a lot easier for both of you.

For example, dogs like to get up at the same time (early) every day. Although many dogs can learn to expect the weekend break in routine, others don't care if it is Sunday morning. They still want to go out at 7 a.m. However you negotiate this difference in sleeping patterns, you will eventually establish a routine that is acceptable or at least tolerated by both of you.

A good routine makes it perfectly possible for working people to successfully keep a dog—as long as the dog is not left alone for very long periods of time. No one should expect a dog be happy at home alone eight or nine hours day. As more and more people realize the importance of companionship for dogs, the doggy day care business is thriving. Day care not only makes the day speed by for your dog, but it will also enhance his social skills.

Doggy Dreamin'

Adolescent and young adult dogs (six months to three years) need the least amount of sleep, but all dogs sleep more than we do.

A Fitness Program

Exercise is critically important to keep your dog fit. Dachshunds are one of the breeds that tends toward obesity, and obesity is extremely dangerous for them, leading to intervertebral disk disease.

For growing Dachshunds, moderation is the key. Before the muscles are sufficiently developed to support the Dachshund's rather unnatural body shape, excess running and jumping can lead to back problems. Try to keep the dog from jumping off furniture (it's easiest not to allow him on furniture at all except by

Caring For Your Dachshund's Back

Dachshunds have delicate backs, and although most Dachshunds do not experience back trouble, about a quarter of them do. To help protect your Doxie against back problems, follow these simple rules:

▼ Select a veterinarian who is well acquainted with the vagaries of the Dachshund back. If an emergency occurs, you will want to have the best immediate care. If your regular vet is not an orthopedist, get him to recommend one to you in case of emergency.

▼ Pick up your Dachshund carefully from both ends at once. Don't allow the rear end to dangle. Pick the dog up with two hands, one hand under the deepest part of the chest, the other supporting the rear legs. Allow the front paws to dangle.

▼ Don't allow young children to pick up the dog. Kids mean well, but they have a tendency to drop the dog.

▼ Don't allow your dog to jump on or off furniture, especially the bed.

▼ If you have stairs in the house, keep your Dachshund away from them. Block them off, and when the dog must get to another floor, carry him.

▼ Keep your Dachshund fit and trim. You should be able to feel his ribs easily. Extra weight puts more stress on the back.

▼ Exercise your dog to improve his muscle tone, but don't engage him in activities that involve jumping or twisting. Some dog sports, such as Agility trials, are not meant for the Dachshund's unusual build.

invitation). Luckily, Dachshunds really enjoy being carried, and I would carry mine up and down stairs rather than have him risk an injury. Dachshunds are just not built for climbing and descending stairs. Much as they may look like Slinky toys—they are not.

Around the House–Literally

Please fence your yard. Even the happiest, most secure Dachshund may be seized by wanderlust at any time, so a sturdy fence is essential to your dog's safety. For a Dachshund, a sturdy fence means one built so that your dog can't possibly dig underneath it to escape. Some people pour a concrete curb along the base of the fence; others bury the fence several inches below ground. You can also bury cinder block a foot underground right by the fence. No matter how dearly he loves you, your Dachshund's nature is to follow his nose, and he will leave home to explore his world if given the opportunity. Thus, make sure that the fence is kept in good repair and that the gate has a lock on it. Don't take any chances with having your precious Doxie stolen by someone awful.

Although some people swear by electronic fences, my own preference is for a conventional fence that not only keeps your dog *in*, but also keeps other dogs and neighborhood bullies *out*. A

English import, Ch. Drakesleat Matt Rimony, second from the left, with three of his offspring. Bred by Zena Thorn-Andrew of England   Photo courtesy of Joella Maser

standard fence doesn't require electric power and special collars, or depend upon electric shocks to confine your dog. (Some dogs, if given sufficient motivation, will even tear through an electronic fence. And once they're out, they tend to stay out, unwilling to risk another shock to get back *in*.) Whatever kind of fence you choose, however, make sure that it is high enough to keep your dog from jumping or climbing over it, and deep enough to keep him from digging under it.

One of the best ways to keep your dog happy at home to make sure he *is* happy. Bored, lonely dogs have the greatest need to escape, so spend plenty of active play time with your pet. When he realizes the best times in life are the times he spends with you, he'll be less inclined to want to leave. If your dog must spend some part of the day in the yard, give him plenty of inter-active toys, and don't leave him out there too long. The free run of the yard is no substitute for your company. Your dog needs both.

Cleaning Up

There's nothing like having a dog to make one aware of the joys and sorrows of good housekeeping. Dog owners need their own special set of housekeeping tools, and I'd like to recommend a few of my favorites. To get rid of stains and odors, nothing works better than Simple Solution Odor and Stain Remover, found in most pet supply stores. This product doesn't just cover odors; it neutralizes them by changing the molecular structure of the odor-causing particles. Simple Solution is a concentrate, so you need to mix it with water according to the directions and soak the stain with the solution. (For the cheap at heart, you can try the time-honored method of using white vinegar and warm water mixed in a one-to-three solution. Check the colorfastness of the target fabric by testing the solution on an inconspicuous place first.)

To protect your carpeted floors, DuPont makes a product called SpillNet, a protective barrier placed just underneath the carpet and on top of the pad. This prevents urine from leaking through the carpet and soaking into the pad (which retains the odor); it also keeps the urine from staining the floor.

Another bane of dog-owning housekeepers is, of course, dog hair. The best tool for removing unwanted household (as opposed to facial) hair is a lint roller. Many varieties are available, but my choice is Evercare's Washable Lint Pic Up. Its big advantage is that it is indeed washable, thus saving you the expense and time of refilling the lint remover with masking tape. This product is available in travel and regular sizes. Of course, if you don't feel like washing lint rollers, simply purchase the kind that can be refilled. They all work equally well. Another product, called Sticky Mitt, works like a glove. It too is washable, but I don't think it works as well as the classic lint roller.

Once you've taken care of the inside of the house, you need to deal with the yard. Several varieties of pooper-scooper are available. The advantage of a pooper-scooper is that it saves your back and keeps your nose distant from the object you are picking up. On the other hand, a pooper-scooper is never around at the right time, and it's silly to carry one on a walk. You can purchase little baggie pooper-scoopers at any discount retailer, but a plain old sandwich bag works about as well and is much cheaper.

Chapter 6
The Dapper Dachshund

Grooming not only makes your dog look good and feel good—it's essential to his well being. One reason for this is that every grooming session is a mini-veterinary exam. It is during grooming that you're most likely to notice something wrong with your dog's ears, eyes, gums, or paws. You will pick up suspicious lumps, small cuts, hot spots, parasites, or other problems you might otherwise overlook. Careful grooming really serves as a kind of health home-check, and the information you learn will be invaluable to your veterinarian. So as we can see, good looks and good health go together paw in paw.

Begin grooming sessions while your puppy is still young, so that he accepts grooming as a normal part of life. The first step with both puppies and older dogs unaccustomed to being groomed is simple touching and stroking, especially around the face, feet, and ears—tender spots that can be troublesome unless your dog is mentally prepared. It is also very helpful if you can train to your puppy both to stand and lie quietly on his side (in case you have to work on a tangle).

No matter what coat type your Doxie possesses, the basic principles of grooming remain the same:

▼ Clean ears
▼ Bright eyes
▼ Pink gums
▼ Sparkling teeth

▼ Trimmed nails
▼ Clean, well-brushed coat

I'll discuss the first five first—and then talk about grooming each coat type separately.

Ear Care

At least once a week, clean your Doxie's ears with a moistened cotton ball. Don't insert anything deeply into the ear, since you could damage the delicate tissues. Because the dog's ears are L-shaped, you can't get to the bottom of them anyway. Use a commercial, alcohol-free cleaner, or a good herbal product (I like ones with mullein, a natural product that grows wild in the mid-Atlantic region). If your dog tends to have serious wax build-up or similar concerns, clean the ears more often.

The ears are an extension of the skin, and so dogs with skin problems often tend to have ear problems as well—and vice versa. Dark, gritty material in the ears may be a sign that your Dachshund has ear mites. You can buy a commercial cleaner to get rid of them. Red, smelly, or inflamed ears indicate a bacterial or fungal infection, in which case you'll need to take your dog to your veterinarian. If your dog pulls away or resists having you examine an ear, suspect trouble. If your dog has repeated problems with ear infections, it may indicate a problem with the immune system.

Eye Care

A healthy dog's eyes should be wide open and bright. The center should be clear and shining, with pupils of the same size. The whites of the eyes should be pure white with no redness. Older dogs may have a greenish tinge to their eyes—this is a normal process of aging and nothing to worry about. The tissue beneath the lower lids should be a healthy pink, although some breeds have a dark tinge on the membrane. To examine your dog's eyes, simply stroke him gently on the head, pulling back the ears—the eyes will naturally open up wide and come clearly into view.

Cleaning the eyes should be a part of regular grooming care; if a slight irritation appears, you can apply a commercial non-

Photo courtesy of Butch & Joyce Sheridan

medicated eyewash. Gently clean away any discharge that has gathered at the corners of the eye. If the discharge is yellow or green and the eye is swollen or red, the dog needs veterinary care immediately. Small dogs often have malfunctioning tear ducts that require constant cleaning around the eyes.

If you have questions about your dog's eye health, you may want to schedule an ophthalmic exam for your Doxie. Usually this simple exam does not involve anesthesia or even sedation, although the veterinarian may want to numb the eye and dilate the pupil. Tear production is measured by the Schirmer tear test, in which a strip of absorbent paper is passed over the lower eyelid. To look for corneal scratches, the vet can use a drop of fluorescent stain to light up suspect spots. He can also use an ophthalmoscope to check the retina, optic nerve, and ocular blood vessels. A tonometer checks eyeball pressure. If anything

Be On the Lookout for Puffy Eyes

A swelling beneath the eye is an indication of an abscessed carnassial tooth, a common condition in older dogs. If the tooth is not extracted, deadly bacteria can escape into the bloodstream and lodge in the heart. My friend's Dachshund died from exactly this condition.

complex or suspicious shows up, your vet may direct you to a board-certified veterinary ophthalmologist.

Administering eye medications can be a daunting task if you are not used to it, but a little practice will soon remove your apprehension. If the medicine is a liquid, stand behind the dog and place one hand on the side of the head to hold the head still and open the eye. Hold the head securely with one hand and drop the required number of drops directly into the eye with the other hand. Use the same technique to apply salves and creams.

Teeth and Gum Care

The average adult dog has forty-two teeth (puppies have only twenty-eight). Every one of these teeth requires care. You should brush your dog's teeth every day. I know you won't, but you should. The more often you brush your dog's teeth, the better his dental health will be and that's a fact. If you don't brush your dog's teeth every day, do so as often as you can, and start when your dog is young. Your puppy may not look as if he needs his teeth done, but getting him used to the process early on will makes things easier later. In truth, studies show that most dogs exhibit signs of gingivitis by the age of one year. The smaller your Dachshund, the more crowded his teeth tend to be and the more dental problems he is likely to encounter.

Look Ma, No Cavities!

Because of the alkaline quality of their saliva and the comparative lack of flat surfaces on their teeth, dogs seldom get cavities. (Properly fed dogs don't get any sugar, either.)

Examine the gums when you brush your dog's teeth. They should be a clean, healthy pink. Gums that are dark red, pale, gray, or yellowish may signal a serious disease. Liver problems, infections, and anemia all reveal themselves in the gums.

If your puppy won't allow you to brush his teeth, start with just your finger inside a cloth. Gradually progress to the brush, which can get under the gum line. Although he may want to, don't allow the puppy to chew on your fingers, which would set

Overtime for the Tooth Fairy

Watch those sharp little baby teeth! They start to fall out and get replaced by adult teeth when a puppy is about four months old. However, sometimes the adult tooth makes a "mistake" and doesn't erupt right beneath the baby tooth to help force it out. When that happens, both teeth can remain crowded in the mouth, causing abnormal placement of teeth. You should check the teeth carefully every week until the puppy is about seven months old. Retained teeth can be extracted by your veterinarian.

a bad precedent. Of course you will use only toothpaste designed for canines; they come in a variety of flavors, including chicken, beef, mint—and peanut butter. Dogs like meat-flavored kinds the best, of course, although people usually prefer mint.

Keeping Nails in Trim

Nail care is unpopular with both dogs and people, but it is an essential part of grooming. Wild canids, of course, don't bother with nail trimming; they just run around on rocks and dig dens and engage in enough other suitable activities to keep their nails short. (They chew off the dewclaw nail when it gets out of hand.) And although most Dachshunds would like to inhabit an environment where they can dig to their heart's content, it's not usually allowed. Some surveys show that only about half of dog owners clip their own dog's nails. Most others let their vets or groomers do it. The bad part about this is that you are putting together the idea of the vet (already stressful for most dogs) with "nail-clipping." Thus the dog becomes increasingly resentful and fearful of the nail-ordeal. A disgraceful minority of owners simply let the nails grow out until they break of their own accord. In most breeds, neglected nails eventually curve into the paw, but Dachshund nails tend to grow straight out. Part of this is due to their digging heritage. (Doxies also tend to put on a greater percentage of their weight on their front feet than most breeds, and so wear the nails down.)

Few dogs positively enjoy having their nails trimmed, but most learn to tolerate it. A very few need to restrained or even (in worst cases), muzzled during the procedure. Whatever it takes, however, you must do it or have it done. Nails that grow too long can split painfully. They can even splay out the foot so badly that it becomes deformed.

Accordingly, you must keep your Dachshund's nails reasonably short. (The nails of some dogs will wear out to the proper length simply by hitting the sidewalk, but you can't rely on this process.) It's ideal to starting trimming (or even pretending to trim) your dog's nails from the time he is a youngster and if you have been handling your dog's feet routinely from puppyhood, you have been preparing him well. Puppies tend to have softer nails than adult dogs, and so are easier to trim. In fact, most puppy nails are so soft they wear down of their accord and so technically don't *need* a trim; however, if you don't "practice" now, you'll be in big trouble when your dog grows older, less active, and hard-of-nail.

If you can hear your dog's nails clicking on the floor, they are too long. Floor-length nails are already putting enough pressure on the toes to distort the shape of the foot. It's time to get out the clippers or grinder. Clippers come in two basic styles: guillotine and scissors-style. Guillotine clippers are usually a little smaller. You can use whatever makes you and your dog most comfortable, but it pays to buy better quality tools. It's also a good idea to invest in some Kwik Stop styptic powder in case your hit the quick by mistake. In fact, Kwik Stop now offers a styptic gel that works better than the powder. As a safe alternative to clipping, try grinding your dog's nails. I have used a Dremel grinder on all my dogs' nails for years. No muss, no fuss, no cutting the quick. As soon as the dogs get used to the noise and vibration, they actually seem to enjoy it. Grinders come in cordless varieties, too.

Choose a quiet and relaxed time to do the nail trimming. Start the process by taking the dog's paw gently in your hand. If your dog seems nervous, praise him gently, and offer a treat. Softly squeeze the paw to extend the nails. Don't try to bully your dog into submission; you are only increasing his stress, and he'll fight harder every time. (The fact that this was the tactic used by many veterinarians has not provided the right model for dog owners. Most veterinarians have historically been interested in getting

Dewclaw Care

Don't forget to trim your dog's dewclaws, which may be on the front feet, hind feet, or both. If too long, the dog could tear them on something. In spite of their name, dewclaws don't really do anything and you might consider having them removed surgically during a routine operation like spaying.

the job done, with not enough regard for the feelings of the animal.

Clip the tip speedily, and be careful to avoid cutting the quick—the blood vessel that runs nearly to the end of the nail. You can't often see the quick in dark-nailed dogs, so you'll need to clip just a tiny bit at a time. The quick has both a nerve and blood supply. If you do accidentally clip it, apply styptic powder right away. The bleeding will stop quickly. If you don't happen to have styptic powder—any flour-based product like cornstarch will work.

Don't feel compelled to trim every nail if the procedure frightens your dog. Do just two or three at a time. However, don't allow your dog to "win" if he objects. If he protests, and you quit, then he will be even more adamant next time. You must finish on a successful note. On the other hand, a working dog—one who is involved in Earth trials, for instance, would not do well with nails excessively short as is common with some show dogs. Dogs need their nails to dig.

Coat Care

Great coat care starts from inside. For example, if your dog is eating low-fat food, his coat will tell the tale. It will be dry and rough. Although frequent and thorough brushing will help bring out the shine; the real secret is good nutrition, particularly the omega fatty acids. There are two basic varieties of omegas: the omega-6 fatty acids, and the omega-3s. The first kind abounds in nature, and in your dog's food, since it's found in plant oils such as sunflower oil. Even dog foods that don't contain sunflower or safflower oil will have their "precursor," linoleic acid. Omega-3s are found in marine fish oil and flaxseed oil and because they're expensive, some cheaper dog foods may not have them. Most nutritionists believe that the omega-6 and -3 acids need to be properly balanced. The current theory is that the ideal ratio of omega-6 to omega-3 is 5 to 1. Quality commercial foods add the omegas in the correct balance.

It's Not the Heat

Even though you can buy many products for coat care (for all types of coat), these products work differently in humid conditions than they do in dry ones. You'll need to experiment a bit.

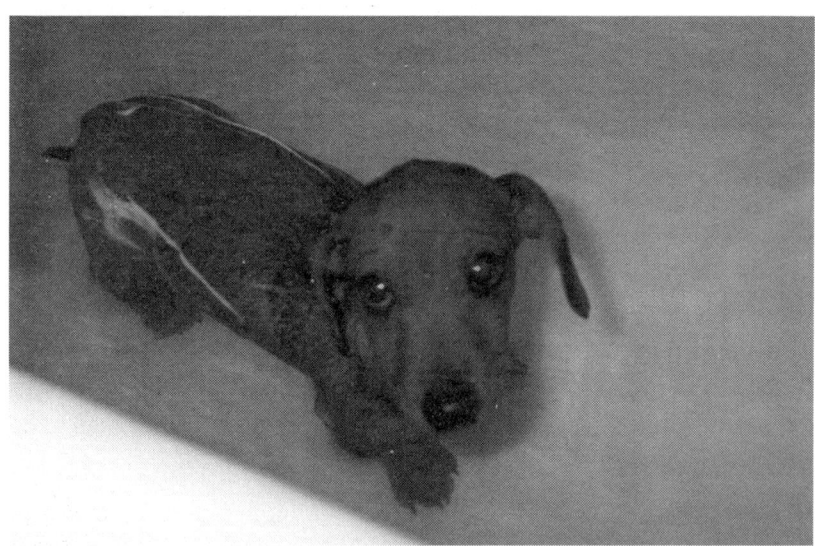

Annie, a smooth, miniature red

Photo courtesy of Daisy & Charles Buchignani
Owners: Cheryl & Steve Lakich

Bathing Your Dachshund

In spite of all that you've heard, frequent bathing does not destroy a dog's coat, any more than frequent shampooing ruins your hair. It is true that frequent use of harsh shampoos can strip away important oils. But this is true with your hair as well. The answer to that is not to use harsh shampoos. I have bathed every one of my dogs once a week for many years—and none of them has ever had a problem with dry skin, dandruff, or hotspots. And as with human hair, many dogs benefit from a conditioner.

Dealing with Dry Skin

An oatmeal bath is the perfect solution for dogs with dry, itchy skin. You can use a colloidal commercial product like Aveeno, which dissolves instantly in water, or even ordinary breakfast oatmeal wrapped in cheesecloth—or a sock! You can use oatmeal soap or shampoo as well, although some of these products contain added substances that may irritate the skin further.

Encourage your dog to soak in a cool tub for at least ten minutes. (Warm water tends to make itching worse.) Bathe your dog every day for three or four days until the itchiness goes away. For dogs who simply won't put up with a bath, use a cool oatmeal compress on the irritated skin. Oatmeal baths and compresses are also excellent for dogs who have been bitten by ants or stung by bees.

In general, Doxies are odorless dogs, so a lack of bathing will not make itself known by an offensive smell, as with many other hound breeds. In large part, how often you bathe your Doxie depends on your personal preference. In general, Longhaired Dachshunds need to be bathed more often than Smooths and Wirehairs. Follow your instinct!

Frequent use of a gentle shampoo will keep your Doxie's coat clean and shining. You can choose either a mild shampoo for humans or one formulated especially for dogs. The pH of dog and human skin is different, but that doesn't really matter much, as far as shampooing goes. I have found that the biggest advantage in using shampoo for dogs is that it doesn't seem to lather as much and so rinses out more easily—a major concern when bathing dogs.

To wash the dog, place him in a suitable container. The kitchen sink is big enough for some Dachshunds, while others require the use of the bathtub. In either case, put a non-skid mat

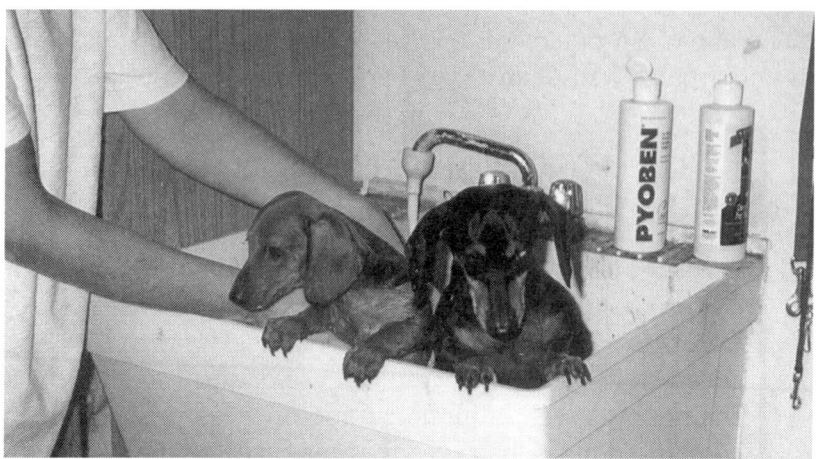

Bath time for Annie and Kallie   *Photo courtesy of Frank & Renee Renwick*

down to assure your dog doesn't slip. A drop of mineral oil in each eye helps protect them against errant shampoo, and a cotton ball in each ear will keep the water out. (Wet ears provide an ideal home for fungal infections.) A handheld shower attachment makes bathing much easier—I wouldn't even attempt it without one. Use no less than three or four units of water for each unit of shampoo; it will lather nicely and rinse out well.

Use warm water, not hot. I start at the head, making a collar of soap around the neck and working backwards. If you do shampoo the head, use a tearless shampoo. There are kinds available for dogs. Lather briskly, and follow with a conditioner (if desired), on the Smooth or Longhaired dog. After shampooing, rinse, rinse, rinse, rinse. It should take twice as long to rinse a dog thoroughly as it did to wash him.

Towel-dry the dog after washing, and make sure he stays inside until he's completely dry. You can also use a hair-dryer, but put it on the lowest setting.

Smooth Coat Requirements

Brush a Smoothie two or three times a week with a hound mitt or a soft, natural bristle brush. Brush in the direction of the hair growth, and work from the skin out. You won't need a comb, obviously. Brushing helps improve circulation, stimulates the skin, removes dead hair, and makes your dog feel healthy and loved. You can even groom your Smoothie while he's lying comfortably beside you as you watch *Animal Planet*. Begin at the head, and work your way gently down to the tail, using short, gentle strokes.

Longhair Care

The silky coat of a Longhair needs daily care or it will mat, especially beneath the ears. Brush in the direction of the hair growth, from the skin out. Use a natural bristle brush or a pin brush. (Both of these are gentler on the skin than a slicker brush.) It helps if you mist the dog's coat first with a water/conditioner mix or tangle remover. To prevent mats, you should comb your Longhair at least every other day. It's easiest to do this if you own a grooming table; they are not expensive and fold up neatly when not in use. Most come equipped with a noose to help hold the dog in position. If you don't have a grooming table, put the dog on the washing machine or dryer for the grooming. The rather slippery surface will encourage your dog to stand still. Or, if you are limber, you can sit on the floor with him. Otherwise, you may need a friend to help hold the dog.

Establish a regular routine for the grooming process. This will prevent you from forgetting any step and your dog will know what to expect. The first thing to do with a Longhair is to seek out any tangles and carefully pull them apart with your fingers.

Photo courtesy of Pamela Joslin

Don't try to yank through them with a comb; you wouldn't care for that yourself. Start with the outer part of the tangle, and slowly progress toward the skin. If the coat is badly snarled, work in short sessions and praise the dog frequently. It's not the dog's fault his coat is matted.

If the dog has hair growing between his pads and around the edges of the foot, trim the excess hair with a pair of blunt-edged scissors. You may want to trim away some hair from under the tail to help in the hygiene area. Hold the tail out straight and scissor out about an inch or an inch and half near the base.

After combing and scissoring, you can begin to brush. Brush in the direction of hair flow and aim for a flat (not wavy) finish. Use long strokes. Start with the legs, and then move on to the tail and under the ears. Finish with the back and sides. These areas are likely to cause the least trouble, so you will finish the brushing on a very pleasant note.

Brush First, Bathe Second

Always brush the dog before you bathe him. If you bathe him first, you will ensure than any mats in the coat will turn indissoluble. Knots tighten when wet.

For a Longhaired Dachshund, use a shampoo especially formulated for a long, silky coat. When bathing, keep a small pair of blunt-tipped scissors on hand in case you come upon a recalcitrant mat under the elbows. After the dog gets wet, snarls are impossible to comb out, so you might as well just snip them. Of course if you have a show dog, you'll have to go through the laborious process of detangling. After bathing your Longhair, pin a towel around him to keep the coat flat. If you like a wavy haired Dachshund, that's fine, as long as you don't plan on showing him. You should brush out the coat while it is still somewhat wet for the best effect.

If your Longhaired Dachshund has an oily skin, use a rinse of half water and half witch hazel or apple cider vinegar. Add just a bit of lavender and chamomile. Try this instead of a commercial conditioner; it does a great job of cutting the oil, leaving the dog with a wonderful coat.

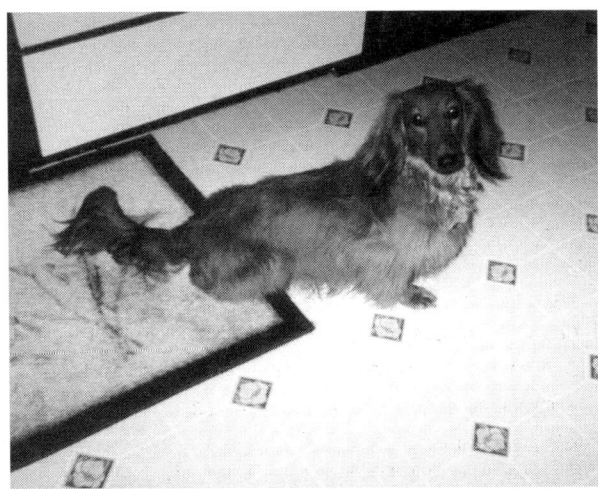

"I don't need a bath, thank you."   *Photo courtesy of Butch & Joyce Sheridan*

Longhaired Dachshunds with dry or brittle coats do well with a daily spray of distilled water mixed with a drop of mink oil or glycerin. Don't use too much or the coat will turn sticky. You can also add a small amount of glycerin to your shampoo.

Wirehair Care

The coat of the Wirehair can vary from soft to harsh, and from rather straight to very curly. The hair should be uniform in length, except for the beard, eyebrows and ears. The hair on the beard and eyes is long and bushy, that on the ears is shorter than that of the rest of the body. There is a finer, softer undercoat interspersed among the wiry hairs of the outer coat. A hard curly coat is preferred in show circles, and is easier to keep, but your pet Dachshund may have a coat of any type. When you comb your Wirehair, don't forget the beard, which can get tangled or messy. Use short, gentle strokes, as with the Smooth. Use a slicker brush and a medium-tooth metal comb.

You may want to thin the beard, the hair around the genitals, or the eyebrows with thinning shears. Show dogs are "stripped," which allows the coat to come back tight and curly, the way most show judges like. The stripper is placed at an angle and run down the back of the dog—gently. If the coat is naturally tight and curly, stripping needs to be done only once or twice a year. You can learn to do this yourself with a stripping blade or knife, although

Stanley, a one and a half year wirehair   *Photo courtesy of V. Jean Trefes*

some owners of Wirehairs prefer to have their dog groomer do it. Show dogs are often "hand-stripped." This is a technique for the experienced person only. Don't try it without expert advice and supervision. It's only used on show dogs, anyway.

Wirehaired Dachshunds generally need to be clipped several times a year, and it may be easiest to go to a groomer for this task. If you want to clip your dog yourself, buy a dog clipper and go to it. Dog clippers come with several, numbered blades. The higher the number on the blade, the closer the blade cuts. Use a number 10 blade on the head, and a number 5 on the body to leave a longish coat, a number 7 for a shorter one. (That will leave the hair about one quarter of an inch long.) It's best not to clip a harsh, tight-coated Wirehair at all, since clipping destroys the coat's desirable harsh quality. With a softer coated Wire, the clipping will help keep the dog comfortable and it won't detract from his appearance.

Wirehaired Dachshunds can get by with less frequent bathing than the Smooth or Longhaired variety. Do not use a conditioner on a Wirehair. Instead use a shampoo designed specifically for the wire coat. You can purchase such a shampoo through the Internet, at a dog show, or in large pet supply stores. Other shampoos can cause the hair to lose its texture.

Professional Grooming

If you have a Longhaired or Wirehaired Dachshund, you may prefer to avail yourself of the services of a professional groomer. This is a good plan, but you should do your part as well. If you don't know a good groomer, ask your veterinarian, dog's breeder, or knowledgeable friend for a recommendation. You may also want to observe a few grooming sessions; the last thing you need is someone who is rough or hard on your Dachshund. One bad session at a groomer's can undo months of careful work on your part.

Most grooming shops require proof of vaccinations, including *Bordetella*. You should also make sure an overactive dog is well exercised before he gets to the shop; he'll be more docile and less "antsy" that way. For the same reason, let your dog go "potty" before his appointment. And if you have a nervous dog, it's kinder to the groomer not to feed your pet beforehand; there's a possibility he might leave his breakfast on the floor of the grooming shop if he gets over-stimulated.

Clearly explain (with a picture if possible) exactly how you want your dog trimmed. If your dog objects to having his nails clipped or ears cleaned, say so. No groomer wants a nasty surprise. If your dog has ever nipped or bitten anyone in similar circumstances, you must warn the groomer, or you might be liable if something untoward happens. A dog groomer is a dog groomer—not a pet therapist, dog trainer, or animal behaviorist. And while most groomers can cope with some resistance on the part of a pet, none expects to be bitten. It is up to you to teach your dog to stand still while being brushed and bathed.

If you are dreaming of a show career for your dog, tell the groomer, but don't expect the average pet groomer to be able to a do a show clip. This is an art that requires extensive knowledge of the fine points of the breed. Most show grooming is done by professional handlers. A show groomer knows how to accent your Dachshund's finer points while minimizing his "faults." Don't expect a pet groomer to do this, although she can certainly give your pet the proper cut for a "show look" if that's what you want.

Shedding

Your Dachshund may shed, so don't be surprised. The Smooth variety sheds more than the Longhaired, simply because the hair growth cycle is shorter. However, the Longhaired Dachshund can shed quite a bit when growing out his new coat. Wires shed the least, and actually require some "help" to remove the dead hair. Dogs tend to shed the most in the spring and fall, although there are plenty of them who pay no attention to this natural cycle and shed whenever and wherever they feel like it. It's not unlikely that you'll own a year-round shedder. Warm baths and frequent grooming may help minimize the damages. A stripping knife, which you can use like a comb, will get rid of an enormous amount of dead hair.

Shedding seems to be triggered by hormonal changes that are tied to day length and light conditions. Unnatural shedding may be caused by poor nutrition, bad health, or stress, including surgery and whelping. In these cases, I always recommend Mrs. Allen's Shed-Stop or a similar product containing the right combination of omega-3 and -6 oils to help the dog's coat regain some oil and achieve its very best look.

Woody, a longhaired Dachshund, waits patiently to have the "snowballs" removed from his coat during a Colorado winter.

Photo courtesy of Lisa Liddy Owners: John & Margie Flynn

Chapter 7
The Dining Dachshund

Dachshunds are not only scent hounds, they are chow hounds as well. It is very tempting to give in to your Doxie's constant desire for food and yet more food, but to do so is dangerous. Obesity is one of modern dogs' leading medical problems, and it is especially serious in Dachshunds. Because of his unusual—and unnatural—physique, extra weight can damage your dog's spine, in addition to all the other problems caused by obesity, including other musculoskeletal troubles, circulatory difficulties, liver diseases, and pancreatic disorders. Overweight dogs are also more prone to heatstroke. Please keep tabs on your dog's weight. He'll be a healthier, happier hound if you do.

Basics of Nutrition

Here are the six building blocks of good nutrition: water, protein, fat, carbohydrates, vitamins, and minerals. Of these six, five are essential to your dog—meaning he will die without them. The one building block that is not essential to dogs (except possibly for pregnant dogs, although the point is debated) is carbohydrates. Although dogs can make adequate use of carbohydrates in their diet, they aren't necessary.

Carbo Candor

Although carbohydrates aren't needed by your dog, they make up a huge component of most commercial dog foods, especially dry foods. Why? Because they're cheap and convenient to include. While they do provide an easy source of quick energy, my own opinion is that many dogs would do better with fewer carbohydrates and more fat and protein. Not only do dogs enjoy such meals more than starchy ones, they are more natural and better for them.

Water

Keep your dog constantly supplied with clean, cool, accessible water. Some people don't leave their dog enough water when they leave home for the day because they feel that the dog will be less likely to urinate in the house. If that's the case, please find another way to protect your home. The best way is to hire a noontime dog walker, or perhaps to install a doggy door. Don't deprive your dog of water. It is cruel and counterproductive. Dogs given insufficient water are much more likely to develop bladder and kidney stones, and your dog needs more water than anything else in his diet. If a dog becomes more than 12 percent dehydrated, he will die.

Protein

About 50 percent of every cell in your dog's body is protein. Proteins are also critical for building enzymes, hormones, hemoglobin, and antibodies. All animals need protein for maintenance and healing, and young animals need it for growth. If a puppy doesn't get enough protein, his tissues and organs won't develop properly. Like fats and carbohydrates, protein provides energy. However, all proteins are definitely not equal when it comes to their value to your Dachshund. Dogs cannot use proteins derived from plants very well; they are carnivores by nature and need high-quality animal-based protein to do their best.

Fats

Fats have twice the number of calories per gram as do protein or carbohydrates; they are packed with energy. Fats keep the cells in good working order, increase palatability, and add texture to food. Dogs digest fats *very* efficiently, and need a higher proportion of fat in their diet than we do to keep healthy. Too much fat in the diet, however, is associated with pancreatitis, especially with overweight, sedentary dogs who aren't used to it. A balanced diet is necessary.

Dogs can use both plant and animal fats with equal ease. However, oils derived from plants provide large amounts of essential fatty acids (EFAs). These acids are essential for many biological functions. In the wild, dogs eat portions of the vegetable matter contained in the prey stomach. It is presumed that this supplies them with some EFA's.

Carbohydrates

Carbohydrates provide energy, and serve as building blocks for other biological components. They are a heat source for the body when they are metabolized for energy and they can be stored as glycogen or converted to fat. Carbohydrates also help regulate protein and fat metabolism.

Nearly all commercial dry dog foods are based on carbohydrates, in the form of grain and cereal products. As I mentioned before, dogs can get along perfectly well without carbohydrates in their diet. (There is some evidence that diets high in grain may be a factor in the development of diabetes, arthritis, and obesity.) What dogs do *need* is glucose, which can be derived from proteins, carbohydrates, or the glycerol found in fats. Your dog needs a steady supply of glucose to keep his central nervous system in good working order. (The body needs glucose so badly that it will get it wherever it can find it, even if it means metabolizing amino acids needed for muscle development.) Thus a dog on a no-carbohydrate diet needs plenty of protein and fat to make up for it.

Vitamins

Vitamins are plant- and animal-derived substances necessary for your dog's health. A vitamin is defined as an organic component of the diet different from proteins, fats, or carbohydrates. Vitamins are critical for normal body functioning and their absence produces a deficiency syndrome. They don't have calories, but your dog needs them to convert calories to energy. They also help with many other jobs throughout the dog's system—everything from helping blood clot to maintaining cell wall integrity.

There are two basic types of vitamins: fat-soluble (A, D, E, and K) and water-soluble (C and the eight B vitamins). Fat-soluble vitamins need dietary fat in order to be absorbed into the body, while water-soluble vitamins need only water. The metabolites of fat-soluble vitamins are excreted in the feces, and excess fat-soluble vitamins are stored in the liver.

Water-soluble vitamins (except B12) are not stored in the body and need to be replaced regularly. Most water-soluble vitamins are absorbed in the small intestine and excreted in the urine. Unlike people, dogs don't have a requirement for vitamin C, because they can make their own. However, under times of duress, extra vitamin C has been shown to be beneficial to dogs.

Minerals

A dietary mineral is any inorganic component of a food. Like vitamins, many minerals are necessary for an animal's health.

Dietary minerals are generally classed into three groups. Macro-minerals (sulfur, calcium, phosphorus, magnesium, and the electrolytes sodium, potassium, and chloride) are consumed in gram quantities per day. Trace minerals such as iron, zinc, copper, iodine, and selenium, are needed in milligrams or micrograms per day. A third class includes the ultra-trace minerals that have been shown to be necessary in laboratory animals, but not in dogs.

Minerals participate in nearly every function of the body. They build teeth and bone, serve as parts of enzymes, and are a vital part of the blood and other bodily fluids. Minerals also play a role in muscle contraction, the transmission of nerve impulses, and in cell membrane permeability.

Dogs can make better use of minerals derived from meat than from plant-derived minerals. This is especially true for zinc, iron, and copper. Plants often contain "anti-nutritional" components such as phytate, oxylate, and certain fibers like beet pulp that can limit mineral availability. (This is one reason that I hate to see "beet pulp" as an ingredient in commercial dog food.)

Unless you really know what you're doing, stay away from mineral supplementation in your dog's diet, especially with puppies. Minerals need to be in a particular balance, so if you supplement one, another becomes deficient. The most important mineral pairs are: calcium/magnesium; calcium/phosphorus; sodium/potassium; zinc/copper. Besides, commercial dog foods have plenty of calcium, iron, copper, and zinc. Speak with your veterinarian or a qualified animal nutritionist before beginning any supplementation program.

Barney enjoys his dinner   *Photo courtesy of Phyllis Grilli*

Commercial Dog Foods

We have only been feeding our dogs processed feeds, at least on a large scale, for about sixty years. (The military played a role in the popularization of processed dog food, since the army needed an easy-to-store food for its dogs of war.) Nowadays, about 95 percent of American dog owners feed their dogs primarily or solely a commercial diet, usually dry kibble. While most of these products contain the minimum amounts of nutrients to be considered "nutritionally complete," none of them is really an ideal food for your dog. Their greatest advantage is that they are convenient.

Prescription Foods

Some foods are specially designed to treat certain conditions like bladder stones and can only be obtained through a veterinarian's prescription. This is one area where commercial foods can be a real godsend. However, because prescription foods are designed to treat a specific condition, they may not be nutritionally balanced for a healthy dog.

Some premium products, including those made by Wysong, Wellness, Flint River, and Solid Gold do approximate top nutrition, but these products can be hard to find—they aren't sold in grocery stores or even in most pet supply stores. (Wellness brand is something of an exception here.) This doesn't mean you can't get them—go to their Web sites to locate your nearest distributor—or have the dog food delivered right to your door.

The Dirt on Dry Food

It is commonly believed that dry food helps keep a dog's teeth in good condition. There is some evidence that a diet of hard kibble does indeed slow down periodontal problems, but it doesn't prevent them. Brushing teeth is what keeps them in good condition.

Although some canned dog food smells unpleasant to us (one reason people prefer to serve kibble), most dogs prefer both the aroma and flavor of canned foods. In fact, some people serve such unappetizing dry fare that they have to anoint the stuff with canned food before their dogs will touch it. To find the best canned food for your dog, check the label. Look for food containing whole meat, fish, or poultry as the first ingredient. Most lower quality canned foods have water as the first ingredient, and many canned foods are over 78 percent water. The best canned foods use whole vegetables, not grain fractions like rice bran, rice flour, or brewer's rice. Canned dog food should look good and smell good, even to you. Mushy, bad-smelling food is not right for your dog.

Disease-free Food

The FDA has recently approved irradiation of all pet food products. (This doesn't mean that pet foods will be irradiated—it means they can be at the manufacturer's discretion.) This practice is designed to ensure that at least 99.9 percent of insects and disease-causing bacteria are eliminated from the food. It is especially designed to eliminate the risk of salmonella. The greatest benefit will come from irradiating dog chews. In 1999, a serious outbreak of salmonella occurred in children who handled salmonella-infected dog chews. Dogs themselves are not likely to get salmonella, although it is possible. Their intestinal tracts are generally too short and acidic for the bacterium to survive.

Unfortunately, the best quality canned foods can't often be found at your supermarket; you must go to the manufacturer, a few pet specialty stores, or dog shows. This is because the shelf rental space of most supermarkets is simply too expensive for many small, premium pet food manufacturers. At any rate, that doyen of high-quality pet care, the *Whole Dog Journal*, provides the following alphabetical list as the top canned foods for your dog: Avo-Derm, Azmira, California Natural, Canidae, Evolve, Innova, Lamaderm, Lick Your Chops, Natural Balance, Pal Chow, Petguard Premium, Pinnacle, Precise Plus, Solid Gold, Spot's Stew, Wellness, and Wysong.

If you have questions about the food you feed your dog, call the 800 number listed on the label. One important query is: "Where does the meat come from?" Ask whether their food is organically grown. Ask if the company does its own feeding trials. (Many smaller companies can't afford them, but larger reputable companies usually perform their own.)

Labels

The label on a package of dog food is a legal document. That means it is subject to certain rules. It also means the average person can't figure out what the rules are. The Principal Display

Panel (on the front) must contain the brand name of the food (Iams) and name of the product (lamb and rice). It also must state that that food is intended for dogs—in case you were looking for a snack for yourself. It will also state what life stage the food is intended for—puppy, adult, seniors—or *all life stages.*

The labeling then becomes more weasel-like. If the label states that it is, for instance, Lamb Dog Food (*food* is the operant word) it must be 95 percent lamb, exclusive of the water sufficient for processing. No dry food meets this standard. But if it uses a word like *dinner* or *entrée*, it needs to be only 25 percent lamb. If the words *with lamb* appear, we are down to only 3 percent lamb, and if the word *flavor* is used it means that merely the flavor of the stuff must be detectable to dogs. So they can get by without any lamb at all really. *Nowhere on the label will you find the actual percentages of the ingredients.* Apparently it's enough for the manufacturers to know—the poor consumer doesn't need to. (Having made this complaint, I should add that the labeling on baby foods is even less informative than on dog foods.)

The dog food package also contains an Information Panel, which includes the guaranteed analysis. That's the *minimum* amount of crude protein and crude fat. It also gives the *maximum* levels for crude fiber, moisture, and ash. The minimum percent of protein for maintenance is 18 percent, while the minimum for growth and reproduction is 22 percent. Again, this doesn't specify the actual quality of the protein, just how much is present.

The Information Panel also includes feeding instructions and the nutritional adequacy claim. Last is the list of ingredients, which for most people is somewhat less than informative.

The AAFCO Seal of Approval

Most dog foods sold commercially in this country bear the seal of the AAFCO (Association of American Feed Control Officials), showing that the food in question has passed either an AAFCO feeding trial or an AAFCO nutrient profile. The feeding trial is a higher standard than the nutrient profile, but neither one tells you much about the actual quality of the food. For example, the feeding trial is simply this:

▼ Eight dogs older than one year must start the test.

▼ At start all dogs must be normal weight and health.

▼ A simple four-panel blood test (not a complete chemistry) is to be taken from each dog at the start and finish of the test.

▼ For six months, the dogs used must only eat the food being tested.

▼ The dogs finishing the test must not lose more than 15 percent of their body weight.

▼ During the test, none of the dogs used are to die or be removed due to nutritional causes.

▼ Six of the eight dogs starting must finish the test.

That's it. This test doesn't take into consideration a slew of other important factors, including the differences among breeds. The test is not multigenerational and tells us nothing about the long-term value of the food. So while an AAFCO-approved food won't kill your dog, there's no guarantee he'll thrive on it either.

Where's the Beef?

Unfortunately, almost any kind of meat can end up in dog food. In many places, pet food manufacturers are free to use road kill, cows dead from disease, or any other source of protein that suits them. Some companies, like Wellness, use only human grade meat. Formerly, companies were not permitted to state this valuable fact on their labels, a regulation obviously not designed to protect the consumer, but the farmer, who had an outlet for his diseased and downed cattle. However, this regulation has now thankfully been relaxed—so you can easily choose human grade meats for your dog.

However, you can avoid the worst food by sticking to some simple guidelines:

▼ Avoid dog foods containing "by-products." Meat by-products are the part of the animal not deemed fit for human consumption, and while some by-products are both healthy and tasty to dogs, many more are not. Avoid them.

▼ Avoid food laden with grain or cereal by-products. These ingredients are the part of the plant left over after the milling process; they are technically called "fragments," but appear in many guises on the label. The carbohydrates in food should be whole grains. Many dogs are allergic to soy; stay away from it.

▼ Good food should not contain sweeteners, artificial flavors, colors, or preservatives. The best dog foods are preserved naturally with vitamin E (tocopherols) or vitamin C (ascorbic acid). Dog food companies used to use ethoxyquin for preserving food. Ethoxyquin was originally developed as a rubber hardener. Then it was used as an insecticide. Although it cannot legally be used to preserve food for humans (with the minor exception of chili powder), since there's some fairly convincing evidence the stuff causes cancer, liver disease, and immune disorders, manufacturers have used it for years to preserve dog food. Because of increasing consumer pressure, the FDA announced in 1998 that ethoxyquin is not safe in dog food either. They have asked manufacturers to voluntarily stop using it.

▼ Select food with the specific name of a meat (beef, chicken, turkey) as the first ingredient. Avoid foods whose label first lists a generic "meat" or "poultry." Unfortunately, just because a product has "beef" as the first ingredient doesn't mean that the product is mostly beef. Some companies engage in a nefarious practice called "splitting." If they can possibly do so, they will divide the cereal products up into separate categories, like "rice" and then "brown rice." Added together, there may be more rice than beef. But because the companies are allowed to list them as separate ingredients, beef is listed first.

Although the label declares the amount of protein in a food, it doesn't say where the protein comes from. Some kinds of protein are much more usable than others. Hair, for example, is just about all protein, but try living on a hair diet and see what happens to you. Plant proteins are much lower in quality than animal-derived protein. For example, protein derived from eggs has a biologic value of 100—the top rating. This means that it has a high ration of essential amino acids (ones your dog can't make for himself) as opposed to nonessential amino acids (the ones he can make in his body). Corn, on the other hand, has a biologic value of only 45. Reading the labels on pet products leaves you guessing about the protein source. It may say the product contains egg protein, but won't tell you how much. Most of the protein might come from plant sources instead. You'll need to check with the companies directly.

Home Cooking

In an ideal world, dog owners would prepare home-cooked meals for their dogs. By doing this, owners can choose the best ingredients, and customize each meal for each individual dog.

If you decide to prepare your dog's food yourself, take the time to learn the basics of canine nutrition. This is not something you can do without adequate information. For example, a dog who is fed meat alone will receive insufficient calcium. If not enough calcium is present in the blood, the dog's body is forced to extract it from the bones, causing a condition called nutritional osteodystrophy. If too much calcium is provided, relative to phosphorus, a dog could develop lameness and bone and joint problems. For more information on canine nutrition, see my book *Feeding Your Dog for Life* (Doral 2002).

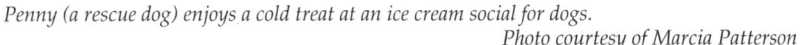

Penny (a rescue dog) enjoys a cold treat at an ice cream social for dogs.
Photo courtesy of Marcia Patterson

More on Mealtime

In addition to the nutritional value of the food you feed your dog, you need to have a good idea about what and when your Dachshund should eat. If you leave it up to him, dinner time will come around every fifteen minutes or so. It's up to you to determine a good schedule.

Variety

The best single thing you can do to ensure that your dog is getting what he needs is to feed him a variety of different foods. This will not only make eating more pleasurable for him, but also, if you start early enough, help protect him from developing allergies. I also strongly urge you to supply your dog with something besides a steady diet of commercial foods. Well-chosen table scraps will not only (this is proved) reduce his risk of bloat, but can boost the quality of every meal.

Frequency

Puppies need to be fed three or four times a day until they are about four months old. Most adult dogs fare best on two meals a day but some thrive on only one meal daily. The latter more nearly approximates what a dog would eat in the wild, but then, our modern Dachshunds live a rather different lifestyle than their ancestors did. Feed your dog a measured amount of food on which he thrives without gaining weight. There are so many variables involved in knowing how much to give, including the activity level of each individual dog, that it's best simply to experiment. If your dog starts getting too fat, cut back, and vice versa. Your puppy should seem eager to eat, but not desperate (although I have some dogs who can make me believe that they haven't eaten in weeks).

Keep your dog on puppy food until he is between six months and one year old.

Managing Your Dog's Diet

Hunger is the natural state of all mammals, including dogs. By natural inheritance, dogs are programmed to run all day long, in honor of the days when they were chasing game around the tundra. Running takes a lot of energy, so dog stomachs tell their owners to eat as much as possible. They never know how long it will be before they catch the next caribou. Dogs almost never say, "No, thanks, I've had enough." Today's dogs have the same instinct to eat and eat as did their ancestors, but almost none of them gets the exercise to justify this dietary imperative.

Unfortunately for Dachshunds, the dietary imperative is a dangerous thing. Dachshunds gain weight extremely easily. The problem is that many people don't even realize how fat their dog is. The dog looks fine to them. Even more unfortunately, some veterinarians are reluctant to tell you outright that your dog may be overweight. There are a number of reasons for this. In the first place, clients get angry at the "weight lecture," especially if they tend to be on the chubby side themselves. Therefore, don't expect your vet to come right out and tell you that your pooch is a fatty. Ask him directly, and be prepared for a truthful answer.

Providing your dog with the proper amount of food for his ideal weight is a key step in keeping him at his ideal weight. Your vet can help you to determine what that weight is, and how much food he should eat. I know you enjoy feeding your dog treats, but they add on pounds. If you do like to treat your dog, cut down on the meals proportionately, or give low-calorie treats like carrot slivers.

In some cases, you may want to resort to a commercial low-calorie food. Pick one that includes specific "weight-loss" directions. (If you feed a dog according to the regular feeding directions he won't lose weight. Regular feeding directions are designed to maintain a dog's weight.)

Another way to keep your dog's weight in check is to provide him with plenty of healthy exercise. Dogs like this option much better than cutting down on their chow, too. If you are starting an exercise weight-loss program for your dog, check with your vet before embarking on anything truly strenuous.

Chapter 8
Dachshunds in Danger

I'm afraid that there is nothing fun about this chapter but it is essential reading if you want to keep your Dachshund around a while.

Everyday Hazards

Some otherwise innocuous items around the home can be extremely dangerous to dogs. Other hazards, such as encounters with wild animals, are pretty obvious. Here is my own alphabet of dangers.

Antifreeze

Antifreeze is remarkably tasty to dogs (apparently it has a sweet flavor) but it is also extremely toxic, even in small amounts. Although less toxic kinds of antifreeze based on propylene glycol are now on the market, many people continue to use antifreeze containing ethylene glycol. When consumed, this chemical depresses the central nervous system and enters the cerebrospinal fluid, making the dog act as if he is drunk. Unfortunately, the symptoms may not appear until twelve or more hours (a day and a half in some cases) after the dog has consumed the stuff. Untreated, dogs who are poisoned by antifreeze almost always die, but if caught early enough, an antidote call Antizol (4-methylpyrazole) is effective.

A tablespoon of antifreeze can kill a small dog, and it doesn't take much more to knock over a mastiff. Dogs who survive antifreeze poisoning may suffer from irreparable kidney damage. Keep your dog away from your garage, and wipe up all antifreeze spills. Of course, if your dog runs loose all over the neighborhood, you have no control over what he might lap up. Almost 10,000 dogs die from antifreeze poisoning every year. Don't let yours be one of them. If your dog does consume antifreeze, induce vomiting, and give him Kaopectate to coat the stomach. Get him to a vet immediately, whether you see any symptoms or not; the stuff takes a while to produce its deadly results. (To obtain antifreeze that is much less toxic than traditional products, call the Sierra Company at (888) 88-SIERRA.)

Battery Acid and Other Lead-Containing Products

Lead is a poisonous substance. Just a few pennies minted after 1983 can kill a dog. Poisonous symptoms include abdominal pain, oral ulcers, bloody vomit, and shock. Do not induce vomiting, and treat for shock if necessary. Make your dog swallow sodium bicarbonate or milk of magnesia.

Bee, Wasp, and Hornet Stings

While all stings are painful, some are deadly. Unfortunately, many dogs consider it the height of summer fun to try to catch bees in their mouths. Dogs stung on the face will try to rub their muzzles on the ground. The nose will swell. If your dog is allergic to bee stings, a sting may cause trouble breathing and/or he may develop hives, vomiting or diarrhea. Give him a dose of Benadryl and take him to the vet right away. If he does not seem to be having an allergic reaction, scrape out the stinger with a credit card. (Don't try pulling it out, because you can squeeze more poison in.) Apply a cold compress and meat tenderizer to the wound. The swelling should disappear in a couple of days.

Bones

Dried or rotten bones pose extreme dangers to dogs. Dogs can choke on them, or they can become lodged in the small intestine. If the intestinal wall is punctured, the dog can develop peritonitis, the seepage of intestinal material into the abdominal cavity. This is deadly. Symptoms of intestinal blockage include acute vomiting, lethargy, and in the later stages, a stiffened abdomen. If this happens to your dog, he needs immediate veterinary intervention. Put cooked or stale poultry bones in the trash and tie it up securely so that your dog cannot get at them. Even large beef bones can splinter or break your dog's teeth. Throw them away too.

Carpet Cleaners and Shampoos

Many carpet shampoos contain perchlorethylene, an agent that can cause cancer, and damage to the liver, kidneys, and nervous system. Others contain ammonium hydroxide, which is irritating to the eyes and nose. While this stuff may not bother *us*, since we stand up tall enough to avoid it, your little Dachshund spends a lot of time with his nose in the rug. Clean your rugs with plain hot water; it works better than you think.

Chocolate

Chocolate, of course, is found naturally in the cocoa plant, and somewhat more unnaturally in your cupboard and refrigerator. It contains theobromine (a compound similar to the caffeine in tea and cola), which can be toxic to canines. This is because dogs metabolize it very slowly. Chocolate can be completely metabolized by people in 12 hours; it would take 35 hours for a dog. Dark chocolate is about nine times more potent than milk chocolate, with baking chocolate being the worst of all.

Even a bit of a chocolate bar can be dangerous to some dogs. And just because your dog has "gotten away" with eating chocolate before, don't assume that the next time won't be the last one. Symptoms of chocolate poisoning include vomiting, diarrhea, frantic activity, rapid pulse, and frequent urination. In a worst-case scenario, coma and death can result. One of my own dogs, a Basset Hound named Mugwump, ate an entire chocolate fudge cake one evening when no one was looking. She spent the night at the vet's being purged. She was fine as fiddle the next day, and on her arrival home immediately began looking around to see if any cake was left. Mugwump is a slow learner.

Madison and Morgan are ready for the holidays   *Photo courtesy of Eileen Scacetti*

Christmas Tree Decorations

Dogs like to steal tree ornaments that they promptly break and/or swallow, to the advantage of neither. Angel hair seems tasty to some dogs, but since it is made spun glass, it is not the best aperitif. Tinsel can clog up the gastrointestinal tract. Pine needles themselves cause irritation to the intestinal lining, and while dogs are singularly unlikely to eat pine needles on trees outdoors, the Christmas tree seems just aching to have its branches eaten. (You can prevent some of this by carefully vacuuming around the tree.) Some people actually use popcorn or gingerbread to decorate the tree. Dogs love this idea. This is not really a problem in my house since I myself devour all the edibles before the dogs can get to them, but with a more discriminating human family, it can be a dangerous practice.

Cold

Dachshunds are small dogs, and none of them tolerate extreme cold very well—especially the Smooth haired variety. Most refuse even to go out when it is raining. Their feet are particularly sensitive. Clean up antifreeze spills, wash paws after walks on chemical-treated sidewalks, and don't allow your pet to languish outdoors in the cold. Smooth Dachshunds do very well in a sweater (designed especially with their long body in mind) and booties during the winter months. If your dog gets too cold, he can develop hypothermia, or low body temperature. If his body temperature drops to 75 degrees, he can die. Symptoms of hypothermia include shivering and fatigue. Wrap up your dog in a coat or blanket, get him indoors, and dry and warm him gradually until his body temperature reaches 100 degrees.

Small dogs suffer from the effect of cold more than big dogs do; it has to do with the body surface area. In addition, dogs can be frost bitten just the same as people can—and the worst effects show up on the same places—digits, ears, and the tip of the nose and tail. Severe cases of frostbite require amputation. In the earliest stages, the skin appears pale or gray as the blood supply decreases; later as the circulation returns it becomes red and inflamed. The dog may lose hair or even skin. A gentle compress of warm water for fifteen to twenty minutes may help mild cases, but more severely affected dogs can suffer serious tissue damage. Don't try to massage, squeeze, or rub the area—you can cause more tissue damage. Try to keep your dog from licking or chewing the affected area also. Your veterinarian may want to prescribe analgesics for the pain and antibiotics for the infection. Improper care can result in gangrene.

Curiously, more dogs are lost in winter than during any other season. And of course winter is the very worst time to get lost. Protect your Dachshund by keeping him on a leash and an ID tag on his collar.

Compost Pile

The friendly garden mulch pile can contain dangerous molds and bacteria. Keep your dog away from it.

Electrical Cords

Puppies are drawn to electrical cords. Tack them up against the wall and behind furniture so they are inconspicuous. You can also cover the cords with spiral plastic covers designed for telephone cords. The symptoms of electrical shock include labored breathing, visible burns, and excess salivation. Electric shock can cause cardiac arrest.

Fabric Softener Sheets

Fabric softener sheets that you toss in the dryer are poisonous to dogs. Keep them out of reach at all times and dispose of them carefully.

Fertilizers and Garden Sprays

Many lawn care products such as fertilizers and insecticides are poisonous. If you must use this stuff in your yard—and you shouldn't—at least wait till it is completely dry before letting your dogs or children out there. Symptoms of fertilizer poisoning include difficulty in breathing, a blue tongue and mucus membranes, and congested lungs. Give the dog mineral oil, and get him to your vet.

Weed killers are poisonous in large amount—your dog can absorb them through his skin. Induce vomiting if he swallows them and call your vet.

Fringes

Puppies adore devouring fringes on slipcovers, pillowcases, and carpets, but fringe and other stringy fabric can clog up your puppy's intestines. This situation can be extremely deadly, so keep your dog away from these dangerous materials.

Getting Lost

Getting lost is a heart-rending occurrence for both dogs and their owners. The best way to get a lost pet back is by making sure he has visible identification. As I mentioned in Chapter 5, statistics show that most dogs with overt identification are returned to their owners—most who don't have ID are not. Wearing a collar is not a risk-free activity but the dangers imposed are extremely slight when compared with the dangers a collar repels.

You have many choices in visible identification. Probably the most visible and simplest is an embroidered nylon mesh collar. You can have your dog's name and your phone number embroidered on it, or if you prefer, just your phone number. An identification collar takes away the worry of your dog losing his tags, something that happens all too frequently. However, since some dogs inevitably lose their collars as well, I suggest a back up method of identification like tattooing, or even better, micro-chipping your dog.

As far as tags go, you can choose anything from a make-your-own to highly elaborate "systems." Petscope, for example, is a dangling ID collar on microfilm. You can fill out all your dog's information (including veterinary information) and the whole form is reproduced on microfilm. Of course, then you have to get somebody to read it. Another fancy choice is the Dog-E-Tag, which digitally stores up to forty lines of information. You can program the device in any of the five languages offered, and update it whenever you like. The Pets Talk talking collar has a tiny recording device attached that lets you record your own message, a message that can be changed as circumstances warrant.

For those who like to bake, you can buy a FastTag—a plastic tag that you write on, and then bake in the oven. The baking shrinks and embeds the writing. Kids love this kind of thing. Every so often, read the tag to make sure that it is still legible. A friend of mine almost gave up trying to locate a dog's owner because the phone number on the tag had all but disappeared.

For those who opt for the more permanent tattoo or micro-chip, the AKC Animal Recovery Program has a database for both methods—the cost is $12.50. For information, call 800-252-7894 or visit the AKC Web site: www.akc.org.

If your dog does get lost, put up color photos of your pet all around the area in which he went missing. Go to the animal shelter *in person* to see if your dog is there. If you just call, they might just say "No" automatically without even bothering to look. (Some of the workers can't tell a Dachshund from a Dalmatian anyway.) Keep checking, every week. Do not give up hope. I have seen dogs reunited with their owners after months have passed.

Grapes and Raisins

In a few cases, grapes and raisins can cause liver damage in dogs. Don't feed them to your Dachshund.

Heat

Dogs suffer from the heat as much as they do from the cold—perhaps more. Unlike us, they are not tropical animals. Their main heat regulator is not perspiration but panting—rapid breathing that exchanges warm air for cool air. If it's blazing hot, there just isn't too much cool air around. The greatest danger comes when dogs are left in parked cars even for short periods—and even with the windows a few inches open. Even in shaded areas cars can soon become blazing hot and heatstroke can occur within minutes. Never leave your dog in the car. If your dog does get heatstroke, move him to a cooler place, and give him cool water to drink. Apply cool wet towels to his head, chest, and thighs.

Ibuprofen

This made-for-people medicine can be dangerous to dogs. The same is true of aspirin (in large quantities) and Tylenol. Keep painkillers in cabinets that your dog cannot get at.

Matches and Mothballs

Matchheads contain potassium chlorate, which can trigger abdominal pain and discomfort. Induce vomiting if your Dachshund consumes them. Mothballs are poisonous to both moths and dogs. Keep your Doxie out of your closet.

Jumping

Jumping from almost any height can be bad for your Dachshund's back. If he needs to get on the furniture or bed, install a no-slip ramp with a gradient the dog can easily manage.

Loneliness

Dachshunds are house dogs and should never be relegated to the back yard except for play and exercise. Dachshunds left alone become depressed and angry. Then they start to bark. Any behaviorist will tell you that barking is one of the most difficult of all habits to break once it gets started, and Dachshunds are known barkers.

Macadamia Nuts

Honestly—I am not kidding. Macadamia nuts contain a substance that can cause rear leg weakness in dogs. Stick to less exotic treats. Dog biscuits are fine. (Ask your friends to bring you something else from Hawaii. I hear that Hawaiian coffee is great.)

Motor Oil

I don't know why your dog might be attracted to motor oil, but if he consumes any, do not induce vomiting. Get him to a vet.

Obesity

A Dachshund of the proper weight will have an hourglass figure when looked at from above. If your dog looks like a rectangle instead, he's overweight. From the side, he should have a slight "tuck up." You should be able to feel (but not see) his ribs. Fat dogs have ribs that are difficult or impossible to feel, and have no tuck-up.

Obesity doesn't just look bad; it *is* bad. It's hard on the heart, bones, spine, lungs, liver, and on the locomotive and endocrine systems. It can be a factor in inducing glucose intolerance, hyperinsulinemia, and diabetes. A fat dog is more likely to be prey to gastrointestinal problems than a thin one. Certain kinds of cancer, notably skin cancers, liver cancer, and cancer of the digestive system, are linked with obesity. An overweight dog is more likely to have constipation, diarrhea, or to exhibit irritable or aggressive behavior. He won't be able to tolerate heat. He may have dental problems owing to sweeteners in the diet. He will have less resistance to illness, will need more anesthesia during surgery, and is more challenging to operate on. Don't risk it.

Onions

Most dogs aren't crazy about onions anyway, but if your dog does chomp down on as little as a quarter cup of them (cooked or raw) he can develop acute hemolytic anemia, a temporary but severe condition. In fact, dogs have been known to need blood transfusions after dining on onions.

Pantyhose

Something about underwear attracts dogs—especially dirty underwear. This propensity may be embarrassing but it is usually harmless. Pantyhose, on the other hand, are deadly to dogs. They clog up the intestines just like carpet fringes.

Pine Oil Cleaners

Cleaners such as Pine-Sol and Lysol may be dangerous for dogs. They contain phenol or phenol derivatives, which have been implicated in liver and kidney damage. Phenols are slow-acting toxins that may affect your dog so gradually that you don't know what's happening. They are especially dangerous to puppies. If ingested, call a vet immediately.

Plants

Not all plants are deadly to Dachshunds, of course, but plenty are. Dangerous plants include almonds, amaryllis, apricot pits, autumn crocus, begonia, bleeding heart, caladium, calla lily, castor bean, choke cherry, delphinium, dumb cane, hydrangea, Jack-in-the-pulpit, Jimson weed, kalanchoe, lantana, marijuana, milkweed, mistletoe berries, morning glory, oleander, peach pits, philodendron, rhubarb leaves, rosary pea, sacred bamboo, shamrock, and yew.

Potpourri oils

Some potpourri oils can be toxic to dogs. I recommend sticking with scented candles.

Play dough, Plaster, and Putty

Although not actually poisonous, this stuff is dangerous when ingested. If your dog swallows plaster, do not induce vomiting. Call for veterinary assistance.

Rat and Mouse Poison

Many of the most common rat poisons contain warfarin, coumafuryl, pindone, valone, diphacinone, chlorophacinone, bromadiolone, or brodifacoum. These are anti-coagulant rodenticides, which cause the animal to bleed to death internally. These names are the chemical ingredients, not the product names. If you even suspect your dog has eaten any product containing one or more of these chemicals, get him to the veterinarian immediately. With vitamin K therapy, which must continue for as long as there are toxic levels of the stuff in the liver (usually about three weeks), your dog will probably recover. Another kind of rat poison contains bromethalin, which attacks the nervous system. There is no cure for the ingestion of this poison, only supportive treatment. Still other rat poisons are strychnine (induces seizures), and zinc phosphide, which damages red blood vessels. There is no antidote poisoning from zinc phosphide.

For the best treatment, your veterinarian must know what your dog swallowed. Bring any suspect package with you to the emergency clinic. Symptoms (especially in the anti-coagulant class) can be delayed for days, and by the time they appear it may be too late. *The best cure is prevention.*

Salmon

I don't recommend sushi for dogs. Raw salmon, for example, can carry a dangerous fluke.

Snail and Slug Bait

Ingested snail bait contains arsenic and is a common cause of poisoning among dogs. Although not usually fatal with good medical care, it often requires hospitalization. Symptoms include drooling, tremors, garlic smelling breath, and seizures. Arsenic can kill quickly, so induce vomiting and get your dog to a vet, who can administer an antidote.

Snakebites

Although there is no actual data concerning how many dogs are killed by venomous snakes each year, it does happen. Since Dachshunds are nosy and interested in things of the earth, they are at risk in areas where poisonous snakes abide. If a snake does bite your Doxie, stay calm. Don't grab a knife, make an X, and start sucking at the (probably) nonexistent venom. (Even when a venomous snakes bites, it does not always release its venom, which is a precious commodity.) Most snakes are not poisonous. A harmless snake leaves a horseshoe-shaped set of teeth marks, but no fang marks. By contrast, a poisonous snake leaves two fang marks. Symptoms of poison include pain, swelling, weakness, and excessive salivation.

To avoid snakebite, keep your dog on a leash in strange areas, and do not let him dig or explore holes or beneath woodpiles—a favorite snake hideout, since woodpiles attract mice, a snake's favorite food. Most snakes are more active at night, especially in the warm weather. If you live in an area where there are poisonous snakes—and that includes every state except Maine and most of Alaska, learn to identify them. This helps not only in avoiding them, but also in recognizing harmless snakes that are helpful to the environment. If your dog is bitten, take him to a veterinarian immediately. Don't bother with a tourniquet, but you can use a pressure bandage. Be sure to muzzle your dog first, who may be in great pain. Call ahead, so the vet can get the necessary antivenin from the hospital. Most vets don't keep the stuff on hand.

Stairs

No dog is meant to climb stairs—and Dachshunds are among the most likely breeds to be injured doing so. It is not only hard for them, but hard on them. If your Dachshund must get to a different floor, carry him.

Swimming Pools

Dachshunds are notoriously bad swimmers, and don't generally like water anyway. Keep your dog away from the pool.

Tar

Although tar isn't likely to kill your dog, it can be a nuisance when he gets it caught in fur or paw pads. If your Doxie does get tar stuck on him somewhere, use mineral oil or petroleum jelly to soften the tar, then wash with a mild shampoo. Never use turpentine or kerosene. They are irritating to the skin, and toxic if your dog tries to lick them off.

Tobacco

Tobacco is a poison, and although it tempts some Doxies, don't allow them to eat it; it can make them extremely sick. (The stuff doesn't do you any good either.)

Walnuts

Fresh walnuts won't hurt your dog, but moldy old walnuts can contain toxins that cause tremors and seizures.

The Good News

It isn't really hard to keep your Dachshund safe from the harmful items listed above. Being aware of the possible problems is really half the battle, and most preventive practices are just common sense. Eliminate dangerous items from your home or put them out of your dog's reach. When outside, keep your dog on a leash. If you believe your dog has ingested something that he should not have, or has been otherwise injured, take him to the veterinarian's office right away.

Chapter 9
Driving Your Dachshund

Dachshunds are singularly portable pooches. They want to go everywhere with you, and most adore riding in cars. Because they are small and easy to carry, there's simply no reason not to take your Dachshund either for drives about town, or for cross-country vacations.

Car Travel

Car travel should be routine for your Dachshund. If he doesn't enjoy riding in the auto it may be because he anticipates getting carsick (which I'll discuss later on in this chapter) or it may be because he fears the destination. If the only time he gets a ride is when he is going to the vet, you can expect trouble. If this is the case with your dog, make trips a joy for him by taking short journeys to fun places. Take him to the park or even to a new block for his daily walk. He'll be thrilled; it doesn't take much to impress a dog.

Safety First

Of course, you are responsible for your dog's safety while en route. Your Dachshund should be safely restrained in a harness or seat belt made for dogs. You wouldn't take a drive without fastening your seat belt, so give your Dachshund the same treatment. Restraining your dog is just as important for your own safety, of course. A loose dog becomes a projectile during a sudden stop, to the detriment of both of you. I heard of a case in which the dog survived the accident—but since she was loose in the car, she escaped through the broken windshield and was killed by the traffic on the road.

Although dogs aren't safe using designed-for-humans restraints, there are plenty of good canine restraint systems on the market. One restraining device I like is the Travel Tether. This product is intended for use in sport utility vehicles, wagons, and vans. Of course, you would never tether your dog in the back of pickup truck! It consists of a fully adjustable harness and tether. The best thing about it is that it safely contains your dog when you open the back of the vehicle, so he doesn't go leaping from the cargo area. Other good seat belts include the Doggie Catcher Pet Seat Belt, and the Kwik Klip Safety Harness. All good restraint devices, of course, are designed for use with a harness rather than a collar, and all should be used in the back seat.

Another easy way to keep your dog safe in the car is to use his crate. If your vehicle is large enough, a crate is probably your safest bet. Your Dachshund is at ease there and his crates serves to both keep him happy and—in case you need to brake quickly— healthy too. Remember to secure the crate in your car—a flying crate is even more dangerous than a flying dog.

A Dachshund-Friendly Design

General Motors has designed an SUV especially for you dog owners. It's called the GMC Envoy Pet Pro, and its special features include vents in the cargo area, storage units specifically designed for pet-supplies, an integrated vacuum cleaner for that pesky dog hair (and a special cover for the second row seats), and a pet safety belt integrated with the human safety belt system. The Envoy Pet Pro has a net barrier between the cargo area and the passenger seats and a pull-out tray in the cargo area so you can slide the dog crate out from the interior. Of particular interest to Doxie fans is a built-in dog ramp, a treat for you and your dog!

Whatever you use to restrain your dog in the car, the safest place for him is the backseat. Even a restrained dog can be killed by an airbag. (A device unsafe for someone as large as a 12-year-old child is not safe for a Dachshund.)

Never let your dog ride with his head out the window, even in the rare instances when he can reach up to do it. Dogs seem addicted to this activity, undoubtedly because it allows them to catch passing scents. It's a dangerous occupation, though, because grit and other debris can get lodged in the eye. You wouldn't allow your child to ride this way—so don't allow your dog to do so, either.

You can buy a window vent guard that can be installed or removed in seconds. It allows the dog to catch the scents without endangering his head or eyes. They are small enough to fold up and stick in your glove compartment. However, don't use these in place of opening the windows all the way if the dog must remain (restrained, of course) in the car. They don't let in enough fresh air to cool down a baking parked car.

Planning Ahead

If you're taking a trip of any length with your Dachshund, you'll need to plan carefully. Make a list of everything you'll need and check it off as you pack the car. Here's a good starter:

▼ Extra leashes. You might lose one, break one, or need one of a different length.

▼ Dog food, especially if you use a "designer brand" not available everywhere.

▼ Water. Puppies in particular are apt to develop diarrhea on a trip if they start sampling different water. This isn't something you want in to happen in your car.

▼ Paper towels. For everything.

▼ Dog dishes.

▼ Pooper-scooper and/or plastic bags.

▼ Veterinary first aid kit and manual.

▼ Any medication your Dachshund takes. A copy of his veterinary records, including his rabies tag and vaccination record.

▼ Dog toys and treats. Familiar objects will make your dog more comfortable.

▼ Dog bed or blanket. Another reminder of home.

▼ A recent color photo of your dog—in case the worst happens. A picture of a lost dog is worth a thousand words. Saying, "I lost my dappled Dachshund" isn't enough.

▼ A flashlight.

▼ The dog. I knew someone who, after carefully packing all the essentials, actually left her dog at home and had to drive back fifty miles to get him.

Car Sickness: Those Travel Time Blues

Gas in the tank. Bags in the trunk. Sammy belted safely in the rear seat. Key in the ignition. Ready to go. Then: B-A-O-F-R-G-H. That sound. That sight. That—that smell. Yes, Sam has just deposited his entire breakfast all over the backseat. And you're not even out of the driveway. Sound familiar?

Carsickness is one of the most common ailments of the modern dog, but you can prevent it with the right techniques. First, however, you need to understand what's causing the problem.

It's possible that the first bout of carsickness was triggered by strictly physical causes. However, the resulting nausea triggered anxiety, which triggered more sickness at even the prospect of getting in the car. Thus is born psychologically motivated carsickness. Dogs suffering from psychologically motivated carsickness become tense at the very sight of a car, and may throw up the minute they get in. They may betray their anxiety by salivating, trembling, and pacing before they are even asked to ride. Dogs who suffer from simple motion sickness have no such symptoms. They just barf when they start feeling nauseated.

The physical cause of carsickness is a stimulation of the vestibular apparatus of the inner ear. The fluid-filled semi-circular canals are connected by nerve impulses to the brain and affect the sense of equilibrium. Some dogs (and some people, like me) are particularly sensitive to the sudden stops, starts, and swaying of cars. Unfortunately, the symptoms are exacerbated in the back seat, where the dog is safest.

Dogs who suffer motion anxiety definitely need retraining, and may also need medication. As I mentioned earlier, if your dog associates riding in the car with something unpleasant, you'll need to counter-condition him with short joy rides. As he adjusts, lengthen the driving periods.

This problem won't be cured overnight. Although some kinds of medication can help, they do have side effects. Tranquilizers can have an adverse effect on blood pressure, and antihistamines, although relatively safe, don't always have the desired effect of making the dog sleepy. In a few cases, dogs treated with antihistamines become hyperactive.

Coping techniques for dogs who suffer from simple, physical motion sickness, can be the following:

▼ Travel light. Most dogs ride better on an empty stomach. Even if it doesn't stop the vomiting, at least you'll have less of it to clean up. Don't feed your dog six to eight hours before a journey—or, if he really puts up a fit—feed him very lightly. (A few dogs actually ride better on a full stomach. If your dog throws up a lot of bile rather than chunks, he's probably one of these.)

▼ Let Sammy ride shotgun. If your dog continues to be violently ill in the back seat, you may have to resort to moving him to the front, although it is less safe. Most dogs prefer riding in the front seat. Front seat riding gives your dog a good view of the horizon, which seems to help prevent nausea. Besides, it's usually less bumpy up there. Just attach his seat belt to the front and put the kids in the back where they belong anyway.

▼ Drive slowly and go easy on those turns. Pretending the family car is a ride at the amusement park is not calculated to relieve either your dog's travel sickness or his nervousness. You'll also be a lot less likely to hit a deer.

▼ Take a break. Stop the car every few hours to give your dog a breather and a walk. A walk will allow your pet to relieve himself. Give him plenty of opportunity to do this.

▼ Don't leave the car running. If your dog must remain briefly in the car, turn off the motor, unless you have to run the air conditioner. Gas fumes make pets sick.

▼ Cool down. Keep the car ventilated with fresh cool air. Crack the windows. Dogs, because of their arctic heritage, like it colder than we do. Crank up the air conditioning and put on a sweater.

▼ Crate your dog. It won't help with the carsickness, but it will localize the vomit and make cleanup easier.

▼ Herbalize. Many people use holistic remedies for carsickness. Chief among these is ginger, which can be bought in extracts at health food stores. (Extracts work better than capsules for dogs.) Give a Dachshund one quarter to one half the dose recommended for a person. Alternatively, give your dog a ginger snap cookie. Peppermint also works well for this purpose.

▼ Medicate. Dramamine (Dimenhydrinate) is a commonly used over-the-counter antihistamine that can reduce or halt canine carsickness. The usual dosage is between 25 to 50 mgs. three times a day, or 1 or 2 mgs. for every pound of body weight. Give the medicine about an hour before traveling. Most dogs tolerate this drug best if you give a little food with it. Dramamine won't help if your dog is already sick, however. *Do not give Dramamine if your dog has bladder problems, hyperthyroidism, seizure disorders, or glaucoma.* The effectiveness of Dramamine diminishes with repeated use, so this "remedy" is best for urgent situations only.

Air Travel

It's a new world we're living in. Considering the uncertain state of travel, I would never put my dog on a plane unless he was going to travel in the passenger area under my seat. If you absolutely must, must, must fly your dog and can't sit with him, and you can't use one of the new door-to-door travel services for dogs, call the airline for the *latest* information. Most airlines require health certificates for all animals transported by air. The health certificate must be provided by a veterinarian within 10 days of transport.

In general, it's best to book a direct, midweek flight or a flight with only one stop. In the summer, select an early morning or late evening flight when the plane is coolest.

Your dog will need to be in a crate that meets the following criteria:

▼ Large enough to allow the animal to stand, turn, and lie down stretched out.

▼ Sturdy, without interior protrusions. It must have handles or grips.

▼ Leak-proof bottom, lined with plenty of absorbent material.

▼ Food and water dishes must be securely attached and be accessible without opening the crate.

▼ Ventilation on opposite sides, with exterior rims or knobs to prevent blocked airflow. According to regulations, the ventilation openings must make up at least 14 percent of the total wall space.

▼ Label "Live Animal," in large (at least one-inch) letters, with arrows indicating the upright position, and your name, address, and phone number.

▼ Instructions for feeding, watering, and administering medications to the dog over a twenty-four hour period must be attached to the crate, in case the plane is diverted from its original destination. The shipper (that's you) is required to document that the animal was given food and water within four hours of transport, and the certification must include the time and date of the feeding. Puppies under sixteen weeks old must be provided with food every twelve hours. Adult dogs must be fed every twenty-four hours and given fresh water every twelve hours.

▼ Except on the advice of your veterinarian, don't tranquilize or sedate the dog before flying. These drugs can interfere with his heat regulatory system.

Dachshunds on Holiday

More than forty million pets vacation with their owners annually. Dachshunds adore spending time with their owners and it's great for both of you if you get away together. To ensure that the trip is fun, some planning is a must.

Vet Care Away from Home

If your Dachshund becomes ill while traveling, you can call the American Animal Hospital Association (AAHA) member services at 1-800-883-6301. They are open between 7:00 AM and 5:00 PM Mountain Time. By using the zip code of your location, a staff member will refer you to the AAHA member veterinary clinic closest to you.

Reserving Accommodations

Be sure to be honest with the hotel about your four-legged friend. When making your room reservations, get confirmation in writing that having a dog in the room is permitted. You don't want to show up and be told that there must be some mistake and dogs aren't allowed. Your confirmation is your security.

At the Hotel, Motel, or Campsite

One of the reasons that dogs cause trouble when traveling is that their much-beloved routine has been shattered. Your Dachshund is in a new place, with strange things happening, and strange people all around. He may get unsettled, nervous, or downright scared. If you have to leave him alone for any length of time, he might also get bored. Any of these emotional states can cause him to behave in a less desirable way.

Rules vary from place to place, but basic etiquette does not. Do not attempt to sneak your dog in. Declare your Dachshund! Of course you will always clean up after your dog, in the room or out, and will respect all rules regarding animals.

If you have to walk your male dog through the lobby, go quickly. Do not stop and allow him to sniff anything. The next step after sniffing something is peeing on it. It's best if you can go directly from your car to the room.

Most motels will not allow you to bathe your pet in their bathtub. They also require your dog to be crated when you are gone. There's a good reason for this. My sweet wonderful dog, who never did anything untoward at home, destroyed the motel room I left him in uncrated. I was only gone five minutes, but that was enough for the dog to tear apart three pillows and chew a hole through the quilt.

Keep your dog clean and well-brushed. The more you brush him outside, the less he'll shed inside, which is good news for the custodial staff. Remember, you don't want the facility to start turning dogs away. Make his stay hassle-free for everyone. And when you leave, give a nice a tip to the cleaning folks. Leave them with a positive feeling.

Health Check

It's always a good idea to have your dog examined by the vet before you leave on a trip and again when you return.

Boarding Your Dachshund

As much as we'd like to, we can't always take our dogs with us. Boarding kennels are a fact of life for most owners. And because there are about 6,500 of them across America—you should be able to find a good one near you.

Get referrals from friends and talk to your vet before deciding on a kennel. If you decide to try out an unfamiliar kennel, ask the management to give you references and call them. Before you board your dog, however, be sure you check the place out personally. When you return from your trip, you certainly want your Dachshund to be healthy and happy.

Cleanliness

The importance of a clean kennel can hardly be overstated. No dog should be left at a place where the floor is littered with dog poop. Use your nose as well as your eyes to assess cleanliness!

Your Dachshund Can be a Wonderful Guest

Happy, social, well-adjusted dogs adapt to boarding kennels much more easily. This is just one more benefit of socializing your dog properly from puppyhood on!

Space

Kennels should provide runs that are worthy of the name "run." Your Dachshund should have plenty of room to exercise. (Rectangular runs save space and encourage your dog to exercise. For some reason, dogs prefer running up and down a rectangle to running around in a circle. Perhaps they think they are getting somewhere.) The best kennels are equipped with connected indoor and outdoor runs. The surface of the run should provide good traction. All exercise areas should have shade and shelter from the wind.

To help prevent the transmission of disease, each run should be separate from the next. Nose-to-nose contact can spread diseases.

Security

All fencing should be strong and in excellent repair. Dachshunds are escape artists, and the last thing you want is to have your dog run away in unfamiliar territory. The best kennel facilities have fences around the *entire* perimeter—not just the kennel runs. And while your Doxie is not likely to jump over a fence, he is remarkably capable of digging under it. If your Dachshund makes a break for it when the door opens, it's important to have another line of safety—just in case. In addition, be sure to inform the kennel management if your Dachshund is a runner. The staff will want to take extra precautions.

Provisions

Examine the water available to the dogs. It should be fresh and clean. The pails should sparkle. Dirty buckets half-filled with drooly water are a bad sign. Good kennels also provide plenty of clean, safe toys for their boarders, or allow you to bring your dog's own favorites.

Comfort

Kennels should be warm in winter, cool in summer, and free from drafts and flies at all seasons. Most good boarding kennels today are heated and air-conditioned. Expect no less. You're probably paying enough for it. Some kennels go even further, and provide your pet with a truly homelike environment, complete with couches and rugs. Even so, bring along your dog's own bed, so he will know he has not been completely abandoned, (although he may do his very best to make you feel like a villain for leaving him).

Good kennels are also relatively quiet. Although all dogs are expected to make some noise, the best kennels cut down on the racket by limiting the number of dogs per building. On the other hand, dogs require socialization. Check to see how the kennel staff provides playtime for suitable dogs.

Services

Inquire about the services the kennel provides. Most boarding kennels hire groomers and some have a veterinary technician on hand. Good kennels have staff available to walk and play with your dog. Some come with extras like massage!

For more information, check out the American Boarding Kennel's pamphlet: "How to Select a Boarding Kennel." It can be ordered from ABKA at 4575 Galley Road, Suite 400A, Colorado Springs, CO 80915. Or you can telephone (719) 591-1113, fax (719) 597-0006 or e-mail: info@abka.com. In addition, the Web site: www.abka.com. provides a list of member kennels, sorted by city and state, along with tips and other information.

Daycare for Dachshunds

If you work all day and your dog is Home Alone—you might consider enrolling him in doggy daycare. Whether he would attend once or twice a week, or every day depends on his needs—and your pocketbook. Most dogs love spending their days playing with other dogs, getting attention, and having their every need catered to. This is also a dream-come-true for busy working owners who know their dogs need more attention than they are currently getting. Instead of coming home to a desperate-to-go-out, anxious, and lonely pet, you'll pick up your happy, tired, and ready to be cuddled love-muffin.

To find a good doggy daycare facility, ask around. Your friends, veterinarian, dog trainer, boarding kennel, groomer, or kennel club may have some suggestions. Of course you will check out the facility before committing your dog to its care. Good daycare has a low staff-to-dog ratio, has sparkling clean facilities, and has plenty for your dog to do. The best places have safe indoor and outdoor play areas, nap spaces, and toys. While you can't expect a doggy daycare center to be totally silent (you wouldn't want it to be) it should not be filled with the sounds of whining, moaning, and shrieking either. Watch the staff interact with the dogs and note the dogs' demeanor. They should seem happy to arrive and not appear frightened or lonely.

Ask questions about how introductions and socialization are handled, health requirements, and what is done about aggressive dogs. Some daycare centers offer grooming and bathing services in addition to supervision. Although doggy daycare isn't cheap, it's within the price range of most people, especially if they use it only once or twice a week. Expect to pay anywhere from $15 to $35 per day depending on your geographic location and the services provided.

Chapter 10

Dachshund Deportment: Training Your Doxie

We all know that a well-trained dog is a delight and pleasure to be around. But a puppy doesn't come into the world already trained, and a Dachshund is going to present you with an exciting challenge in that department. Start your training regime early—very early. Dachshunds are hounds, and hounds were bred for perseverance, determination, and confidence in their own abilities. Dachshunds think for themselves, and dogs who think for themselves are more challenging to train than "robo-dogs" whose main thrill in life is to stand around waiting to be

Your Attention Please

One of the most useful tactics in training your dog is to observe him. The better you know your dog, the more carefully you actually look at him, the better experience you will have in training him. In fact, dogs are a lot better in reading us than vice versa. They can even pick up signals we don't know we are sending. Much of what is mysterious in dog training could be solved if we paid as much attention to the signals we are giving as to those we think the dog is getting.

Rosie "breakdancing" in the grass   *Photo courtesy of Karen & Rickie Maddox*

told what to do next. Dachshunds always know what to do next without any directions from their owners. Unfortunately.

Socializing Your Puppy

Because behavior, good or bad, is habitual, the main thing to do is get your Doxie started early in the habit of behaving well. That means puppy classes.

Puppy Classes

Puppy classes are important for several reasons. First, they socialize your dog. Dogs who aren't accustomed to being around other dogs can become aggressive toward them when they do meet. Dogs used to being around other dogs take more cheerfully to meeting new playmates. This is why even very experienced dog owners take their pups to puppy kindergarten.

Second, puppy classes help you bond with your dog. Working together toward a training goal gives you quality time together. You will learn not only what to teach your dog, but how to teach him. This time together will help you understand how he thinks, what's important to him, and what motivates him.

Third, your dog will actually start learning those basic commands! Of course, you can also teach them to your dog yourself, and I'll show you how, but individual obedience lessons are not a replacement for socialization. If you can't find a suitable puppy class, you'll need to undertake his socialization yourself by taking him out for frequent walks to meet others—both human and canine, and by inviting people into your home so you're your Doxie can learn the joys of entertaining company. (Even if you do go to puppy class once or twice a week, you'll still need to expand his horizons.)

Learning in the Litter

Socialization is the first and most critical element of training. In normal circumstances, the mother dog takes care of the first step. In the first three weeks of life, the mother *is* the puppy's life. A puppy's eyes don't even open until he is ten days old or more, and the ears open a few days later. A blind, deaf puppy is primarily interested in touching and feeling his mom near him. (Interestingly, it's been shown that close and frequent handling by human beings seems to have not only socialization value for puppies—but it also appears to help them resist disease.) During the fourth week, when the ears and eyes are fully open, the first real socialization begins. Frequently picking up and holding puppies is essential for this purpose. If breeders are too "busy," and skip this step, both the puppies and eventual owners will pay for it later.

The fifth to seventh weeks of life are crucial for puppy development. The puppy is learning to differentiate himself from others—and also learning to find his place in the litter and family hierarchy. He is learning how to interact with his littermates in complex ways. At this stage, a puppy will respond to sounds and appears to be able to tell one person from another. A dog who is removed from the litter too early may never attain proper socialization skills, and he may struggle for dominance over his human owners. This is simply because he was separated from the litter before he attained proper "appeasement" skills from his mother.

Your Job as Social Director

During the eight to twelve week period, a puppy is able to form lasting bonds with people. Any bad experiences during this time can permanently damage his psyche and his ability to trust others. It is during this critical period that most puppies go to their new homes.

Now that the mother and breeder had done their part, you must do yours. Your dog is approaching adolescence, and the thirteen to sixteen week period can be a challenging one. For your dog to be a welcome part of his family and the larger community, he needs to view his world as a friendly place. It's your job to make this his reality. You have two goals in this endeavor. First, to have him make friends at home, and second, to help him make friends abroad.

Too many dogs today live isolated lives. The less often your dog leaves home, the more likely he is to regard the house and yard as his sole domain—one he must guard from any and all intruders. Dachshunds are natural watchdogs, and yours will undoubtedly alert you to the presence of visitors regardless of his lifestyle. To let him know that visitors are friendly and welcome, practice with your long-suffering friends. Have them ring the bell, use the knocker, or just open the door and yell, "Anybody home?" the way we do around my house. The "visitor" should carry treats in hand, and everyone should praise the dog when he acts in a friendly way, neither shy nor hostile. If your letter carrier is friendly (largely determined by how big a tip you leave him at Christmas) you can ask him to drop a dog biscuit in with the mail if you have a mail-slot. Leave one taped to the door.

When going out, take your dog everywhere, and have him meet people of both genders, all ages, of all races and sizes and dress, bearded and bald. Get him accustomed to people with all sorts of accoutrements, such as canes, bikes, wheelchairs, skateboards, and grocery bags. I have known dogs suspicious of people wearing hats, sunglasses, or overcoats. If your dog seems skittish around new people, obtain the assistance of friendly strangers by asking them to give your dog a small treat. (You'll have to hand it to them first, of course. Believe it or not, not everyone carries dog biscuits around all the time.)

Restrict the number of field trips with your new puppy until he has had his second set of shots. That doesn't mean you shouldn't take him out at all, but to prevent him from contracting a contagious disease, you should limit his contacts with other dogs. Be particularly careful when going for a walk in the park, because some people do not clean up after their dogs, and many viral diseases are carried in feces (and your curious puppy will want to investigate everything he finds). Make it a habit to check your own shoes when returning from a walk—you may have stepped in something unpleasant yourself.

When you do make your first venture away from home, don't feed your puppy immediately before leaving. The intense excitement of going on a trip may cause an upset stomach and subsequent upchuck—not the best way to impress your friends with your adorable new Doxie. It's also a good idea to exercise your puppy before bringing him to a new place. The thrill of being in a new house may well make him wish to christen it. Or worse. This brings us to the next topic.

Dachshunds in Diapers: Housetraining Your Doxie

Dachshunds are hounds. I've said this before, and I'll say it again. Although this seems like a neutral, value-free statement, it isn't. Hounds have certain characteristics, such as determination and resolution, that set them apart from lesser breeds. While many of these qualities are admirable, they don't always translate well into ease of housetraining.

However, you can housetrain your Dachshund, as long as you pay close attention to your dog's perspective. One way to do this is to follow my C.R.A.P.S. system of housetraining. Here it is—in a nutshell:

C	Crate
R	Reward
A	Attention
P	Patience
S	Schedule

Crate

If your dog accepts his crate as his sleeping den, he will be less likely to use it as a toilet. Dogs simply don't like to eliminate where they sleep. This is why a large crate can be a handicap in housetraining; it may give a dog a place to "go" other than the place he sleeps. If your dog does tend to eliminate in his crate, it could be that he is drawn to do so by an absorbent mat or bedding. Use plain newspapers until he gets the idea.

Of course, you can't keep your dog in a crate longer than his bowels and bladder can stand! Remember that puppies have tiny bladders, and that their sphincters are insufficiently developed to hold waste for an inordinate period. I would never keep a puppy in a crate for more than two hours, except at night, when he is supposed to be sleeping anyway. Keeping a dog in a crate for long periods is extremely detrimental to his physical, mental, and spiritual health. Sooner or later, he will also start eliminating in the crate—and if he doesn't, he may be well on his way to developing bladder stones. Further, excessive crating turns a happy, curious puppy into a bored-out-of-his-skull monster waiting to break out and get into trouble. The frustrated owner then responds by crating the puppy even more, and the vicious cycle continues. Crating should be done for housetraining purposes only.

Reward

Always reward your puppy, or for that matter, an untrained older dog, with praise or a treat when he eliminates outdoors. If he responds to praise, that's best. Overwhelm the dog with praise—jump for joy! Let him know that you are *thrilled* with his behavior. Most Dachshunds are truly eager to please you (even if they try to hide it). Another treasured reward is a walk. Some people take the dog out, let him eliminate, and then immediately bring the dog back in. The message the Doxie is getting is that as soon as he eliminates, it's back in the house. As a result, he may try to hold it as long as possible. Then the owner decides the dog doesn't have to go, gives up, and brings the dog inside. Then the dog poops in the kitchen. Instead, give your dog a walk or a play session as soon as he's successful, and let him see that as a reward. (If you do take your Dachshund out for a long walk and don't get a result, try bringing him in and then *immediately* taking him out again. He may have forgotten his duties during the excitement of the walk and doesn't remember until he's back inside.) *Never punish your dog for making a mistake. Don't yell, strike him (even with a newspaper) or rub his nose in it. These practices are cruel and ineffective.*

Attention

Your dog will give you signals that he needs to go out, but it's up to you to learn how he sends this message. Sometimes, it is true, a dog will do something refreshingly obvious like actually going to the door. But don't expect that, at least not at first. It's more likely that your dog will give you more subtle signs, such as licking his lips, circling, looking puzzled or, if you're really lucky, actually whining. The instant you notice these signals, grab the leash and take out the dog. Don't simply put the dog out and hope all will be well. Go out with the dog, so you can praise his success. If you don't go with him, he will assume that he is being punished with exile or for giving a signal that he needs to eliminate. Soon he'll stop giving the signal.

Patience

You wouldn't expect to toilet train a child in a week—so don't expect your Dachshund to be reliable after only a few days either. By properly using the crate, watching your dog like a hawk, and keeping to a schedule, you'll encourage the proper response from him. A puppy will inevitably make some mistakes. If you don't find it until after the fact, simply clean it up without comment. If you catch the puppy in the act, scoop him up, tuck the tail between the legs (this helps prevent "spillage"), and say, "Out!" or "Quick!" Don't say "No." Dogs learn quickly that "No" is a negative word, and the puppy may think that eliminating is wrong, regardless of where it occurs. If he gets that idea, he'll start hiding it, and that's the worst.

Schedule

Dogs not only like a routine, it's also good for them. Put your puppy on a regular feeding and elimination schedule as soon as possible. The more regular the schedule, the easier it will be to housetrain your dog. This may mean you will have to take some time off from work or hire a puppy sitter during the housetraining process (which usually takes about two weeks if you do everything right). This may seem like an extreme measure—but believe me, it makes all the difference. Although some dogs have a different schedule, your puppy usually needs to eliminate after naps, after meals, after playtime, first thing in the morning, and last thing at night. You may have one who needs to go out when you're eating, when you're in the shower, when you're on a conference call, during the last five minutes of *The West Wing*, in the middle of the night, and during moments of most intense interaction with your significant other. This is part of the wonder of owning a Dachshund. There's something psychic about them.

Keep Housetraining Simple

Paper-training can be confusing for your dog and I don't recommend it. It's better to begin the way you want your dog to finish—completely housetrained. One exception to this rule is for people who live in high rises. You may want to paper- or litter-train your dog in addition to taking him out. If you do this, think of it as a permanent alternative, not a temporary step, however.

Housetraining Helpers

At my house, we are lucky enough to have a dog door. (With eight dogs, we really need it!) This is the ideal circumstance for most dogs and owners. If you are comfortable with the idea of an autonomous dog, you can't beat the dog door. Of course, they are not practical (or possible) for every household.

Summertime Tip

On hot summer days, your Dachshund will be drinking more water. Consequently, he'll need to go out more frequently. Don't even considering limiting his access to water at these times; it can be dangerous. Dogs are frequent victims of heatstroke.

Some people hang bells or other devices on the door—encouraging the dog to let them know when they need to go out. Although this technique works, the dog soon figures out that ringing the bell translates into an outdoor excursion on demand. Soon you may be traipsing outside every fifteen minutes.

One of the latest rages is litter-training for small dogs. It really does work and is convenient if you live in an upper-level apartment or are gone for a large part of the day. However, this practice does have disadvantages. Dachshunds are great diggers and will tend to scatter the litter everywhere. (I recommend putting the litter tray in a marginal area of the house, such as a utility or laundry room. Besides, who wants a litter tray in the kitchen?) Another potential problem with litter- or paper-training is that it "breaks the taboo" of not peeing indoors. Some dogs get very careless over time about this, and start eliminating everywhere! And because it really isn't natural for dogs to eliminate inside, don't expect litter-training a dog to be as easy as litter-training a cat. Sadly, some people think that because their dog is litter-trained, they needn't take him out regularly. Not true! Dachshunds need to get exercise and need to out and explore the world, regardless of where they eliminate. Don't punish your dog for good behavior!

A Toilet for Toto

One of my favorite products along this line is Wizdog—not so much a litter tray as an "indoor toilet." It comes in two parts—a tray, and a grid. The grid drains away the urine and allows it collect at the bottom of the tray. Solid waste can be easily removed as well.

Accidents Happen...

If your puppy has an accident on the carpet, dilute the spot with a dampened cloth. Then clean the area with an acid solution. You can make it yourself using a solution of one quart water mixed with one teaspoon white vinegar. You may also wish to use a bacteria/enzyme digester like Nature's Miracle. These get rid of the both the stain and the odor. The latter is very important—even if you can't smell the urine, your dog can, and will only be encouraged to re-use the spot. For best results, make sure you use enough of the product to penetrate both the carpet and the pad. And leave it on for the required length of time. Enzyme digesters work very well, but they are not quick fixes. After you put down the solution, cover the area with plastic and step on it a few times to ensure the spot is well-saturated. Keep the plastic in place so the digester doesn't dry out.

Never use an ammonia product to clean up urine. Ammonia smells like urine to dogs and it will only encourage them to use that spot again.

Yard Care

It's best to choose one area of your yard to use as your Dachshund's elimination area. Doing so reinforces the notion that there is a right place to go. And it reduces the damage to your yard—those ugly yellow and brown spots you see all over your lawn are burns from urine and feces. A good chemical remedy is K-9 Turf, which is safe for both pets and kids. It's an all-natural product that doubles as a lawn fertilizer. Use it once a month and your problems should be over.

Besides keeping your yard picked up regularly, you can add products like Grassaver or G-Whiz to your dog's diet. They act to neutralize your dog's urine and control odors. However, don't use these products without an okay from your vet. The urinary tract tends to be acidic for a reason, and raising the pH of your dog's diet might lead to bladder stones. Other products like Spot Check, Dogonit, and Green-Um, sprayed or sprinkled on the damaged area, will help re-establish grass. If you actually catch your dog in the act, rinse the grass (but not the dog) immediately with two or three gallons of water.

Basic Obedience Training

The basic rule of dog-obedience is this. You are a *kind boss*. Successful interactions with your pooch depend upon your developing equal skills in both the kindness and the boss departments. Kindness is essential. Without it, your dog will become an angry, fearful, dysfunctional mess. But being boss is important too. Unless you are willing to become leader of the pack, *you* are the one who will turn into the angry, fearful, dysfunctional wreck.

Dachshunds love kindness and appreciate good leadership. Because they are social animals, dogs understand that getting along in the world depend upon these things. You show your kindness by frequent praise, patience, rewards, and reasonable expectations. You show your leadership by setting consistent goals, responding firmly, and letting your dog know his natural place in the hierarchy—which is always below all humans.

To get the most out of working with your dog, you'll need to find out what most strongly motivates him. Usually, this is food, although some Doxies respond well to simple praise or a moment of playtime.

Treat Tip

If you use food as the primary motivator when training, remember that treats add calories to your dog's diet—and Doxies are one of the breeds most prone to dangerous obesity. So, when I mention using a morsel of treat as a reward, that's what I mean—a morsel. If you're giving a lot of treats, you'll have to cut back on his meals. And if that's the case, the treats must contain the necessary nutrients to make up for going light on dinner.

Dachshunds do not respond well to punishment. Punishing a dog is a negative behavior on your part that *reinforces* rather than changes your dog's actions. If your Dachshund is exhibiting a Dachshund Moment ("I'll Do As I Like, and to Heck With You") simply stop interacting with him. Some Doxie trainers put their dog in his crate for a brief time while they are (apparently) having a joyful time sitting, staying, and rolling over. Soon the Dachshund is rethinking his attitude, and will want to join the fun.

To be effective, training must be fun, and it must always take advantage of the Dachshund's native desires to hunt and chase, as well as to please. (Unlike some other hounds, Dachshunds do enjoy pleasing their owners, as well as being the center of attention.)

Here are my five basic principles of successful dog training, the TRAIN system:

T   Timing
R   Reward
A   Attention
I   Individualized
N·   Natural

Timing

One of the most overlooked, yet critical, elements in dog training is timing. Good timing has many aspects. First, it means starting to train your puppy early. The earlier you begin working with him (while knowing his limits, of course) the faster and more reliable your results will be. Young puppies are more dependent on their owners than older dogs and this is the age when they most eagerly seek their owner's approval. Take advantage. As your Doxie ages and becomes more independent, he'll be more difficult to train. You *can* teach an old dog new tricks, but no one ever said it would be easy.

A second aspect of good timing is deciding when in the day to schedule lessons. You want to pick a time when you yourself are relaxed, of course. A tense, tired trainer is by definition not a good trainer. You also want to choose a time when your dog is neither exhausted nor hyper, and a time when he is hungry enough to want to work for treats, but not too hungry to listen.

A third part of good timing is the amount of time you allocate to lessons. Puppies get bored easily, so don't work for more than five minutes at a time when you start. Later on, you can work up to fifteen minutes or so. You can include several short training sessions throughout the day. Training is much more effective when the session ends on a successful note—in other words, quit while you're ahead.

Reward

All dogs like working for rewards, and Dachshunds appreciate rewards more than most. So your goal in working with your hound is to convince him that what you want him to do is more rewarding than any alternatives. "Rewards" in this case can

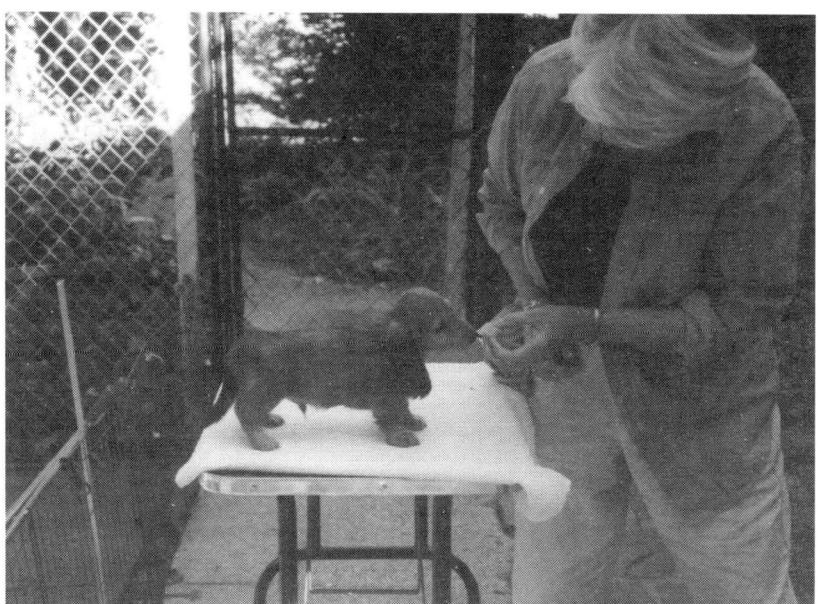

A reward for good work   *Photo courtesy of Edith Colaneri*

mean food, praise, clicks (if you do clicker training), playtime, or caresses. Laboratory dogs work for food best, but a well-socialized, happy Dachshund at home should also respond to praise.

Attention

In terms of dog training, "attention" runs two ways. One of the most important (and trickiest) parts of Dachshund training is to get your dog to look at you. This is important because if the dog isn't paying attention, you can't get him to respond. Looking up at you is harder for Doxies than for most dogs, because frankly, Dachshunds have to look from a lot further away. But it can be done, for all that. The trick is to reward your dog whenever he meets your glance. At first you may have to use treats as a reward, but soon he'll respond to praise, clicks, or even a smile and nod. Once contact is established, training can proceed.

You also have to pay attention to your dog. By carefully noting his responses and progress, you'll be able to hone your training program to suit him—which brings me to the next element.

Individualized

Every dog is different. Some dogs respond to treats, some to clicks, some to praise. Some dogs need a firmer hand than others. Some dogs won't fetch. Others have problems staying in a long down. Some can't stand the idea of coming on command. What works with one dog may fail with another. Always keep your options open, and be flexible. If you work with a trainer, look for one who is willing to modify her trainings methods if they aren't getting results.

Natural

Successful trainers study canine behavior and use natural behaviors to help train. For instance, dogs naturally follow a leader—so good trainers become good leaders. Dogs have a natural prey drive—this drive can be harnessed to teach them to "fetch." They have a natural desire to please their pack leader, as well. The more you study the natural behavior of dogs, and the more closely you can link training to natural tendencies, the more successful your training efforts will be.

Dachshunds on Leashes

Dachshunds are safest outside when in a securely fenced area or on a leash. Even a Doxie who has excelled at obedience training is likely to ignore his schooling if he is confronted with a delectable scent of rabbit, squirrel, or the dog next door. Your Dachshund may be one of the *few* who is always reliable off-lead, but is it worth risking his life to find out? My friend Melinda and her husband went walking along the beach with their Dachshund Chloe. Chloe's favorite occupation was to chase the waves, so she was allowed off lead to enjoy her game. Melinda's attention was distracted for a few minutes with one of her other dogs—and when she turned around, Chloe had disappeared. Melinda and her husband looked endlessly along the beach for her. Envisioning the Dachshund having been swallowed up by the ocean (or one of its denizens) they returned sadly home. Happily, Chloe was sitting on the front porch waiting for them—but they didn't let this turn of events happen again.

When Dachshunds were first developed, there were no cars and few busy roads—just acres and acres of fields. Times have changed, but your Dachshund's propensity to wander off in search of that ever-elusive badger has not. To keep your Doxie safe, keep him leashed. You cannot begin leash-training too early, either. The sooner you begin, the more successful you will be.

To train your puppy to a leash, allow him to walk about dragging a short leash to his buckle collar. (Watch him, of course.) He'll soon get used to it and ignore it. Then take the end and call gently to him. He will toddle up (and you'll be teaching the "Come" command at the same time.) Walk along and urge him to follow you—with treats if need be. Use the reward system. Most dogs learn to walk on a leash very quickly. To help keep his attention, change directions frequently as you walk. If your Dachshund is a puller, it is usually because he is anticipating his walk with great pleasure. To keep the situation under control, wait until the dog is sitting or standing quietly before you attach the leash. If he starts pulling on the walk, stop walking and wait for at least fifteen seconds. When the dog stops pulling, you may resume the walk. Soon your Dachshund will get the idea. He's not stupid.

Teaching Commands

The real purpose of training a dog is to make him a pleasant companion. But training serves other purposes as well—and can sometimes save your dog's life. The following pages discuss some of the most important commands (or "cues" as they are often called nowadays).

"Come!"

Dogs are natural followers. When you first start teaching the "Come!" command, move away from your dog, and encourage him to follow by calling softly to him. (Dogs can see a moving target more clearly than a stationary one.) Chances are he'll follow you. Just in case, however, keep a leash attached to him for all the early lessons. For more directed training, you'll need a long lead or piece of rope. This is not to force the dog, but to encourage him. And if you need to use a treat, do so. That doesn't mean you always have to give him a treat; in fact the intermittent-reward system is more effective than consistent rewards. It's one of those psychological things; it works with people too.

When Not to Call Your Dog

Never call your Dachshund for anything unpleasant like punishment, baths, or medication. When you have to give your dog a pill, you'll need to go after him yourself. You don't want to teach him that coming to you may not be a good idea.

To encourage your Dachshund to come, you must make yourself the most enchanting object in the vicinity. Move, jump, sweet talk, initiate play, offer a treat—anything get him to make the right move. Then praise him extravagantly.

When your dog approaches, praise him with every step. If he doesn't come, gently draw the leash toward you, still encouraging him. Don't jerk on it. The purpose of the leash is to help him focus. You don't want your dog to get the idea that it's even thinkable to go in a direction other than the one you're calling him to. When he responds by taking some steps in the right direction, praise him. When he reaches you, treat him. If he seems reluctant, try kneeling down so you are at the same level. Lean back and open your arms as you call him. This inviting gesture usually elicits a positive response.

Run Away–Not After

Never chase your dog, not even in play. You can't catch him, and it only encourages him to run in the opposite direction. Get him to chase *you*.

Practice calling your Dachshund to you several times a day. When he gets really good at it (at least two weeks of perfect behavior), experiment off lead in a secure area. (His response to the "Come!" command should be absolutely foolproof before you call him in an unfenced spot.) Don't practice (yet) in times of high excitement or lots of distractions. He won't be able to concentrate, and that will practically guarantee a failure. It's all a matter of simple psychology. You need to be more interesting to your dog than anything else.

"Leave it!"

Young dogs are always getting into trash, diapers, and expensive shoes. Start teaching your Doxie to drop such objects by waiting until he is chewing on something he really doesn't care *that* much about. (It should also be an item that's not important to you, either.) As he's chewing away, say "Leave it!" Offer him a tasty treat in exchange, something he likes better than whatever it is he's got. (Bacon and liver are great favorites.) If he doesn't let go, place your hands gently near the jaw-hinges and deftly remove the article. Give him a small treat as a reward and praise him when he accepts the exchange. Make sure you "win" the article. If you allow the puppy to win even once, you've set a bad precedent. Food and possession guarding is instinctive behavior (wild canids who were lackadaisical about their meals went hungry and died), and the only way you can overcome it is to apply equally instinctive "I'm the alpha around here, Fido! Now surrender the article!" Dogs who are territorial are likely also to be food and possession possessive, although the reverse is not necessary true.

In real life, you'd be most likely to use the "Leave it!" command when the dog has gotten into something really irresistible like a deer carcass, so your established reward needs to be very powerful. Of course, you probably won't have any bacon actually on hand when the infraction occurs, but it's okay to cheat that one time. Afterward, practice "Leave it!" several more times with your accustomed treat and plenty of praise.

"Stay"

Although some folks, teach "Stay" as a separate command, I prefer to use "Sit," which means "sit there until I say 'OK!'" I believe that teaching "Stay" as a separate command is confusing to dogs, since you're not asking them to do anything new—you're just asking them to keep doing what you have already asked them to do. However, other people believe that saying

Photo courtesy of Butch & Joyce Sheridan

"Stay" signals to the dog early that he'll be sitting for quite some time. At any rate, never ask your dog to sit-stay for more than a few seconds when you are starting out. You want to make success easy for him.

"Sit"

Although "Sit" is not a really critical command, dogs learn it easily, and it's fun to teach. Consequently you both feel as if you have accomplished something. To teach your Dachshund to sit, take a tasty morsel and hold it just above his nose. Say "Sit" in a gentle, encouraging way and move the treat back over the dog's head. He will sit on his own. Don't attempt to push down his hindquarters. This use of force is unnatural and can even injure a Dachshund. Remember this is a breed whose back is very susceptible to injury.

"Down"

While the dog is sitting, hold the treat in front of his face and gradually lower it to the ground between his front legs. The Dachshund should lie down as well. Some dogs resist this position because it makes them feel vulnerable. However, if your dog has confidence in your leadership, you should be able to teach him to lie down.

Do Not Teach "Beg!"

Please don't teach your Dachshund to sit up straight and beg. This action compresses the spine and puts your dog in serious danger of intervertebral disk disease. (It also is not a behavior you want to encourage. Begging is not particularly charming.)

Formal Training

It doesn't hurt to reinforce what you've learned at home by taking your Dachshund to formal obedience classes. Obedience classes also double as socialization events, so you'll really be getting a lot for your money. Before you go, know exactly what you are looking for from the class. Some classes focus on household manners and basic commands, while others prepare you for formal obedience work. Choose the class—and the teacher—that best fits your needs. It may be worthwhile to visit the class first, and observe the teacher in action. You want someone who understands the Dachshund's unique psyche—a combination of willfulness and sensitivity that requires very enlightened teaching. Avoid any teacher who relies on force, choke chains, or harsh or punitive methods.

The most "advanced" level of trainer is probably someone who has been certified by the Animal Behavior Society. Most of these people are veterinarians or Ph.D.s, and there are fewer of fifty of them in the entire world, so don't count on running across one soon. Someone with a graduate degree in animal behavior may use the title "animal behaviorist." Trainers without the degree but with the experience may call themselves "behavior consultants" or "behavior counselors." More important than the degree is the style of the trainer. Don't be afraid to shop around and find someone whose styles "clicks" with your dog (even if they don't use a clicker.)

You want an instructor who is willing to listen to you, and to help you achieve the goals you have set for yourself and your dog. You may want to contact the Association of Pet Dog Trainers at 800-PET-DOGS, to find a trainer in your area.

Ch. Von Maser's New Heart, a miniature, red longhair   *Photo courtesy of Joella Maser*

Chapter 11
The Difficult Dachshund

Although most Dachshunds are perfect in every way, it does appear that (admittedly on rare occasions) a tiny minority of them can be difficult dogs. Perhaps "difficult" is not the word. I have heard them described in even harsher language, if you can believe that. Demanding. Dysfunctional. Depraved. Demented. But this is unfair.

Sometimes Dachshunds get placed in situations they just can't manage comfortably. This is not their fault, but a failure of their owners to understand their needs and capabilities. Some of the behavior humans object to is simply natural dog-behavior. Sometimes it's a response to a trying situation. Dogs have a selection of rather limited, but truly distressing ways of acting out their tribulations—as you may have had the misfortune to discover already. This repertoire commonly includes aggression, house soiling, destruction of property, and barking. Creative dogs can think of other things.

Remember this. Dachshunds were bred for a specific purpose: to hunt badgers and other game. Even though it is extremely unlikely that you obtained your Dachshund in order to rid your property of varmints, he stands ready to do just that. Some of the behavior that you may find annoying—or even impossible—is a relic of his irresistible urge to help out around the yard.

155

Dogs don't have a moral sense. They don't see ripping apart a pillow, nipping a child, peeing in the house, or barking all day as "wrong." They don't look at obeying their owners, heeling on a lead, or behaving nicely around other dogs and people as "right." They are free of a sense of guilt. This light-hearted, pleasant attitude makes dogs really easy to train, actually. You don't have to waste time imbuing in dogs a moral code. All you need to do is to show them what works best for them. Problems arise when dogs have discovered this on their own; they have already decided what works best and you haven't been on the ball to show them differently. Almost every single problem behavior a dog presents is traceable to ignorance, neglect, or mistakes in training on the part of the person who owns him. So go whack yourself on the head ten times with a rolled-up newspaper.

Dachshunds are scent hounds, and while all dogs are exceptionally good smellers, scent hounds are the olfactory Old Masters of the species. Perpetually hunting for badgers, your Dachshund will make other discoveries—tiny particles of food, lost in supposedly inaccessible corners of cabinets, mice in the walls, moles in the yard, and who knows what? Dachshunds know that it is their genetic mandate to seek out, find, and kill these pesky annoyances, even if it means destroying the kitchen or the backyard to do so. Your Dachshund only wants to be of service.

Other kinds of bad behavior occur when a dog's need to be a full partner in the family activities is ignored. Basically, you have four possible approaches to training your dog. You can apply *positive reinforcement*—rewarding a dog for doing as you ask. The reward can be verbal praise, treats, play, or petting. This works best when teaching a dog a new behavior. You can apply *negative reinforcement*—ignoring bad behavior by turning your back or walking away. This works best with unwanted attention-seeking behaviors like inappropriate barking or begging. You can also apply *positive punishment* such as whacking him, jerking his collar, using an electric shock, and so on when he misbehaves. This kind of response "works" in that you can get quick results, but it can be detrimental to your relationship with the animal. You can apply *negative punishment* by simply not allowing him to continue with his chosen behaviors. You might bring him inside when he's barking, confine him when he is tearing up the living

Are you talking to me?

Photo courtesy of M. Brown

room, and so on. As a rule, reinforcement methods work better than punishment, especially if you want a happy, positive dog with a bright outlook on life. The earlier you work on training a dog using positive and negative reinforcement, the more success you will have.

The Magical Hour

Your dog needs a minimum of one hour positive interaction with you every day. Those sixty minutes could include exercising together, playing, training, or grooming. That's every day. (It doesn't include merely being in the same room as the dog.) I promise that simply spending one hour of "quality time" each day will eliminate at least half the problems you may experience with your dog. It is much better if you can spend a couple of hours or more, but most people can't. This magical hour will help prevent many of the problems I discuss next.

Aggression

Aggression is a normal part of canid behavior. Canids use aggression to find and keep their place in a pack, defend their young, food, or territory. Although most forms of aggression are not productive in contemporary dog life, the genes that are responsible for it are still there and can prod a dog into action. Unfortunately, without proper socialization and training, some dogs forget they are supposed to be civilized and reasonable. They revert to more wolf-like behavior.

Some kinds of canine misbehavior stem from your failure to take your proper role as leader of the pack, the so-called alpha position, held by the most dominant animal. That's you—or should be. Every pack must have a leader. Dogs are hierarchical creatures, and the proper hierarchy is "All human beings, including children" are above all dogs. When this rule is not clearly enforced by the owner, and hence not well understood by the dog, the animal may decide that *he* should be leader. He will do what is takes to obtain that position, even if it means snapping or biting. (That's how his ancestors did it, after all.) Most commonly a Dachshund will decide that his adult owners are his superiors, but their children are not. Or he may decide that no stranger has precedence over him. Most dogs with this idea were not sufficiently socialized as puppies.

Aggressive behavior is the most serious problem dogs present to humans and to themselves. Every year about 800,000 people in the U.S. are bitten seriously enough to require documented medical attention. Thousands more bites go unreported. To reduce these unhealthy statistics, we need to take action. Carefully monitor your dog around children (who make up the majority of the victims). Children should be taught to stand tall, speak low, and move slowly around strange dogs. A running, screaming child and an excitable puppy is a recipe for disaster, even though playful nipping is part of normal puppy play. Everyone should learn to read dog-language, so as not to misinterpret a slowly wagging, half-mast tail as a sign of friendliness.

Supervise your Dachshund with children and other pets. If you do find that an aggression problem is developing, don't try to hide it from yourself or others. Do not make excuses for your dog. Seek professional help immediately. Most aggression can be corrected, but you need to deal with it as quickly as possible.

It's important to show the dog quite early that you are the alpha dog—the pack leader. Never allow your Dachshund to nip or bite you or your clothes, even in play. You must establish dominance in ways that a dog understands:

▼ Pet the dog on your initiative, not his. If he paws or nudges you, he is demanding, not asking for your attention. Don't give in. Get up and walk away.

▼ Feed the dog after you have finished eating. Stand and watch him eat. He should learn that all food comes from you. If he's possessive over his food bowl, make him sit and do various things to "earn" his food, such as asking him to sit or lie down first. In severe cases, you might have to remove his food bowl for a while and hand-feed him. This will clarify for him that you are the source of dinner.

▼ Don't allow your dog to beg from the table. Doing so allows him to think he has some sort of legitimate claim on your food.

▼ Go in and out doors first. Do not allow your Doxie simply to barge ahead of you.

▼ Don't allow a dominant dog to sleep on the couch, and certainly not on your bed. Dogs think that being high up is the same as being boss. (In addition, Dachshunds should not be encouraged to jump on or off beds; it's too hard on their backs.) Even if you're short, you're taller than your Dachshund. Stand up straight.

▼ Don't use baby talk with your dog. Dogs respond best to intelligent commands, not insipid gurgles.

▼ Make sure you take your dog for a walk, not the other way around. Let him understand that walking on a loose lead is a privilege he earns by good (submissive) behavior.

▼ Teach your children not to place their faces near that of the dog. It's just asking for a bite.

None of the above conduct is designed to be cruel or to hurt your Doxie's self-esteem, one of the most charming features of the breed. Quite the opposite. Dogs are actually happiest when they know their proper place. Like adolescent children, they may

Woody (longhair adult) attempts to let Wheeler (Golden Retriever puppy) know who is really boss (they got along great).

Photo courtesy of Lisa Liddy

challenge your dominance occasionally, but are secretly pleased to know where the boundaries are. This relieves them of a great deal of responsibility. They can now relax, and go on with being well-behaved, happy pets.

It is incumbent upon all dog owners to make sure their dog is well trained. Potentially biting dogs should be confined and controlled by their owners. For more information about dog bites, see the American Veterinary Medical Association's Task Force on Canine Aggression and Human-Canine Interactions. You can see the report at the AVMA's Web site: www.avma.org.

Barking

The typical Dachshund "finds his voice" when he is about eighteen months old. He'll never lose it. Although most dog owners seem to view barking as a problem, barking is just one way a dog communicates. And Dachshunds are barkers! You can't eliminate this perfectly natural behavior, but you can control it. When your dog barks once or twice to let you know about something, praise him. Then turn his attention to something else.

A dogs has many reasons for barking, including:

▼ To express his joy in living
▼ To protect the yard
▼ To warn you of approaching strangers
▼ To tell you he's bored and lonely
▼ To contact or respond to another dog

As a rule, the more space your dog has to exercise in, the less likely he will be to bark. The worst barkers are dogs kept on a chain. Dogs left outside at night also tend to bark; it's probably spooky out there and full of weird sounds that need to be responded to. If your dog is barking because he is bored or lonely, change his environment. Play with him, take him on walks, exercise him, get him a companion. But don't reward the barking by doing any of these things *in immediate response* to the barking. If the only time you pay attention to your dog is when he barks, you are rewarding his behavior and encouraging the barking.

Baffling Barking

Elderly dogs suffering from canine cognitive disorder often bark for apparently no reason at all. Your senior dog might also be suffering a hearing loss, and not even be aware that he is barking. This is a medical condition for which treatment is available.

If your dog barks outside when you are away from home, keep him inside. If he barks while he's inside the house, shut the blinds to reduce the stimulation. Dogs who are over-stimulated by the outside environment may be calmer with the shades pulled, and some dogs barking from nervousness may feel more comfortable if put a crate.

If your dog is barking from sheer happiness, allow him about six barks, then bring him inside. He will soon understand that joy barking, when overdone, brings an unintended result. You might also try giving the joy barker a cheese- or peanut butter-filled Kong toy. Dogs can't bark and chew at the same time, and by the time he finishes the Kong, the thrill of the backyard may have worn off.

If he's barking because he's bored, ignore the barking if you are out of earshot of the neighbors until he is quiet for a few minutes. Under no circumstances should you allow a barking dog to remain outside and bark his head off. You, via the agency of your dog, are disturbing the peace. After the dog has been quiet, you can bring him in. Don't let a problem barker get the idea that continued barking brings results. Remember that any dog will begin to bark or whine if ignored long enough. The plan is not to ignore the dog.

Never use physical punishment to stop barking. In the first place, it won't work. Punishment never teaches a dog anything except to try to avoid the punishment. Using a punishment to suppress a natural behavior will encourage a dog to resort to other, perhaps more destructive actions to get his point across. It can make dogs neurotic, or even aggressive.

Remember that any attention you pay to barking rewards that behavior. This doesn't mean you should never pay attention to barking. It means you should respond only to barking that is done for a "legitimate purpose." Don't worry about confusing your dog. Except in the case of confused, elderly dogs, your dog knows why he's barking. He can easily discriminate between the kinds of barking that gets rewards (attention) and those that don't. For example, if you come out and yell at or play with a barking dog, you will encourage him to bark at you whenever he wants you to come out. The dog is then calling the shots.

If your dog barks at a visitor, say in a mild tone, "Good boy, no bark." Then touch him, and ask him to "settle." This acknowledges that his warning has registered and that you see the danger and will deal with it appropriately. After all, it's a good thing for dogs to announce to arrival of guests. It is part of their inheritance, after all. He will soon see that a friend has arrived, and there's no need to give continued warnings.

Teach the "no bark" command by saying "no bark" and rewarding your dog with a treat the instant he stops. If he continues to bark, turn your back and walk off. If possible, let him know that strangers are nearly always full of goodwill. If your letter carrier agrees, ask her to speak reassuringly to Oliver, or even hand him a dog biscuit. In an earlier chapter, I suggested taping a dog biscuit to the door and asking the mail carrier to drop it through the letter slot (if you have one) along with the mail. It may not stop him from barking, but at least he'll feel better about the carrier. If nothing else works, close the blinds and keep the dog out of the room with a baby gate.

Dogs operate on the reward system. If your dog learns that you allow him in the house when he is bored but not barking, he'll learn to ask to be let in by a quieter method, such as scratching at the door, or even ringing a little doorbell. (This may make you crazy, but the neighbors will appreciate it.) Most problem barking occurs because the dog is ignored no matter what he does. So he barks, hoping that at least you'll stick your head out the door and scream at him. From a dog's point of view, that's better than nothing. The longer you allow the barking to continue by rewarding it in any way (including negative rewards like yelling), the harder it will be to extinguish the behavior.

Many people have had success in quieting their dogs by teaching them to "speak." Paradoxical as it may sound, the point is to teach the dog to bark appropriately. The reward is given on the command, "Shush." Soon the dog learns to associate the reward with the word "shush" and the correct response, silence. You must be consistent in teaching this behavior, and always use the same commands.

Other people have had success with a startle approach, which is pretty much what it sounds like. When the dog begins to bark, and is presumably not looking over his shoulder, you toss a water balloon near him or use a noisemaker. Ideally, the dog should not recognize you as the person responsible for the water balloon or noise. He should merely understand that barking brings evil results from out of the blue. This idea is correct in theory, of course, but it's not as easy to sneak up on a dog, especially a Dachshund, as you might imagine.

Anti-barking Alternatives

I don't approve of the so-called "anti-bark" collars for most dogs. They are punishment devices. Some of them work by subjecting the dog to various levels (one to eight kilovolts) of "harmless" electrical shock. Although electronic anti-bark collar manufacturers use words like "stimulation," "pulse," "vibration," or even "tickle" to sell their wares, don't be fooled. These devices give your dog a jolt of juice. Even trainers who think these collars are effective caution that they shouldn't be used for long periods. We also really have no idea how much pain they cause the animal. In addition, anti-bark collars are also completely ineffective when used on a dog with separation anxiety or a neurotic condition. The most effective use for these collars is to curb "joy barkers," and although they tend to work, what a nasty means to an end. What if someone gave you a shock every time you laughed?

Another kind of anti-bark collar contains citronella oil, which dogs hate. The collar sprays citronella mist in the dog's face when he begins to bark. Although his device is somewhat more humane than an electrical shock collar and more effective than a vibration or awful-noise collar, it's a poor second best to real training. And at about $100 per collar, it's the most expensive of the anti-bark devices.

Some experts recommend "debarking" a dog when all else fails. This is a surgical procedure to remove the vocal cords. Debarking does not completely silence the dog, however; it merely "tones" down the noise, leaving the dog with a hoarse, whispery, muted voice. Debarking and electronic collars should be reserved for truly intractable cases.

Some kinds of barking, particularly those caused by psychological problems, such as separation anxiety, depression, canine cognitive dysfunction, and obsessive/compulsive disorder, respond well to drug treatment. (Medication does not work for "normal" barking.) Some drugs that have been used successfully include amitriptyline (Elavil), clomipramine (Clomicalm), buspirone (Buspar), methylphenidate (Ritalin), fluoxetine (Prozac), and selegiline (Anipryl). Each drug works on a different cause of barking.

Begging

Begging is a completely natural behavior, and even cute in a little puppy. It becomes less charming as the dog gets the idea he can scramble onto your lap and eat your dinner. The best way to avoid a begging problem is to never let it get started in the first place. If it already has, your choices are pretty simple: ignore the behavior in hopes the dog will give up, say "No!" sharply and scowl while continuing with dinner; tie the dog up, crate him, or lock him in another room until he gets the idea.

Digging

Dachshunds are for digging. At least, that's what they'd say. It's part of their heritage, and they were bred to do it well and easily. Doxies enjoy digging, and it is not fair to expect them not to dig just because you may not care for the result.

You have several approaches when it comes to digging, all of which involve management. First, you can encourage the dog to ‑

"Why would you think I'm going to dig?"   *Photo courtesy of Edith Colaneri*

dig where you want him to by supplying him with an "earthbox," which is simply a child's sandbox filled with attractive, soft, diggable earth or sand. You can encourage him to dig in it by hiding one of his more precious toys there. Restrict your dog's access to valuable real estate by a fence, or if this is not practical, simply watch him like a hawk. When you see the front legs going, put him in the earthbox—perhaps with a great toy anchored to it to encourage his presence. Never punish your dog for doing what comes naturally.

If your dog digs inside the house, he may be looking for mice or other home invaders. It's also common for dogs to dig at new carpeting. The new material hasn't yet absorbed the familiar odors of the house, and your Dachshund digs at it to find out just what this strange new stuff is made of. You'll need to keep the dog separated from the new material until it has lost its mystery. Digging in the sofa is commonly regarded a kind of "nesting behavior," but I have seen males do this as well.

Strange Behavior

If your dog exhibits a sudden or unexplainable change in behavior for which you can devise no reasonable explanation (a scary experience, change in schedule or family pattern, an injury or the like) take him to your vet for a thorough workup. Many diseases can be responsible.

The Fear Factor

Many Dachshunds have inherited a "shy" gene, which can manifest itself in several different ways. One of the most common is in "thunderphobia," a condition that plagues many members of the hound group. (As dogs bred to work outside, they instinctively know, perhaps, that thunderstorms can be dangerous!) No one is sure what causes it, but dogs who come from shelters are especially likely to be fearful. They may tremble, pant, or hyperventilate. In some cases, they may pace or even become destructive, ripping up fabric or even furniture. Treating thunderphobia can be difficult. Most desensitization programs are only moderately successful. You can help by not coddling your dog during a storm (that convinces him that something really is terribly wrong.) You can also close the windows (wouldn't you anyway?) and let your dog go to a safe place. Most dogs prefer the bathroom, behind the toilet or even in the tub!

Many dogs respond very well to melatonin, a natural hormone, while some require a mild dose of Valium, Xanax or Clomipramine (Clomicalm) before the anticipated storm to keep them from freaking out. Try a combination of techniques and see what works best for your dog.

Escape Artistry

As hounds, Dachshunds have a propensity to wander. They cannot be reliably trained to stick around the old ranch basking in the sun. They want to be out and about, and while it is not their intention to run *away* per se, they have no objection to wandering off and expecting you to come find them. This is one reason why you need a good fence and permanent ID on your dog.

Foraging

The ability to find food is an evolutionary advantage, and Dachshunds are uncommonly skilled at it. They are much too clever to find food only in their bowls. They can find it on top of counters, under sofas, in children's hands, and in the trash. It's amazing how a short dog like a Dachshund can get on a table (or even a refrigerator) but it has happened. Although a dog can be trained out of grabbing food from a child's hand, it is not possible to reliably train your Dachshund from un-absconding with readily available treats. In other words, it is not wise to turn your back on your Dachshund when food is available. To do so is to fly in the face of generations of selective breeding.

Discourage foraging and food stealing by never feeding your dog from the table or counter. Do not give in, no matter how adorable he looks. Put all food directly into his dish rather than into his mouth. This technique is no guarantee, but it won't hurt, either. To prevent your Dachshund from stealing food, make it unavailable. Put it away. In the dog world we call this "management." It's just as effective as training, and a heck of a lot easier. In other words, if you train *yourself* not to leave food around the house, the dog ceases to be a problem. Dachshunds are *much* more agile than they look and are unaccountably adept at climbing on top of tables when it suits them. If he finds food in the trash, keep the trash out of his way. (We keep ours behind the door leading to the cellar.)

Predatory Behavior

If raised together, or correctly introduced, cats and Doxies can get along quite well. However, smaller or more defenseless pets like bunnies, hamsters, birds, or guinea pigs are not safe around Dachshunds. You must keep them firmly separated. (It is particularly difficult if you have more than one dog. Dogs tend to gang up on the unfortunate gerbil. ...) Don't even try to "train" the Doxie out of such behavior. You *may* get lucky and succeed, but the Doxie may just bide his time and wait until you're not looking. This is a survival imperative for the breed, an imperative that is likely to be stronger than anything you might do to persuade him otherwise. If you fail, your small pet's life will be lost.

Separation Anxiety

According to one estimate, 14 percent of the dogs in this country suffer from separation anxiety. Dogs are social beings, and were never meant to spend hour after hour away from kith and kin. *Dogs need at least one hour of close human companionship a day to be happy and healthy.* Walking, grooming, training, playing, and cuddling all count as "close companionship." As I mentioned earlier, co-existing in the same space does not. If you've ever found yourself watching someone else watch television, you have an idea of how unrewarding some "time together" can be.

Remember that although a dog may not be the center of your life, you are certainly the center of his. A lonely dog can become stressed, despondent, and destructive. Some dogs seem to manage well enough by themselves, but most dogs need companionship—preferably yours. If that is not possible, adding another dog (or even a cat) to the family can soothe anxious moments. Dogs from shelters who have experienced abandonment suffer most.

Drug therapy is a new and very promising treatment for severe separation anxiety in dogs. But before medicating your pet, see what behavior modifications you can make in your own lifestyle. Luckily, neither you nor your dog has to suffer through separation anxiety. Treatment, both medical and behavioral, is available. Try the following methods of alleviating your dog's separation woes:

▼ **Get up**. Get up a little earlier than you have to, and spend some time with your dog. Play with him, run with him, groom him, brush his teeth.

▼ **Sleep in**. If he doesn't already, let your dog sleep in your bedroom with you. He'll enjoy your company even while he's asleep.

▼ **Go to work—with Rascal**. Try sneaking the dog into work with you once in a while. I did this for years under the pretext that the animal was having medical problems and needed frequent medical attention. It was sort of true.

▼ **Desensitize**. Start desensitizing your dog gradually to being left alone. Of course you can't take your dog with you to the opera, but it is not unreasonable to expect to be able to leave him alone for a few hours without returning to a war zone.

▼ **Be calm**. Don't make a big to-do about either departing or returning. Pay no attention to your dog for about fifteen minutes or so before you leave. This means you should avoid even looking at your dog, as strange as it sounds. It actually has a calming effect.

▼ **Prepare to leave, but don't actually do so**. Jiggle the door-knob and jangle your keys. Do this several times a day, and soon Matilda won't necessarily associate your getting out your purse with her being left alone.

▼ **Change your routine**. Stop giving the dog cues about when you'll be leaving. The cues allow him to set himself up for misery. One dog I knew began panting when his owner put on her deodorant.

▼ **Don't over-stimulate the dog**. This means you shouldn't *soak* him in attention when you're home—then suddenly depart. The contrast is too much for him to bear. Sometimes it works better to be rather distant with a separation anxiety sufferer until he improves. This advice seems to conflict with the hour of attention I want you to give him, and it may. A lot depends on the individual dog.

▼ **Leave your Doxie unsupervised for very gradually lengthening time periods**. Get him used to the idea of your being gone. At first, leave and come back within a minute or two. Give him a special toy, perhaps filled with peanut butter, as you depart, and collect it upon your return. Soon, he'll understand that you'll always come back, and he won't become destructive, at least not from separation anxiety. (That doesn't mean he won't get bored, however.) He will also learn that there is at least one good thing associated with your departure, a very special toy.

Most people make the mistake of not being gradual enough in their separation training. If your dog behaves well for one hour alone, do not assume he can be safely left for eight hours. Increase his periods alone by only fifteen minutes a time. Get your dog used to being on his own, even when you are at home. Discourage him from following you around the house, and give him his own chores to do (like chewing a bone). This doesn't mean ignore him;

the concept is to build up his confidence that he's part of your life even though you are not paying exclusive attention to him.

Another way of helping the dog cope is by placing him in his crate. Crating may create a sense of security, and even if it doesn't, while he's in the crate he won't be chewing the furniture. (It's not safe to leave a puppy under four months of age alone and unconfined; he simply does not have the psychological poise to keep from ripping things into shreds.) Don't leave him in the crate for more than four hours a day, tops, however. He needs both mental and physical stimulation he can't get in a crate. In addition, some dogs get worse with being crated.

Getting another dog can also alleviate the problem. Dogs are pack animals. Even though we have successfully bred them for thousands of years to think of *us* as their pack, there's no substitute for the real thing. Another dog is a natural playmate and a natural stress reducer. (After all, the other dog won't ask him to sit, or tell him to fetch. They'll just run around and be doggy together.) Your new dog doesn't have to be another Dachshund; however, it usually works best if the two dogs are approximately the same size. If two dogs are too much for you, or forbidden by the landlord, consider getting a cat. Even a cat who steadfastly ignores a dog will draw his attention.

If you must be away from home for an extended period of time, hire someone trustworthy to entertain your dog. A visit from a pet sitter or time with a dog walker gives your dog something to look forward to. When you return, you'll find a much quieter, happier dog. This does not have to be an expensive proposition. A responsible child in the neighborhood might be happy to walk your dog for a nominal fee. You might also leave on the radio or television. It's not much, but better than nothing. (I suggest the Animal Channel.) You can also call your dog on the phone, and leave him a nice message on the answering machine.

If your dog does not respond to behavior-based methods, get professional help, and medication. The best of all the new treatments for separation anxiety is the antidepressant Clomicalm (clomipramine hydrochloride), developed by Novartis. Clomicalm is the first behavioral drug approved exclusively for canines. It comes in pill form, and is amazingly effective for both separation anxiety and obsessive/compulsive disorders.

Some people seem to object on principle to "drugging" their dogs, although these are often the same people who cram their dogs with unneeded vitamin supplements and garlic (which contains one hundred chemicals). Although I empathize with those who want to treat their dogs "naturally," there are times when modern pharmacology is a good answer.

Clomicalm is a godsend for those people whose dogs do not respond to conventional behavioral therapy alone. It is neither a sedative nor a tranquilizer, and it won't change your dog's personality. It will calm him down and enable him to learn positive behaviors more easily. It costs about $1 a day. This drug is designed to be used along with behavioral therapy; it's not a replacement for it. Owners using Clomicalm have noticed an improvement in their dogs in about a month. Although a few dogs—those with obsessive/compulsive disorders in particular—will have to remain on Clomicalm permanently, most can be weaned off the drug in three to six months.

Territoriality

Dachshunds are natural watchdogs and they can be protective of their own turf. The good news is that Dachshunds have never been known to kill anybody, and are unlikely to cause serious damage even if they do nip at someone. The bad news is that this is no excuse for an over-protective dog, and even a tiny nip can cost you more than you want to spend.

Unfortunately, the very fence we buy to keep our dogs safe is a primary cause of territoriality. The dog soon learns that whatever the fence encloses in some way belongs to him, and as a possession, it must be protected. Owners sometimes unwittingly reinforce the undesirable behavior by being secretly proud of how well the dog is protecting his home. At least the owner thinks it's a secret. Unfortunately, the Dachshund has read his mind, and is only trying to fulfill the unspoken expectations. Likewise, people who are fearful of strangers unconsciously communicate their fear to the Dachshund, sometimes by giving off chemical messages. No much we can do about that—except work on our own fears.

The best way to curb territoriality in a dog is start early. As part of his socialization training, your dog should learn that

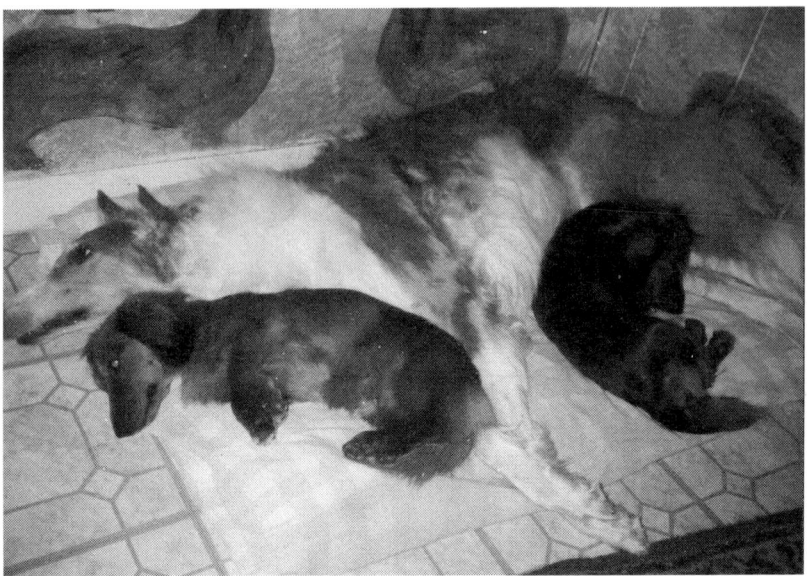

Hanging with the big dog…   *Photo courtesy of Edith Colaneri*

visitors are welcome and fun and usually have dog treats to hand out! If you don't want your dog to bark at all upon the arrival of strangers, don't make a big deal of them. If you are excited, even in a happy way, your Dachshund will copy you—by barking. The calmer and quieter you are, the more likely your Dachshund will agree that company is no big deal. If he barks, reward him when he ceases.

Chapter 12
Dachshunds on Display

Although most people are perfectly happy keeping their Doxie at home as a pet and boon companion, others like to expand their own and their dog's horizons. Today, there is a plethora of canine activities to enjoy with your pooch. It's no longer necessary to have a "show dog" to have a winner!

Conformation

A conformation show is a beauty contest. You probably shouldn't consider entering this kind of competition unless you bought a show-quality dog from a reputable breeder. In any case, it's best to get a second opinion from an experienced Dachshund conformation competitor as to whether or not your Doxie has what it takes to be a success in the ring. (Show judges can get really picky.)

The goal for a conformation dog is to win his Championship, which means earning fifteen "points." One to five points are awarded to the best male and female Dachshunds of each coat type in the show, and a dog must win under at least three different judges. At least two of the shows have to be "majors," (shows worth three or more points) which means your dog is facing a lot of competition. How many dogs it takes to comprise a major is fluid, depending upon how many Dachshunds are registered in that area at the particular time the show is held. If there are a lot of Dachshunds around, more dogs are required to "build a major."

Showing "Exquisite," a standard, red longhair　　　*Photo courtesy of Daisy Buchignani*
Owner: Jean Trowe

Each show offers several different classes. There are classes for puppies, classes for dogs bred by their exhibitors, classes for dogs bred in America, and Open classes that anyone can enter— these classes also have the stiffest competition. Standard and miniature Dachshunds are shown together except in the Open classes. In an all-breed competition, the winners of the three varieties (coat type) compete in the hound Group. In a Dachshund specialty show, the three Best of Variety winners compete with each other for Best of Breed.

Obedience Competitions

In an obedience event, a dog must qualify with a score of 170 out of a perfect 200 points, plus earn at least half the points possible for each exercise at one of three levels: Novice, Open, or Utility. At the Novice level, the dog must heel on a lead for a figure eight, stand for examination, heel off lead, recall, and do a long Sit and long Down. Titles offered in Obedience include Companion Dog (CD), Companion Dog Excellent (CDX), Utility Dog (UD), and Utility Dog Excellent (UDX).

Dachshund Shows Abroad

In Canada and Great Britain, Dachshunds are divided by size as well as coat type, so there will be six Dachshunds in the hound ring! Under international (FCI) rules, however, Dachshunds are put into their own group altogether—Group 4. Here three sizes are recognized—as well as three coat types. The three sizes are: *Zwergteckel* (miniature), *Normalgrossteckel* (standard), and *Kaninchenteckel* (Rabbit). So there are nine different types competing. Under FCI rules, these sizes are determined by chest circumference rather than weight, which makes a lot of sense to me. The standard has a chest circumference of 35 cm; the miniature a chest circumference of 30 to 35 cm, and the rabbit has a chest circumference of up to 30 cm. The last two must be measured when the dog is at least fifteen months old. The reason for using circumference rather than size is telling: it's the circumference of the chest that allows (or does not allow) a Doxie to proceed down a certain hole.

It is the rare Dachshund who excels at obedience. First of all, they have a hound's independence, and second they have a Dachshund's physique. The former gives them a mind of their own; the latter makes it rather difficult for them to perform some of the common obedience requirements. For example, obedience judges are unduly picky about having a dog sit *straight*, as if that makes a difference in the real world. Well, Dachshunds find it hard to sit straight. Their long bodies tend to place them at an angle for comfort, and that's just the way it is in Dachshund land. It's a silly requirement, anyway.

Rally Obedience, known affectionately as Rally-O by its supporters, is a new kind of obedience competition that is becoming very popular. Rally-O combines classic obedience with the more exciting elements of agility. In addition, Rally-O handlers are free to talk to and praise their dogs in ways that are disallowed in classical obedience trials. To learn more about Rally-O competitions, go to the Web site of the Association of Pet Dog Trainers, www.apdt.com.

A just-for-fun obedience test is the Canine Good Citizen certificate. To pass, a dog must successfully complete the following ten exercises:

▼ Accepting a friendly stranger
▼ Sitting politely for petting
▼ Appearance and grooming
▼ Walking on a loose leash
▼ Walking through a crowd
▼ Sit, Down, and Stay on command
▼ Coming when called
▼ Reacting appropriately to another dog
▼ Reacting appropriately to distractions
▼ Supervised separation

Canine Good Citizen tests are conducted from time to time by many local kennel clubs. Contact the one nearest you for more information. Dogs of any age can take the test, and dogs do not have to have AKC papers (or even be purebred) to pass. All dogs should have the necessary immunizations, however. For a copy of the Canine Good Citizen pamphlet, contact the AKC at (877) 252-2665 and ask for it or e-mail orderdesk@akc.org.

Peanut on parade   *Photo courtesy of Daisy & Charles Buchignani*

Field Trials

Dachshund field trials were modeled after Beagle and Basset Hound field trials, and they are indeed often held on the same grounds—usually owned by the local Beagle Club folks, who are generally much more attuned to this sort of thing than Dachshund owners. The area is very large and always fenced, for all hounds have a propensity to wander off, even when supposedly engaged in their favorite pursuit.

In the highly competitive world of field trials, Dachshunds must go after rabbits. In all fairness, if you are seriously interested in catching rabbits, you're really better off with a Beagle. But if you're interested in competing in this friendly sport, it's a great way to spend a fresh spring or autumn morning with your Doxie. Never fear, no blood is spilled—except possibly yours as you pick out the thorns from your flesh. (My own experience with field trials reminds me that there are a great many more ticks in the world that you would think possible—get tick repellant for you and your dog.)

The Dachshund is not supposed to actually "engage" (attack) the rabbit, but merely to track the animal and follow it to its den. The dog is supposed to use his keen nose in this endeavor. Any dog who *sees* the rabbit is picked up by the handler. Often a human sees the rabbit before the dog is aware of its existence. (The Beagle Club will undoubtedly keep a large rabbit supply on hand—they provide them with plenty of food and sheltering bushes and everything a rabbit could desire.)

Two Dachshunds (a brace) are paired by random draw. When a rabbit is flushed from the bushes by the "beaters," someone yells out "Tally-Ho!"—fake British accent optional. Two judges observe the rabbit and note the spot where it is last seen. At that time the brace is "called up" and shown the "line" or scent trail. The leashed dogs are given a three- to ten-foot distance to follow; the handlers are allowed to speak to and encourage the dogs. When one dog picks up the scent, both are released. The handlers must then stop giving instructions to the dog, and must follow well behind. (The judges get to follow the dog.) Winners are determined by accuracy in trailing. Observers traipse around after the dogs in what is called the gallery. (Pointing breeds

Chloe tracking   *Photo courtesy of Melinda Brown*

engaged in hunting trials have galleries, too, who follow along on horseback.)

Dogs usually begin formal field trailing when they are between nine months and one year old. The following is an excerpt from the Dachshund Field Trial Rules and Standard Procedure, which explains what positive qualities are expected, and how demerits can be acquired.

4-B Definitions–Desirable Qualities

Searching Ability

> Searching ability is evidenced by an aptitude to recognize promising cover and by an eagerness to explore it, regardless of hazards or discomfort. Dachshunds should search independently of each other, in an industrious manner with sufficient range. In field trials Dachshunds should remain within control distance of the handler and should be obedient to the handler's commands.

Pursuing Ability

Pursuing ability is shown by a proficiency in keeping control of the trail while making the best possible progress. Game should be pursued rather than merely followed, and actions should indicate a determined effort to make forward progress in the surest, most sensible manner, by adjusting speed to correspond to conditions and circumstances. Actions should be positive and controlled, demonstrating sound judgment and skill. Progress should be proclaimed by tonguing. No hound can be too fast provided that the trail is clearly and accurately followed. At a check Dachshunds should work industriously, first close to where the loss occurred, then gradually and thoroughly extending the search farther afield to regain the line.

Accuracy in Trailing

Accuracy in trailing is demonstrated by consistent control of the line while making the best possible progress. An accurate trailing Dachshund will show a marked tendency to follow the trail with a minimum of weaving on and off, and will display an aptness to turn with the trail and to determine direction of game travel in a positive manner.

Obedience to Commands

Obedience to commands is demonstrated by the Dachshund's attentiveness and responsiveness to the handler. A Dachshund should, at all times, be under the control of the handler. If, in the opinion of the judges, the Dachshund is unresponsive to the commands of the handler, the Dachshund should not be considered for top placing. Allowances must be made by the judges only when the Dachshund is in hot pursuit when called by the handler.

Proper Use of Voice

Proper use of voice is the proclaiming of all finds of scent and announcing all forward progress on the scent line by giving tongue. The Dachshund should keep silent when not in contact with the scent line. Giving tongue on a sight chase is not a fault, but it is also not an indication of proper use of voice. Proper use of voice is a highly desirable trait in the Dachshund, but it should not be allowed to compensate for faulty work in other categories of performance. Judges may, at their discretion, place a silent Dachshund above an open trailer, provided that the silent Dachshund's performance was superior in other respects.

Willingness to Go to Earth

Willingness to go to earth is evidenced by the Dachshund's eagerness to enter the earth without encouragement. Should a rabbit lodge in any earth or run through any drain large enough for the Dachshund to enter, the Dachshund should be expected to enter without hesitation or encouragement. Failure to follow the game to earth should automatically render the Dachshund ineligible for first award, even though its performance is in all other aspects outstanding.

Endurance

Endurance is the demonstrated capacity to compete through the duration of the trial and to go on as long as it may be necessary.

Determination and Courage

Determination and courage are the qualities that permit a Dachshund to succeed against the severest odds. A determined Dachshund has a purpose in mind and will overcome, through sheer perseverance, many obstacles that will frustrate less determined running mates. Courage is displayed by the willingness to face punishing coverts with almost total disrespect. Courage and determination keep a Dachshund at its work as long as there is a possibility of achievement and quite often long after its body has passed the peak of its efficiency. Determination is desired in its most intense form.

Patience

Patience is a willingness to stay with any problem encountered as long as there is a possibility of achieving success in a workmanlike manner, rather than taking a chance of making the recovery more quickly through guesswork or gambling. Patience keeps a Dachshund from bounding off and leaving work undone, and ensures that it will apply itself through the surest and safest methods in difficult situations.

Adaptability

Adaptability means being able to adjust quickly to changes in scenting conditions and being able to work harmoniously with a variety of running mates. An adaptable Dachshund will pursue its quarry as fast as the conditions allow or as slowly as conditions demand.

Independence

Independence is the ability to be self-reliant and to refrain from becoming upset or influenced by the actions of faulty bracemates. The proper degree of independence is displayed by the Dachshund that concentrates on running its game with no undue concern for its running mate, except to hark to it when it proclaims a find or indicates progress by tonguing. Watching the other Dachshund is indication of lack of sufficient independence. Ignoring bracemates completely and refusing to hark or to move up with running mates is an indication of too much independence.

Cooperation

Cooperation is demonstrated when a Dachshund works harmoniously with others, doing as much of the work as possible in an honest and efficient manner and yet being aware of and honoring the accomplishments of running mates without jealousy or disruption of the chase.

Competitive Spirit

Competitive spirit is the desire to outdo running mates. It is a borderline quality that is an asset only to the Dachshund that is able to keep it under control and to concentrate on running the game rather than on beating other Dachshunds. The overly competitive Dachshund lacks such qualities as adaptability, patience, independence and cooperation, and in its desire to excel such a Dachshund seldom does accurate work.

Intelligence

Intelligence is that quality which helps a Dachshund apply its talents efficiently in the manner of a skilled workman. The intelligent Dachshund learns from experience and seldom wastes time repeating mistakes. Intelligence is indicated by the ability to adapt to changes in scenting conditions, to adapt to and control its work with various types of running mates under a variety of circumstances.

The Dachshund that displays the aforementioned qualities should be considered the ideal Dachshund as a single hunter or as a running mate for trailing either rabbit or hare.

4-C Definitions–Faulty Actions

Quitting

Quitting is a serious fault deserving severe penalty and, in its extreme form, elimination. Quitting indicates lack of desire to hunt and succeed. It ranges from refusing to run, to such lesser forms as lack of perseverance, occasional letup of eagerness, and loafing or watching other Dachshunds in difficult situations. Quitting is sometimes due to fatigue. Judges may temper their distaste when a Dachshund becomes fatigued and eases off, if such a Dachshund has been required to perform substantially longer than those with which it is running. During the running of a class, a Dachshund may have to face several fresh competitors in succession. In such instances a short rest period is in order. Otherwise, judges should expect Dachshunds to be in condition to compete as long as necessary to prove their worthiness, and no Dachshund that becomes unable to go on should place above any immediate running mate that is still able and willing to run.

Backtracking

Backtracking is the fault of following the trail in the wrong direction. If persisted in for any substantial time or distance, it justifies elimination. However, hounds in competition sometimes take a backline momentarily, or are led into it by faulty running mates. Under these circumstances judges should show leniency toward the Dachshund that becomes aware of its mistakes and makes creditable correction. Judges should be very certain before penalizing a Dachshund for backtracking and, if there is any doubt, take sufficient time to prove it right or wrong. Backtracking indicates lack of ability to determine the direction of game travel.

Ghost Trailing

Ghost trailing is pretending to have contact with a trail and to be making progress where no trail exists by going through all the actions that indicate true trailing. Some Dachshunds are able to do this in a very convincing manner and judges, if suspicious, should make the Dachshund prove its claim.

Pottering

Pottering is behavior that produces little progress on the line due to a lack of effort or desire. Hesitating, listlessness, dawdling, or lack of intent to make progress are marks of the potterer.

Babbling

Babbling is excessive or unnecessary tonguing. The babbler often tongues the same trail over and over, or tongues from excitement when casting in attempting to regain the trail at losses.

Swinging

Swinging is casting out too far and too soon from the last point of contact without first making an attempt to regain scent near the loss. It is a gambling action, often indicating over competitiveness or an attempt to gain unearned advantage over running mates.

Skirting

Skirting is purposely leaving the trail in an attempt to gain a lead or avoid hazardous cover or hard work. It is cutting out and around true trailing mates in an attempt to intercept the trail ahead.

Leaving Checks

Leaving checks is the failure to stay in the vicinity of a loss and attempt to work it out, and instead to go bounding off in hopes of encountering the trail or new game. Leaving checks denotes lack of patience and perseverance.

Running Mute

Running mute is the failure to give tongue when making progress on the line.

Tightness of Mouth

Tightness of mouth is the failure to give sufficient tongue when making progress. This will often be evidenced by the Dachshund tightening up when pressed or when going away from a check.

Racing

Racing is attempting to outfoot running mates without regard for the trail. Racing Dachshunds overshoot the turns and generally spend more time off the trail than on it.

Running Hit or Miss

Running hit or miss is attempting to make progress without maintaining continuous contact with the trail, or gambling to hit the trail ahead.

Lack of Independence

Lack of independence is a common fault that is indicated when a Dachshund watches its running mates and allows them to determine the course of action. Any action that indicates undue concern for other Dachshunds, except when harking in, is cause for demerit.

Bounding Off

Bounding off is rushing ahead when contact with scent is made without properly determining the direction of game travel.

4-D Credits

1) Dachshunds shall be credited principally for their positive accomplishments. The extent of any credit should be governed by the magnitude of the accomplishment and the manner in which it is achieved. Credit is earned for searching ability, pursuing ability, accuracy in trailing, obedience to command, proper use of voice, willingness to go to ground, endurance, determination and courage, patience, adaptability, independence, cooperation, competitive spirit, intelligence displayed when searching or in solving problems encountered along the trail, and success in accounting for game.

2) When crediting Dachshunds for working style or methods used to accomplish their work, judges should keep the purpose of the breed constantly in mind and be alert for Dachshunds deficient in ability that make simple problems appear difficult. They also should guard against becoming impressed by fascinating actions that do not produce results. Credit for working style should be used chiefly to differentiate between successful performers, and should never be applied to a degree which might indicate that style or method should be preferred to accomplishment, except in cases where excessive faultiness is involved. Credit for any accomplishment should be in proportion to its importance in getting work done. Mere lack of fault is not grounds for credit. While faultiness is not to be considered lightly, the slightly faulty Dachshund should be preferred to the stylist that fails.

4-E Demerits

1) Faults, mistakes, lack of accomplishment, and apparent lack of intelligence shall be considered demerits and shall be penalized to whatever extent they interfere with or fail to contribute to a performance.

2) Faults are undesirable traits indicating lack of sound quality and shall be penalized in proportion to the degree of commitment, the frequency of repetition, and the distraction they afford running mates, as well as for the interruption or lack

of progress they cause during performance. Quitting, back-tracking, and ghost trailing are serious faults. Running mute, pottering, swinging, skirting, leaving checks, running hit or miss, babbling, tightness of mouth, and lack of desire or ability to find and move game shall be considered demerits.

3) Mistakes are erratic judgments, sometimes committed under pressure of competition and prompted by a desire to excel and sometimes due to influence of faulty running mates. Where mistakes are not committed with a frequency that would indicate lack of sound quality, consideration should be shown according to the Dachshund's aptitude for realizing its error and its efforts to overcome them.

4) Lack of accomplishment is the failure to get enough done to compare favorably with the competition, and is often due to lack of such qualities as determination, patience, intelligence, or endurance. In instances where this is apparent the penalty should be severe. Judgment on Dachshunds that fail to accomplish as desired should be based on the circumstances under which the failure occurred and the determination and intelligence displayed in the effort to overcome it. Where failure is no fault of the Dachshund, such as in cases of interference with the game or trail, or in a case where a worthy Dachshund encounters an especially hazardous or abnormal circumstance unlike anything that the majority of the contestants are expected to overcome, new game should be provided without penalty. Lack of intelligence is apparent in the Dachshund that does not portray sound judgment and skill during its performance.

Tracking

Tracking is a non-competitive event open to all breeds of dog. All your Doxie needs is a harness and a twenty- to forty-foot lead, and you're set to go. Dogs can compete in the Tracking, Tracking Dog Excellent, or Variable Surface Test. A dog who earns all three titles is a Champion Tracker. At the Tracking level, a dog follows a 440- to 500-yard long track that is between thirty minutes and two hours old. The track contains between three and five turns.

Chloe tracking   *Photo courtesy of Melinda Brown*

The track is not made by a rabbit, however, but by a person dragging a glove or wallet. The American Kennel Club requires that a dog must first pass a certification test before a qualified judge or handler before officially competing for titles; the point is to ensure that only dogs with a reasonably good chance of passing will be competing. (Tracking takes up a *lot* of room—as each entrant needs his own field.)

Earthdog Competitions

Dogs can compete in earthdog trials at three levels: Junior, Senior, and Master. Unlike field trials, the dogs do not compete against each other, but try to pass the test (as in obedience and tracking). At the Junior level, the dog travels a thirty-foot tunnel with three ninety-degree turns. The goal is a rodent (safe inside a cage). When the dog reaches the prey, he must "work" it by barking, digging, or pulling at the cage. He must continue to try to get the prey for one minute. The rodents, of course, aren't thrilled with this event, but they aren't harmed by it either.

Agility

The sport of agility has become extremely popular among dog owners these days, although it is not without its detractors (like me). Agility has three levels: Novice, Open, and Excellent. Two types are offered at each level: "standard" or "jumpers with weave poles." For example, at the Novice "standard" level, a dog dashes through an obstacle course consisting of ramps, seesaws, "dog walks" tunnels, jumps, and a "pause table." The weave pole level adds the weave poles and omits the pause table. There are other minor differences.

Dachshunds are not cut out for agility (except possibly for the tunnel part). It is stressful on all dogs, but Dachshunds run a *serious risk of paralysis* from intervertebral disk disease owing to the stresses of this activity. Dr. Robert Cody, an orthopedic veterinary surgeon for over thirty years, explains that the jumping and twisting involved in agility can result in disk herniation, and strongly advises against Dachshund owners from stressing their dog's backs in this way. If you really want to participate in this sport, my advice is to choose a breed more suited to its rigors. (I personally think that agility is stressful for any dog.) No Dachshund should jump off anything higher than himself. If you are bound and determined to compete in this sport, please don't begin training until your dog is seven or older, when risk of intervertebral disk disease substantially decreases.

Dachshund Club of America Events

Versatility is the name of game these days. More and more dog clubs are rewarding owners not only for encouraging their dogs to participate in what they were originally bred to do, but also to expand their horizons. The Dachshund Club of America (DCA) offers two ways your Dachshund can show his versatility: the DCA Triathlon and the Versatility Program.

The DCA Triathlon

To win the DCA Triathlon, a Dachshund must pass a conformation evaluation by two judges at the annual national specialty and also distinguish himself in three performance events. These may include obedience, field trials, tracking, agility, and earthdog. The dog with the highest combined score is awarded the title: DCA Triathlon Dog of the Year.

The Versatility Program

In the Versatility Program, a dog must earn a total of eighteen points. Some of the points must be conformation points. The rest must be obtained from three of the following five groups: field trials, agility, obedience, tracking, or earth work. Any dog who is a triple Champion, however (conformation, field, and obedience) is qualified to win a Versatility Certificate. Of course, I strongly believe that anyone engaging in this event or the DCA Triathlon, should avoid the agility option.

Racing Dachshunds

For reasons unknown to me, some people have taken up the idea of racing Dachshunds. I suppose that a Dachshund race in one's backyard, among one's own friends might be a lot of fun, but what I'm talking about is commercial Dachshund racing. And I'm not kidding. The DCA has condemned such a practice—which usually takes place at Greyhound racing tracks. The problem began with a Miller Lite commercial depicting two racing Dachshunds; later the Miller Brewing Company started a public relations campaign sponsoring these events. Dachshunds are not designed for racing, and that's all there is to it. If you love this breed, please do not support the continuation of this ridiculous and possibly cruel activity.

Chapter 13

Debugging Your Dachshund—
the Problem of Parasites

Dachshunds are not alone in the world and unfortunately some of their closest companions are not ones good owners approve of.

Fleas

Thanks to modern science, these fleas aren't the problem they used to be. This is so true that I can tell you unreservedly that there is no reason for any modern dog to be afflicted with them. But it still happens—and even one fleabite is enough to transmit tapeworm, or to cause an allergic dog to develop flea dermatitis. Fleas even carry bubonic plague, and although we seem to have gotten that pretty well under control, why allow your dog to run that risk?

Your Head in the Clouds

One great reason to live in Denver is that fleas can't stand high altitudes. Heat and cold, however, don't bother them. However, their favorite kind of climate is hot and moist.

There are over 2200 species of flea worldwide, and luckily most species are not interested in your dog. The most common flea to attack dogs in the cat flea (*Ctenocephalides felis*). I know this doesn't make much sense, but there you are. (One other kind of flea, the sticktight flea, is also fairly common on dogs.) But the cat flea is bad enough. It can lay fifty eggs a day for one hundred days. You do the math. (I was never very good at it—it's a lot of fleas, I'm sure.) The smooth tiny eggs usually fall onto the carpet (or your furniture, car seat, or your dog's bed). A few days later they hatch out into larvae. The larvae live largely on flea feces, which is really a model of recycling, isn't it? About a week later, the larvae spin themselves neat little cocoons and sleep away for a variable period of time, usually a few weeks, but occasionally several months.

As I mentioned, even one bite is enough for your poor Doxie to develop flea allergy dermatitis. This painful, itchy condition is caused by enzymes in flea saliva. Once the dog starts scratching at the spot, he can get hot spots, hair loss, and secondary seborrhea. In many dogs, the condition becomes chronic.

We used to handle fleas by spray treatments, powders, dips, collars, and yard sprays. And while some people still resort to these old-fashioned methods, most up-to-date owners choose to control fleas by capsule or use a spot-on liquid applied to the skin between the shoulder blades. More holistic owners rely on various combinations of herbs, although these are more effective as repellents than killers. Some people swear by garlic as a flea repellent. No scientific evidence shows that garlic is efficacious against fleas. At any rate, you really want to kill fleas—not just repel them—when they might decide to take a bite out of you or some other hapless dog. Some effective products, such as Frontline or Advantage, are available from your veterinarian, although you can get others at the pet supply or grocery store.

Ticks

Ticks are bigger, nastier, and more dangerous than fleas. There are hundreds of species and nearly every one of them can do damage to your dog. Ticks carry Lyme disease (borreliosis), Rocky Mountain spotted fever, a rickettsial disease, ehrlichiosis, *haemobartonellosis*, babesiosis (which causes red blood cell destruction and anemia), tick paralysis, *hepatozoonosi*, and a host of other woes. Ticks don't visibly annoy dogs as much as fleas do, they don't scamper around, and they don't leave feces everywhere—but these are some of the reasons why they're easy to overlook. The tiny deer tick, which is most responsible for Lyme disease, is especially hard to see, only the size of a pinhead in some stages. However, it takes between twenty-four and forty-eight hours for the disease to be transmitted, so careful prevention, grooming, and examination should keep your dog free of this arthritic-like disease.

Most ticks live about two years, and require three different hosts. Each stage of development requires a blood meal before the tick can progress to its next life stage. If the tick doesn't get the meal, it can go into a state of suspended animation to wait for it, thus interrupting the normal lifespan. In fact, some ticks have been to know to wait for seventeen years! So-called hard ticks have four life stages—egg, larva, nymph and adult; an adult tick can lay two thousand to eight thousand eggs, usually in dense, piled up vegetation. There reproduce best in a moist, warm environment. The juvenile lives in the soil, and climb to the tip of a blade of grass to await their first victim.

Ticks tend to hang out around a dog's head where it's difficult for dogs to reach them. You may also find them between the shoulder blades. Never touch a tick with your bare hands. The organism responsible for many tick-borne diseases can sneak in through microscopic cuts in the flesh.

If you find a tick on your Dachshund, remove it immediately with tweezers and throw the tick in the toilet. Flush. Don't try to burn the tick (too dangerous) or smother it with petroleum jelly (takes too long). Also be careful not to squeeze the tick; it might disgorge all the disgusting contents of its body, including bacteria, into your dog's bloodstream. Wash your hands thoroughly afterward, because ticks can give you the same diseases they can give your dog. After you pull off the tick, you may notice some red encrustation near the site of the bite. This is very common, and doesn't mean you left the tick's head in the skin. Clean if carefully with an antibiotic lotion and watch it see that it doesn't turn into a hot spot.

You can protect your dog from tick bites with several excellent products. The best ones contain a residual insecticide, such as fipronil (Frontline), permeththrin (Defend), or selamectin (Revolution). The last named chemical is efficacious against only one species of tick, however. Talk to your vet, and start using them.

There's no really good Lyme disease preventative for humans, but there is one for dogs: amitraz, a monoamine oxidase inhibitor. Amitraz both repels ticks and paralyzes the mouthparts of those ticks that manage to climb aboard and try to bite. It also kills many species of tick, although it has no effect on fleas. Amitraz has been used topically for many years to kill mange mites, but an amitraz-treated collar, such as Preventic, is equally effective against the deer tick *Ixodes scapularis*—the tick that carries the organism (*Borrelia burgdorferi*) responsible for Lyme. Don't confuse an amitraz collar with the more conventional kind of flea collars that don't last as long and usually don't work on ticks at all. Three Lyme disease vaccines have been approved for use in dogs.

It's also important not to double or triple up on insecticides. Many kinds are absorbed into the system, and too much can be toxic to your dog. So if you use a monthly spot-on, don't add another product to be "safe."

Lice

Even seen in the kindest of lights, lice are nasty creatures. *Trichodectes canis* is the variety of chewing louse that attacks canines. This pest spends its entire life cycle—about one month from egg to adult—on the dog. Lice cause intense itching and irritation. As the dog scratches, he opens the way to bacterial, viral, or fungal infection. These lice can be discouraged with ordinary flea products. By the way, the human head louse or crab louse can also infect a dog, if it can't find anything better to munch on.

Mosquitoes

There are over one hundred-seventy species of mosquitoes in North America alone, but only half of them bite—the female half. (In case you were wondering, the average female mosquito needs to eat only every three or four days.) Mosquitoes carry heartworm disease, and a number of other conditions, including the notorious West Nile virus. West Nile is a strain of encephalitis, genetically similar to St. Louis encephalitis. It causes a swelling of the brain that, left untreated, can be fatal. The disease is carried by birds, especially crows. It is transmitted by mosquitoes that bite an infected bird and then bite a person or other animal, including dogs. Veterinarians are not sure whether the disease can be transmitted to dogs that eat an infected carcass. No one knows at the time of this writing how long a dog can carry the virus (in humans it's about fifteen days). A serum test conducted in the New York area showed a surprising 5 to 11 percent of tested dogs near where the virus has been detected were infected; none, however, showed sign of illness. We just don't know enough about the virus yet to know how dangerous it may prove to dogs.

The West Nile virus-carrying mosquito tends to bite at twilight. They also do not travel far from their original birthplace, which is always standing water. Disposing of mosquito egg-laying places is your best prevention.

Regardless of where you live, it is imperative that your dog be protected with heartworm preventative, and, in mosquito-infested areas, it wouldn't hurt to use a mosquito repellent on your dog as well. Many are available in pet supply shops. Although some people claim DEET is safe to use on dogs, I have my doubts, since dogs tend to lick whatever you spray on their skin. Citronella, a natural repellent, is a safer choice.

Mites

Mite infestations are treatable, but of course, they're highly unpleasant. There are several types of mites that hassle our dogs and you should have an idea of how to know whether Mitzy has a mite problem.

Mange Mites

Demodex canis is the mange mite. It is nearly always present (you have them too—in your eyebrows), but they don't usually cause trouble. Mange mite problems come in two forms—localized and general. The localized form usually appears on puppies, while the more serious, generalized form usually shows up on older dogs. When the disease is present, the mites crowd out the hair follicles, causing them to fall out. The result is hair loss and itchy, swollen, red skin. The localized form often resolves itself

without treatment, but the generalized form takes intensive therapy, involving dips in the mite and tick killer amitraz or with oral
ivermectin. A complete cure may take up to six months. Generalized demodex is very often a sign that the dog has another
problem: an autoimmune condition or a serious underlying disease like cancer.

Scabies

The sarcoptic mange, or scabies mite (*Sarcoptes scabei*), is also
called "itch mite," and with good reason. The lady mite burrows
into the skin and lays her eyes there. When the eggs hatch into
larva, the larva dig around even more. The results are lesions on
many parts of the body and secondary infections are common.
Both humans and dogs can get sarcoptic mange. People can get a
temporary case (lasting about a week), from their pets, although
these mites do not actually reproduce on humans. Puppies and
young children are more likely to be affected than adults of either
species. Affected dogs have a yellowish crust on their skin and
matted hair, while human beings get itchy red bumps and a rash.
Moist, enclosed areas like between the toes are most likely to be
affected. The mites burrow into the skin and cause itchiness, redness, and hair loss in both people and dogs. (This mite can affect
almost any kind of animal, by the way, are particularly fond of
livestock.) This mange is treated with special shampoos, pills, or
injections. A good insecticide needs to be applied to the entire
area where the dog lives to prevent reinfection.

Walking Dandruff

The cute name of this mite—walking dandruff (*Cheyletiella
yasguri*)—is indicative of its not so cute habit of producing crud
and hair loss on your dog. It doesn't cause the severe itchiness of
the other mites, nor is it as dangerous. Your vet can treat it easily
with amitraz.

Ear Mites

The ear mite (*Otodectes cynotis*), infests both the external ear
and the ear canal, nibbling away at the loose skin there. Dogs
with ear mites shake their heads and dig at their ears. There will
be a nasty discharge, or even a hematoma from self-mutilation.

The ear needs to be thoroughly cleaned and then treated with a good commercial ear-mite killer. They are available over the counter.

Don't Bother with Dips

In former days, people attempted to kill mites by using various dips. I don't recommend this. Most mites live too deep in the skin to be affected by dips, and some dips can be pretty toxic to dogs.

Internal Parasites

You can do a lot to prevent your Dachshund from being the victim of worms, but you should also know the warning signs of a worm problem.

Tapeworm

Dogs can acquire tapeworms from eating infected fleas (or more rarely, lice). A tapeworm infestation doesn't have many symptoms, and you probably won't even know your pet is affected unless you notice the segments of the worms in his feces. They look like grains of white or pinkish rice. Your veterinarian can prescribe a special dewormer to rid your dog of them.

Roundworm

Roundworm or ascarids *(Toxocara canis)*, are the most common of all internal parasites. They are usually harmless in adult dogs, but can be dangerous when they are passed by mother dogs to her puppies. Nearly all puppies are born with roundworms, and severely affected puppies can die from them. Puppies as young as two weeks can start deworming treatment, which is continued every few weeks until the eggs are no longer found in the samples of the puppies' stools. Infected puppies typically have a rough coat, bad breath, diarrhea, vomiting, and a potbelly. They are usually infected through the placenta before birth and afterward from the mother's milk. (This is true even if the mother has been dewormed. Some of the roundworm larvae have lain encapsulated in the liver, kidneys, and muscle. On the forty-second day of pregnancy, they "wake up" and migrate through the placenta to the puppy fetuses. There should be a law against this sort of behavior, but there is not.)

Whipworm

A severe whipworm infestation can kill a dog—I've seen it. Whipworms live in the dog's large intestine and are present in the dog's feces. The things can survive in the ground for years, so it's important to keep your yard picked up every day.

Hookworm

Hookworms can't be seen by the naked eye, but these tiny little devils are all the nastier for that reason. They can penetrate the skin and cause diarrhea and anemia. Hookworms are found mostly in warmer climates.

Heartworm

Heartworm *(Dirofilaria immitis)*, has been identified throughout the world, from South America to Australia. It prefers warmer climates, and in the United States is found primarily (but not exclusively), in the Southeast. Its natural host is the dog, fox, and wolf, but it has also occurred in cats—and even in humans! The disease is spread by mosquitoes, in whose digestive tract the *microfilaria* mature. Then they molt. After two molts, the third larval stage develops into an infective agent. (For the process to work right, the temperature must stay over sixty-five degrees for a month's time, which is why the disease is seasonal.) Although tiny when they enter the system, heartworms can grow to be a foot long! After about five months in the body, they enter the large vessels of the lungs and heart. Some dogs have been identified with more than two hundred worms. They cause fatigue, coughing, and heart disease, but signs of heartworm disease may not be apparent until after several years of infection. Untreated, the condition is always fatal. A good heartworm preventative can prevent not only heartworm but also roundworm, whipworm, and hookworm! I advise everyone in heartworm areas to keep their dogs on heartworm preventative all year long.

Treatment for heartworm disease involves first destroying the adult worms and then eliminating the *microfilaria*. Risks of therapy are directly related to the number of heartworms and the degree of lung involvement, which increase the incidence of pulmonary thromboembolism.

Giardia

Giardia is a common protozoan parasite that can infect any mammal, including people. (In fact, it is possible for dog owners to contract it from their pets.) *Giardia* has two life stages—the cyst and the trophozoite. Dogs can become infected if they drink cyst-contaminated water, lick cyst-contaminated feces, or devour cyst-infected prey. When the giardia enters the dog's gastrointestinal systems, it develops into the trophozoite stage, which rapidly reproduces.

To protect your pet, keep your yard picked up, and prevent your dog from drinking contaminated water sources. This is tougher than it sounds—even pristine mountain streams and tap water can contain the organism.

The main symptoms of *giardiasis* are vomiting and diarrhea in dogs. Humans report cramping and nausea also, but these symptoms are difficult to detect in dogs. If the condition is not treated, infected animals can suffer weight loss and continued periods of vomiting and diarrhea. A stool sample is sometimes used for diagnosis, although even that can be hit-or-miss. The ELISA blood test is more accurate, because it looks for a specific protein particular to *giardia*. This test is quite a bit more expensive than the fecal test, however. Several drugs are available to treat *giardiasis*, and there is also a vaccine available. Talk over your options with your vet.

Viruses, Bacteria and the Vaccine Controversy

Other loathsome life forms—viruses and bacteria—prey upon your Dachshund. Most of these can be kept at bay by a sensible vaccination program. This isn't as easy as it sounds. As the American Veterinary Association now declares: "Medical decisions about vaccine selection and protocols have become complex." That's an understatement. What used to be a simple annual procedure is now fraught with questions. This is partly because we now know more about the immune system than before; partly because our animals are no longer "pets" but full-fledged family members; and partly because our dogs are living longer lives so that we can observe the efficacy of immunizations over long-term use. We also know more about adverse effects associated with vaccinations, and understand more about infectious diseases. (Some people prefer to use titration tests to determine antibody levels rather than routine vaccinations for their dogs; however, optimum levels of antibodies have not been established—you're still playing a guessing game.)

We know that vaccines have played an important role in helping all of us live longer and healthier lives. But we also know that there is *no single best protocol* for vaccination or revaccination. The one-year revaccination frequency recommendation has been based on historical precedent and U.S. Department of Agriculture regulations, not on scientific data. Some vaccines provide protection for more than a year, no matter what the label says.

Making Vaccines More Valuable

Studies have shown that puppies undergoing vaccinations directly benefit from antioxidants in the diet following vaccinations. The antioxidants increase antibody titers and so boost the response rate to the puppies' shots.

Revaccinating an animal with sufficient immunity doesn't significantly increase his resistance to disease and may increase the potential of an adverse reaction. These adverse effects can come from one of the components of the vaccine—an antigen, adjuvant, carrier, preservative, or a combination of these. Further, vaccines don't always "take." A vaccine is never a guarantee that an animal will not get the disease it was vaccinated against. Some animals develop a reaction to a vaccine and some develop immunosuppression or autoimmune disorders after vaccination. Some can develop transient infections, or even long-term infected carrier states. Researchers are currently investigating whether vaccine sites can lead to the growth of malignant tumors.

Despite all this possibly scary information, we do know that by and large vaccines work really well to protect your pets and you. Vaccines have eradicated smallpox, and are responsible for getting rid of most distemper as well. However, what vaccines *your* dog needs, and when he should be vaccinated or revaccinated, is a decision for you to discuss with your own veterinarian. Today, vaccines are often divided into two groups: *core* vaccines (against diseases that pose the most serious threat) and *non-core*—obviously, the rest of them. Usually, core vaccines are considered to be those against distemper, adenovirus (hepatitis), parvovirus, and rabies. In some places leptospirosis is also considered to be a core vaccine.

The following is a list of the common diseases for which vaccines are available—which ones you use are up to you and your veterinarian.

Rabies

Although rabies is not common and not very catching, it's always fatal. Vaccinating dogs against rabies is always a good idea, because rabid dogs may bite people and then humans contract the disease. Rabies is transmitted through saliva into the blood stream, usually by a bite. It affects the central nervous system with lethal precision. Once symptoms appear, the victim—canine or human—is sure to die. (People don't get rabies vaccinations, though, at least not most of the time.) In fact, all mammals are susceptible to rabies, although some (foxes and raccoons, for example), are more likely to get it than others (like squirrels and groundhogs). Anyway, it is the law in most places that you must get your dog a rabies shot at about four months of age. Rabies shots must be renewed periodically. How often depends upon the type of vaccination and the law in your state. Some states require yearly boosters, while other states mandate them only every three years.

Distemper

Distemper, a highly contagious viral disease, is a worldwide killer of unvaccinated puppies and even of older dogs. (Wolves, foxes, raccoons, and mink get it too.) Distemper is airborne, but it can also be spread by contaminated objects. About 80 percent of puppies who contract the disease will die, as will about 50 percent of older dogs. Even a dog who survives a bout of distemper may have a permanently damaged nervous system. He might lose some of his vision, hearing, or even his sense of smell. Puppies who contract distemper usually lose significant tooth enamel, resulting in a brown band around the tooth. The disease is very difficult to treat, and often fatal.

Distemper manifests in two stages. In the first stage the dog will exhibit fever, loss of appetite, discharge from the eyes and nose that gets progressively thicker, cough, diarrhea, vomiting, and pustules on the abdomen. It may just look like a bad cold. Many dogs experience a temporary recovery from this stage. The second stage affects the brain and nervous system, and manifests itself by convulsions. There is no excuse whatever for failing to vaccinate against this dread disease.

Adenovirus

This disease is spread by body fluid contact. It primarily affects the kidneys and liver. It begins as a cough, and can progress to extreme thirst. Symptoms include vomiting, diarrhea, and something called "hepatitis blue eye" as fluid accumulates in that organ. This virus, and the disease it causes, canine infectious hepatitis, is not widespread, and not all veterinarians include it as a core vaccine.

Parvovirus

Parvovirus is a terrible killer of puppies, characterized by severe, odorous, bloody, yellowish diarrhea as well as vomiting, high fever, and lethargy. It can involve the heart as well, causing congestive heart failure months or even years after an attack. Even puppies who survive parvo infection often remain somewhat unhealthy and weak ever after. There is no cure for parvo. (In fact, there's no real cure for any viral disease. All that can be done is to give the stricken animal supportive care.) All dogs should be vaccinated against parvo and not permitted contact with strange dogs until two weeks after their last vaccination. Immunization against parvo is often included in the distemper vaccine. This shot gives protection against several potentially fatal canine diseases all at the same time.

Leptospirosis

Leptospirosis is a bacterial infection of the kidneys, and although not usually fatal, it can damage the kidney, liver, or heart. Infection occurs when a bacterium passes from the urine of an infected host through an open wound. The agent is a spirochete that exists in at least six interesting varieties. Recently, the disease has returned in a new and virulent strain, one that was previously seen only in horses and cows. Over one hundred dogs on Long Island died from this new strain in 2000. Dogs typically contract leptospirosis through direct contact with the urine of infected animals, but not all dogs who encounter it will be become sick. They may turn into carriers, shedding the virus in their urine and infecting other animals in turn.

In its most dangerous form, lepto can affect and shut down the kidneys. Treatment includes antibiotics and, in cases of kidney failure, dialysis. A vaccine is available for some forms of leptospirosis; however, many veterinarians do not recommend its use, especially for young puppies. The older forms of lepto are seldom seen nowadays, and the vaccine can cause reactions in some dogs. A vaccine against the new lepto strain is being tested.

Parainfluenza/Bordetella

Because of its extremely contagious nature, parainfluenza is commonly known as kennel cough. It affects the upper respiratory system. Although not too serious in older dogs (it's like a bad cold), it can be very detrimental to puppies. Most grooming shop and boarding kennel staff want to see proof of vaccination before they will take your dog.

Coronavirus

Coronavirus disease bears a superficial resemblance to parvovirus, but it is not nearly as serious. Usually coronavirus is spread when a puppy samples some infected feces. It is generally self-limiting, and vaccination for it is relatively uncommon and usually unnecessary.

Lyme disease (Borrelia)

Lyme disease is found everywhere in the country, but it is most prevalent in the mid-Atlantic region. Symptoms include arthritis-like pain and swelling, fever, and loss of appetite. Vaccination may be recommended for dogs who spend a lot of time in the woods.

Chapter 14
Dachshund Diseases

Standard and miniature Dachshunds fall prey to pretty much the same set of problems. This is to be expected, since they share the same body structure and genetic pool.

Spaying and Neutering: Please Don't Breed

Spaying and neutering are veterinary procedures designed to make the world a better place. You'll not only spare your dog the pains of parenthood but also the many diseases that plague intact animals. Not incidentally, you'll also make your own life easier by doing so.

Spaying your female dog early significantly decreases the risk of mammary cancer, one of the most common types of cancer in dogs as well as in people. You'll also avoid the spectacle and annoyance of all the neighborhood stray males howling at your window. One of the main reasons to neuter, of course, is to help prevent the ever-rising tide of unwanted dogs. Statistically, nearly half of all puppies born end up homeless or are euthanized.

Neutering a male dog eliminates the risk of testicular cancer, reduces propensity to wander, and may help diminish aggressiveness. Aging male dogs are more likely to develop prostate problems if they were never neutered, or neutered late in life. Most veterinarians recommend neutering between the age of six months and one year. However, there is a growing trend toward so-called juvenile neutering. It has been shown that young dogs experience less trauma than dogs with a mature reproductive system. The only reason not to neuter is if you have a show dog—AKC rules presently forbid altered animals from participating in conformation events. Of course people who breed Dachshunds cannot neuter their dog, but breeding is such a bad idea for most people that I never recommend it.

There are too many dogs in the world right now that need homes. To flood the market with more puppies is unethical. This is especially true in the Dachshund world, where quality puppies are difficult to breed unless you know precisely what you're doing. This entails more than having a couple of unaltered dogs around the house and wondering if they would "make cute puppies." Having puppies is serious business—your mother dog could die during the process. Do you want to risk that? And if you are under the impression that you will "make money" out of breeding your dog, you're wrong—in fact, you shouldn't own one. A dog is a companion and partner in your life, not a profit center.

Barney, a smooth, red miniature   *Photo courtesy of Phyllis Grilli*

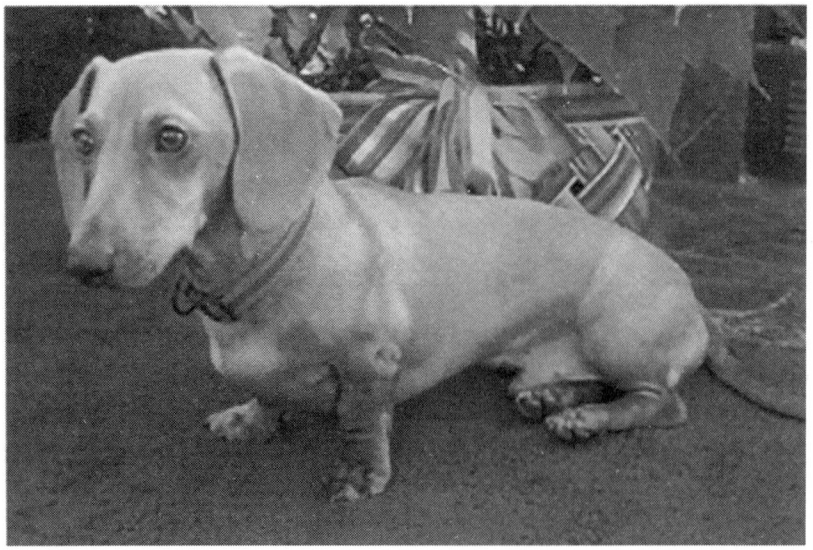

Basic Home Health Care

If your veterinarian prescribes a medication for your dog, don't leave the office without a clear understanding of what you're supposed to do with it. Here is the minimum of what you need to know about each medication your pet gets:

▼ What it is. You should know both the generic and trade name.
▼ What it's for.
▼ When to give it, and for how long.
▼ How it should be administered.
▼ What side effects it may have.
▼ How it interacts with other medications your pet is getting.

Administering Medication

The easiest way to give a Dachshund a pill is to stick it in a piece of bread of a piece of American cheese. Sometimes you can just coat the pill in butter. But for those times when this is impossible, it's still not hard to pill your dog. Simply put the dog on a small table, open the little guy's jaw and place the pill as far back on the tongue as possible. Hold his jaws gently closed, and stroke his throat. Bingo! The pill is gone. You can also try this: while holding the dog's mouth closed, blow gently into his eyes. The natural blink reflex will also cause the dog to swallow the pill.

Liquid medications can be given with an oral syringe. (Luckily most medications are in another form nowadays.) Tuck the syringe neatly down the "pocket" of the dog's mouth, and hold the jaws closed, with the lips held firmly together. Don't cram the thing directly down the Doxie's throat, because you might get the medication into his lungs by mistake. Keep the dog's head tilted upward. After giving the medication, stroke your dog's throat gently.

If you are giving your dog a homeopathic remedy in pill form, be careful not to touch the capsule, because contact with your skin is said to neutralize the remedy. Don't feed your dog for fifteen minutes before administering a homeopathic medication, since tiny food particles in the mouth can interfere with the action of the remedy.

Taking Your Dog's Temperature

Although you won't be taking your dog's temperature every day, it's a good skill to learn in case you suspect that something is wrong. So the first time you try it, it's best to work with a healthy animal. Buy a canine a rectal thermometer, because thermometers for people are too delicate. (Unfortunately, those stick-it-in-the-ear probes don't read accurately for dogs due to the L-shape of a dog's ear canal. You'll have to do it the old fashioned way.)

▼ Put your Doxie on a small table. It's best to have a friend hold the front while you tackle the rear.

▼ Clean the thermometer with alcohol and shake it down until it reads about 96 degrees F or 35 degrees C. (Keep a moist towelette nearby to clean it afterward.)

▼ Lubricate the thermometer with mineral oil or petroleum jelly.

▼ Lift your Doxie's tail gently and place the end of the thermometer into the rectum. Slide it slightly upward about until it's halfway inserted, and let it remain for about two minutes.

▼ Remove the instrument, wipe it, and read it. Normal canine temperature should read at 100.5 to 102.5 degrees F and 38.1 to 39.2 degrees C. Variation of more than a degree may warrant a call to your vet, especially if combined with other symptoms.

Recognizing an Emergency

An emergency is a situation in which you need to get your Dachshund to the vet as quickly as possible. Of course, not every ailment needs professional treatment, and even professional treatment can usually be scheduled somewhat at your convenience. But these symptoms require *immediate action*:

▼ Bleeding from the nose or mouth
▼ Spurting blood (arterial bleeding)
▼ Eye injuries
▼ Paralysis
▼ Seizures or disorientation
▼ Problems with breathing or swallowing

▼ Repeated vomiting
▼ Diarrhea lasting more than eighteen hours
▼ Refusal to eat for forty-eight hours
▼ Burns
▼ Bloated stomach
▼ Muscle tremors
▼ Broken bones
▼ Unusual swellings, especially sudden, hard, or fast-growing ones

Bleeding

If your dog is bleeding, apply pressure to the site. Don't stop for at least five minutes. Place one bandage on top of another as the first becomes soaked with blood. Don't remove the old bandage, because you may pull off a forming clot. It's best to use a sterile bandage, of course, but if you don't have one handy (and in serious cases you won't) use *anything*. Dirty towels, rags, old shirts, bare hands—whatever it takes to stop the bleeding. You'll be taking the dog to the vet anyway, and he'll administer any needed antibiotics. The most important thing is to stop the blood loss.

Much more serious than regular cuts, of course, are cuts that slice across arteries. Arterial blood is usually very bright red, and comes in spurts, rather than the steady flow of darker blood characteristic of venous cuts. In case of arterial bleeding, you must stop the blood flow at once. Apply strong pressure to the wound site. If the bleeding continues, apply pressure to the pressure point closest to the wound, between the wound and the heart. Pressure points are located in "armpits," the groin, and just below the base of the tail, on the underside. Press firmly until the bleeding slows. You will have to relax the pressure for a few seconds every few minutes, so you don't cause tissue and nerve death.

Broken Bones

If your dog breaks a leg, the important thing is to get him to a vet. If you know how to immobilize the dog and set a splint, do so—otherwise, simply try to keep the dog quiet while you transport him to the clinic. If you think your Doxie's spine has been damaged, slide a board beneath him very carefully and try to keep the dog immobile throughout the transport.

Choking

Dogs, especially puppies, will try to eat any number of odd items. Sometimes these can lodge in the intestine—sometimes they don't get that far. If your Dachshund is choking, gently open his mouth. If you can see the object, pull it out. If you can't, try the canine Heimlich maneuver. Place the Dachshund on his side, and press both hands down just below the last rib. Use short, quick thrusts.

Constipation

There are many causes for constipation, including insufficient dietary fiber, and foreign material in the intestines, such as hair or bone. Other factors could include fractures of the pelvis or hind legs, rectal lesions, prostate trouble, spinal cord or disk disease, tumors, and metabolic disorders. Even changes in a dog's daily routine can result in constipation—as can plain old lack of exercise. The easiest way to prevent constipation is to make sure your dog gets plenty of water and sufficient exercise. If symptoms continue, see your vet.

Canine Coughing

Coughing can be caused by anything from a tickle (or obstruction) in the throat to heartworm or congestive heart failure.

Diarrhea

Like vomiting, diarrhea can be a sign of many diseases, including a virus or worm infestation. (Bloody or extremely smelly diarrhea is particularly serious.) It can also result from something comparatively harmless, like anxiety or from eating a new food. In puppies, however, diarrhea is always serious, even if it is caused by something relatively benign. This is because a puppy can dehydrate very quickly. A puppy with a diarrhea needs to see the vet immediately.

Dogs with diarrhea should be given Imodium, Pepto-Bismol, or Kaopectate. Do not feed the dog for a day to allow his intestines to rest. In mild diarrhea, the dog should be allowed plenty of water, but serious cases require veterinary care and IV fluids. In these cases, giving the dog more water can make the diarrhea even worse.

Lameness

First things first. Check the pads of your Dachshund's feet to make sure there is no thorn lodged there or other irritation. *If* it's a pulled muscle, your dog will probably feel fine after a few days of rest. If you suspect a torn ligament or a break, however, you'll need to take him to the vet.

Paralysis or "Slipped Disk" (Intervertebral Disk Disease)

Get the dog to a Dachshund-competent vet immediately. Quick action can reverse many cases of paralysis. *Do not wait* in the hope that the dog will get better on his own. Do not use herbs, homeopathy, flower essences, magnetism, or *anything* as a replacement for immediate veterinary care. Sincere prayer or chanting is acceptable—but do it in the car on the way to the vet. Time is of the essence. Every hour that passes results in more damage and treatment within three hours of the injury or event greatly improves the chances of regaining spinal cord function. After twelve hours it may be too late. Your vet will probably prescribe steroids to get the circulation back to the spinal canal. Surgery is a viable option for many cases, and paralysis can often be completely reversed—if you hurry.

Disk problems can be classified as follows, and one stage may progress to the next:

▼ Pain on being picked up
▼ Lethargy and pain when moving
▼ Weakness and some pain in rear legs
▼ Weakness in rear legs without pain
▼ Paralysis of rear legs, bladder and bowl control retained
▼ Paralysis of rear legs with no bladder or bowel control

Poisoning

Your dog can be poisoned by ingesting, breathing, or merely coming in contact with a toxic substance. The symptoms vary according to the toxin, but common signs include vomiting, labored breathing, abdominal pain, and a bad body- or breath-odor. Obviously this is an emergency. Try to identify the substance and call your vet and the National Animal Poison Control Center hot line: (800) 548-2423 or (900) 680-0000. There is a charge, so have your credit card ready. It will be worth it.

Vomiting

Because dogs are by nature scavengers as well as predators, it's easy for them to devour things that are nasty, inedible, or downright poisonous. Luckily, dogs are gifted with the ability to vomit easily (and apparently with little discomfort) so vomiting can often be seen not as a sign of sickness, but as a way to prevent it. Repeated vomiting, however, may signal something more sinister, especially if the vomiting is accompanied by diarrhea and fever. These symptoms could signal a virus. If the dog vomits repeatedly but has no fever or diarrhea, he could have an intestinal blockage. Dachshunds swallow many things that aren't good for them—including socks, rocks, and clocks. All can and have caused blockages. Get the dog to a veterinarian for X-rays or barium tests (many soft objects won't show up on X-rays). Vomiting can also be a sign of poisoning.

Don't be squeamish about taking a good look at the vomit—the presence of blood, grass, or foreign objects can be a tip off as to the cause. Most experts believe that dogs ingest grass to cause vomiting and because dogs lack the enzyme to digest grass, it works, too.

Diseases and Conditions

In addition to the truly critical health care concerns I've mentioned, dogs can suffer from a variety of afflictions.

Allergic Dermatitis

About 15 percent of all dogs today are afflicted with chronic allergic reactions to inhaled particles—ranging from maple tree emissions to dust mites. Allergic dogs exhibit intense itching and hair loss. Allergic dermatitis can affect dogs as young as six months, but commonly appears later, between the ages of one to three years. Allergies can't be cured, but they can be managed.

The most effective treatment involves removing the allergen from the dog's environment (which is not always possible) or submitting the dog to a series of hyposensitization shots. The shots are effective about 60 percent of the time. Another approach is the use of antihistamines or alternate-day glucocorticoid therapy. Heska Corporation has developed an in-clinic test, Allercept E-Screen, than can determine in five minutes whether your dog has an allergy. The test is not expensive, and can be valuable in helping your vet determine what is ailing your dog.

Acanthosis Nigricans

Acanthosis nigricans is a skin problem to which Dachshunds are particularly susceptible, often developing it at a young age. In fact, primary *acanthosis nigricans* is found almost exclusively in this breed. (Technically, this condition is not a disease, but a "clinical reaction pattern.") It is characterized by a darkening and thickening of the skin, seborrhea, and baldness. The problem is not curable, but early cases can be treated with shampoo therapy and topical treatments. For advanced cases, a more aggressive systemic therapy may be useful.

Arthritis

Although arthritis can result from trauma, it is most usually associated with the aging process. For more information about managing arthritis in your Dachshund, see Chapter 15.

Bladder Stones

Dogs can develop several different kinds of bladder stones, each of which may require different medical treatment. Common types include struvite, calcium oxalate, urate, cystine, calcium phosphate, and silica. And some bladder stones can be a mix of types! In addition, different breeds seem prone to different kinds of bladder stones. Struvite stones, the most frequently seen type, are often associated with a bacterial infection. Sometimes the stones can be dissolved; at other times surgery is needed. Non-surgical treatment includes controlling the urinary tract infection and acidifying the diet.

A Word About Genetics

At one time, most of the problems veterinarians saw were due to trauma or infections. Now most of them are genetically related, the result of inbreeding and linebreeding in purebred dogs, including Dachshunds. Purebred dogs are an "island population," whose loss of genetic diversity over the past few generations has led to a host of health problems. This is as true of "popular" breeds like Dachshunds as in rare breeds like Canaan dogs, because of the comparatively few founders of the breed. It is now believed that the average inbreeding level in purebred dogs has reached 14 percent. (Notably, in commercial livestock deleterious health effects are seen at 9 percent.) The purebred dogs of this world are in serious trouble, and the back problems of Dachshunds are a case in point. Until breeders get together and decide to reverse the trend, there can be no solution.

Cancer

Cancer is the major disease-related killer of dogs in the United States today. Although any dog can develop cancer, it is most common in dogs aged ten or older, so I'll be talking about it in Chapter 15.

Color Mutant or Color Dilution Alopecia

This is a genetic deficiency of the hair coat, and is seen primarily in blue Dachshunds. (The gene at the D locus is diluted, if you want the explanation.) Clinical signs include bacterial folliculitis, hair loss, and scaling, mainly over the back. It generally occurs during the first year or two of life.

Cushing's Disease

Dachshunds are predisposed to Cushing's disease, a fairly common condition caused by excess production of cortisol by the adrenal cortex. Cortisol is an essential hormone released in times of illness, stress, pain, and injury to help the body cope with these stressful events. When too much cortisol is produced, however, the effects can be harmful and even fatal. For example, cortisol can reduce the kidneys' ability to reabsorb water, which in turn causes the loss of dangerously large amounts of water in the urine. Complications of Cushing's disease include increased risk of infection, high blood pressure, congestive heart failure, pancreatitis, diabetes, and blood clotting abnormalities. If the disease is left untreated, the animal will probably die.

Most naturally occurring cases result from pituitary corticotroph tumors or hyperplasia over-secreting ACTH. This is a multi-systemic disorder, but most obvious symptoms concern the skin and urinary tract. Most commonly this disease is seen in middle-aged and older animals. The severity of the disease can vary greatly, and treatment must be life-long; the drug of choice is Mitotane. For properly treated dogs, the prognosis is good.

Cutaneous Vasculitis

Cutaneous vasculitis is a disease to which Dachshunds (and Rottweilers) appear to be disposed. It is an inflammation of the blood vessels and usually affects the paws, the edge of the ears, lips, tail, and mouth. It can be the result of a disease like lupus, a stress like frostbite, or even a vaccine reaction or spider bite. Your veterinarian will do a skin scraping for a diagnosis and may do a biopsy of an early lesion. The prognosis depends upon the cause.

Cysts

Cysts are harmless lumps that form under the skin. However, sometimes something that looks like a cyst could be something more serious like an abscess or even a tumor. Have your veterinarian examine your dog should you see anything suspicious.

Deafness

Canine deafness can be a result of many things including: age, drug toxicity, noise, infection, or trauma. However, we are also seeing increasing numbers of cases of congenital deafness, particularly in double dappled Dachshunds. Blue-eyed dogs have a greater incidence of deafness than those with brown eyes. The mechanism of inheritance of deafness is not known. In many cases, hearing seems to develop normally until the puppy is three or four weeks old, when the vascular supply to the cochlea degenerates, so the hair cells of the cochlea die. There is no treatment, and the deafness is total for each affected ear. The degeneration *seems* to result from a lack of pigment cells, but no one knows for certain. Some experts believe that the pigment cells are suppressed by the piebald gene that produces white in the hair coat.

Bilaterally deaf dogs soon give themselves away, but deafness in only one ear may go undetected as the dog responds to sounds with his good ear. These dogs do have trouble localizing sound, but they soon learn to adapt. The only way to be *sure* about a dog's hearing is to have it tested by the BAER (brainstem auditory evoked response) test.

Dehydration

A dehydrated dog is in serious danger, but a water-deprived dog can be restored quickly. To test, take up a fold of skin and then release it. The skin should return quickly to its normal place. In a dehydrated dog, however, the skin stays loose. Supply the dog with cool water.

Diabetes

Diabetes mellitus is a condition characterized by a deficiency of, or insensitivity to insulin. Insulin is a hormone produced in the islet cells of the pancreas. It controls blood concentrations of glucose, the main fuel for the body. Normally, insulin does this by preventing glucose production by the liver and ensuring that excess glucose derived from food not needed for energy is put into body stores. However, in diabetic animals there is not enough insulin to switch off glucose production by the liver or to efficiently store excess glucose derived from foods. This means that the blood concentration of glucose eventually exceeds a level beyond which the kidneys let glucose leak into the urine. This loss of glucose in urine takes water with it and causes larger volumes of urine to be produced than normal. The main signs of a diabetic animal are therefore excessive urination and drinking. Diabetic animals often lose weight because they break down fat and protein to make glucose and ketones (an alternative fuel) in the liver. Other clinical signs of diabetes may include cataracts, increased appetite, exercise intolerance, and recurrent infections.

The treatment of choice for diabetes mellitus is insulin. Nowadays, dogs can have their glucose monitored at home. You can collect a small blood sample from the ear, either with a conventional lancing device or by means the newer Microlet Vaculance. After the blood collection, a portable glucose meter can determine the blood sugar level within just a few minutes.

Hot Pepper Healer

Jamaicans long ago found that something as zesty as hot peppers may have a role in curbing diabetes—at least in dogs. Researchers discovered that the active compound in hot peppers, capsaicin, effectively lowers the blood sugar level in diabetic dogs and also causes an increase in insulin secretion. Traditional Jamaican healers have used hot pepper for years in treating diabetes, and now it looks as if they had good reasons for doing so. This is not to say you should start feeding your diabetic dog hot peppers. He won't like them.

Dry Coats

Most dry coats are caused by dietary inadequacy, although certain diseases can also manifest themselves in a harsh coat. If your veterinarian has ruled out a medical problem, try giving your dog extra oil in his dinner—cod liver oil, or a commercial preparation. Keep giving him the oil for some time, improvement will not be immediately apparent.

Epilepsy

No one knows what causes epilepsy, either in dogs or in people. Its symptoms can range from the unnoticeable to the truly terrifying, in which the dog loses control of his legs and appears within the grip of a powerful unseen force. This is called a grand mal seizure. (Less severe seizures are now called simple or partial seizures.) In fact, in early days, it was thought that people who suffered from epilepsy were possessed by demons. Now, of course, we know that is not the case. Seizures can be caused by numerous conditions, including head injury, liver or kidney dysfunction, tumors, infections, and too little blood supply to the brain. Veterinarians can perform a variety of tests (including blood cell count, chemistry profile, liver function and thyroid hormone level tests, and magnetic resonance imaging) to discover what causes may underlie a seizure.

Sometimes, however, we don't know why a dog has seizures, and the technical medical term for this condition is idiopathic epilepsy. (Of course epilepsy does have a cause—we just don't know what it is.) Affected dogs are either younger than one year or older than five years. It appears to be more common in unneutered and unspayed dogs. (Because epilepsy can be passed on from generation to generation, no epileptic dog or dog with epilepsy in its family should be bred anyway.) The apparent agony of the seizures can go on for a few seconds or for more than fifteen minutes. A dog may suffer multiple seizures within a short time (cluster seizures) or from one long seizure (*status epilepticus*). This is a medical emergency; get the dog to the vet at once.

The typical seizure has four stages:

1) The *prodome* may precede the actual seizure by hours or days. It is characterized by mood and behavioral changes.

2) The *aura* signals the start of the true seizure. Your dog may whine, cry, or pace. He may try to hide or salivate excessively. He may begin to tremble.

3) The *ictus* is the actual seizure, characterized by sudden increase in tone of all muscle groups. It will last for one to three minutes.

4) The *postictus* phase is characterized by confusion and disorientation. The dog may be conscious but not functional.

Traditionally, veterinarians have recommended that only dogs who have one or more seizures per week should receive medication for epilepsy. New research, however, suggests that the sooner therapy is begun, the more successful it will be in controlling seizures. The most commonly used drugs to treat epilepsy are Phenobarbital and bromide. If these inexpensive drugs fail to do the trick, new medications such as felbamate, gabapentin, phenytoin, and valproic acid may be prescribed.

Although seizures may never completely stop, good drug therapy can reduce their frequency and severity. Never withdraw a dog suddenly from his epilepsy medication. To do so may bring on longer, more frequent, and more severe seizures. The Canine Epilepsy Research Consortium is trying to find ways to genetically screen for this disease. To learn more about canine epilepsy, and how you can help wipe it out, see www.canine-epilepsy.net.

Food Allergies

In dogs, food allergies are less common than those caused by inhalants. (If the allergy is seasonal, it's not a food allergy.) In addition to the typical redness and itching characteristic of most canine allergic reactions, a food allergic dog may also have vomiting or diarrhea. In order to trace the offending ingredient, you need to conduct a food trial of at least four weeks, giving nothing (including treats) except the recommended diet—usually a novel form of protein (like herring or emu) and a bland carbohydrate like rice. Alternatively, you could try eliminating beef, wheat, and corn from your allergic dog's diet, for these are common allergens. Remember to check treats for the forbidden ingredients.

Fungal Infections

Besides ringworm, considered separately, your Dachshund can fall prey to a variety of fungal infections. These include *Coccidioidomycosis* (*Valley Fever*), *Blastomycosis, Cryptococcosis, Aspergillosis, Candidiasis,* and *Histoplasmosis.* Many of these fungal infections are hard to pin down and diagnose, and microscopic examination is critical to making an accurate diagnosis. In addition, many fungal diseases are restricted to certain areas of the country, so it's important when you take a sick dog to the vet to mention any trips you've recently taken with your dog. Treatment for serious fungal diseases is expensive and time-consuming, but you know your dog is well worth it.

Gastric Torsion (Bloat)

The technical name for this terrible condition is Gastric Dilatation Volvulus (GDV). Dachshunds are one of the very few small breeds with a disposition to this dread disease, probably due to their narrow but deep chests—a body configuration that is a chief indicator of bloat-potential.

In bloat, gases or air builds up in the stomach. After a certain point, the stomach twists (torsion), cutting off contact with the esophagus and trapping the gas. This puts pressure on the large blood vessels of the abdomen, leading ultimately to organ failure.

This disease attacks suddenly—often at night. A stricken dog can die within two hours of onset, and more than one owner has come home to the tragic sight of a bloat-killed dog. It is an agonizing and painful death. Symptoms of bloat include:

▼ Pacing and discomfort
▼ Repeatedly lying down and getting back up
▼ Salivation
▼ Panting
▼ Attempts to vomit
▼ Extended abdomen in most cases as the condition progresses

These signs indicate an emergency. Get your Dachshund to the emergency vet clinic immediately, even if it's 3:00 AM. (It probably will be.) *Do not wait!* Left untreated, even for a few hours, your dog will probably die. The first twenty to thirty minutes of bloat's onset are most critical. The vet will X-ray your dog to see if torsion has taken place. If it hasn't he can insert a tube into the stomach to let out the air. If torsion has occurred, a tube is inserted directly through the abdominal wall into the stomach. Once the situation is stabilized, the vet will perform surgery to reposition the stomach.

Even now, there is no cure for bloat and no surefire prevention. But things have made a dramatic turn around. Until the 1990s about 80 percent of dogs who developed bloat died. Now about 85 percent of them live. That's something to cheer about!

No one really knows what causes bloat, or how to prevent it. Many factors combine to create a risk environment for the disease. They include breed, size and shape of the dog, age, genetics, diet, and (rather surprisingly) personality.

▼ **Age:** The older the dog, the higher the risk.

▼ **Gender:** Male dogs have a *slightly* increased risk.

▼ **Personality:** Fearful, nervous, and aggressive dogs have the highest risk for bloat; low-key, happy, easy-going dogs the least.

▼ **Weight:** Underweight dogs are most at risk. Researchers believe that chronic underweight may indicate a permanent problem with the gastrointestinal system that leads to the disease.

▼ **Fast eating:** Gobblers are at a much higher risk of bloat. This is probably because they gulp air. If your Doxie is a fast eater, try placing a rock or heavy chain (no kidding) in the middle of his food dish to force him to slow down as he eats around it.

▼ **Genetics:** Dogs with close relatives who have bloated are at significant risk.

▼ **Food type:** Dogs fed solely on dry food are at increased risk of bloat. Dogs fed with table scraps added are at lower risk.

▼ **Feeding schedule:** Dogs fed only once a day are at greater risk of bloat. The more frequently you feed your dog, the lower the risk.

▼ **Flatulence or belching:** Belching dogs have an 80 percent increased risk of bloat. Flatulent dogs are at a 20 percent increased risk.

Gastropexy is the treatment of choice when a dog is subjected to one or more bouts of bloat. In this surgical procedure, the vet will stitch the stomach to the abdominal wall in an attempt to prevent it from twisting. This procedure will not stop bloat, but it will prevent the accompanying torsion.

Glaucoma

Dogs suffer from this painful and blindness-inducing disease just as people do. It comes in several forms. Primary glaucoma, which is inherited, usually starts in one eye, but later affects both. (Secondary glaucoma usually results from injury or trauma to the eye and is thus not inherited.) To make things more complicated, primary glaucoma also comes in two forms: closed angle and open angle. Dogs with closed angle glaucoma, the most common form in Dachshunds, have eyes with a shallow anterior chamber and a narrow angle. Because the iris partly blocks the angle, an increase in intraocular pressure can develop. (In open angle glaucoma, the angle of the anterior chamber remains open, but filtration of the aqueous humor is gradually reduced, causing (again) an increase in intraocular pressure.)

Glaucoma can appear very suddenly. The affected eye is swollen, red, and cloudy. It is obviously painful. The pupil will be abnormally large, and may weep. The dog may be sensitive to light. *This is an emergency; your dog needs immediate professional care.* Your vet will make an accurate diagnosis with a tonometer to measure the pressure. He may try to relieve the pressure with eye drops or diuretics. The immediate goal is to relieve the pressure as quickly as possible. The veterinarian will need to reevaluate the dog every few days during the first week. In many cases, surgery to remove the affected eye is the only option. Other surgical options include diode laser surgery and cyclo-cryosurgery. Unfortunately, the prognosis for glaucoma is poor.

To test whether or not a dog is prone to certain types of glaucoma, the vet can perform what is called a gonioscopy, an examination of the iridocorneal angle for abnormalities that may predispose the eye to glaucoma. For more information check with the Canine Eye Registration Foundation: www.vmdb.org/ or the Veterinary Ophthalmology Information Center at www.eyevet.ca.

Heatstroke

Heatstroke is deadly. In heatstroke, your dog's internal body temperature soars from its normal 99.5 to 102.5 degrees F to a dangerous 104 degrees. Symptoms include high fever, collapse, panting, and grayish lips. If your dog is affected, relieve him in a cool (not cold) bath and supply water to drink. If he won't drink, wipe the inside of his mouth with a cool wet rag. Fan and massage him. And get him to the veterinarian.

Heatstroke Hazard

Never leave your Dachshund in the car on a warm day—even if you open the windows and put the car in the shade. It's not enough. Dogs do not tolerate heat as well as people.

Hemorrhagic Gastroenteritis

Dachshunds are one of the breeds most disposed toward developing hemorrhagic gastroenteritis. This dangerous condition appears quite suddenly in previously healthy dogs. Its most characteristic symptom is bloody, often explosive, diarrhea, and vomiting. Internally, the dog is also experiencing hypovolemia, a decreased volume of plasma circulating in the body. No one really knows what causes it, but if not treated aggressively, the dog can die from shock. The veterinarian will replace fluids and electrolytes; he will also put the dog on a course of antibiotics. When the dog recovers, he'll be put on a bland, low-fat, low-fiber diet for several days until he can resume normal eating.

Hip Dysplasia

Although Dachshunds are not as prone to hip dysplasia as some other breeds, it's important to know that this condition is inherited, and can be passed to any dog. Hip dysplasia is complex, and can show up in varying degrees—from mild to completely crippling. The easiest way to think of it is as "joint looseness." In dogs with hip dysplasia, the femoral head does not fit snugly into the socket. Symptoms may include difficulty in getting up, stiffness, "bunny hopping," reluctance to climb stairs, and restricted movement in the hind legs, but only an X-ray can definitively detect the disease.

Many treatment surgical options exist for hip dysplasia and each procedure has its place. You can determine in consultation with your veterinarian which, if any, is right for your dog. Drug treatments include buffered aspirin (which alleviates pain but can cause gastric ulcers), steroids (works wonders against the pain, but can actually worsen the condition), and non-steroidal anti-inflammatory drugs (NSAIDS) such as Rimdayl, EtoGesic, and other, newer medications. These drugs are much safer than aspirin but can cause adverse effects in some animals. Nutraceutical supplements, which are categorized as something between a drug and a food, also show great promise. Chief among them is a combination of glucosamine and chondroitin. One such supplement, Cosequin, has proved very popular over the years. Similar, less expensive versions are available, but since the nutraceutical market is not well regulated, it's often best to follow your veterinarian's advice. Other nutraceuticals may also be beneficial, and some companies are now experimenting with combing glucosamine, chondroitin, and antioxidants in a new formula.

Hypothyroidism

Hypothyroidism develops when the thyroid produces insufficient amounts of the thyroid hormone. Nearly all primary hypothyroidism in dogs is caused by a genetic condition called thyroiditis—an autoimmune destruction of the thyroid gland. (Secondary hypothyroidism, which is less common, is not genetic.) Hypothyroidism is common in Dachshunds, and manifests itself in harsh, dull coat and hair loss on the trunk and thighs. Many dogs gain weight, and many become sluggish and lethargic. Most indicative is the development of a hairless "rat" tail. Dogs with low thyroid function may also suffer repeated skin and ear infections.

If left untreated, hypothyroidism can lead to goiter, or even heart failure. Treatment is inexpensive and simple—a daily dose of thyroid hormone replacement. You will notice improvement within a few months, but the dog will need to take his pills for the remainder of his life. Dogs should be tested for this problem once a year during the first four years of life, and every other year thereafter.

Impacted Anal Sacs

No one is absolutely sure what use dogs have for anal sacs, but whatever it may be, the things sometimes fill up and become impacted. This problem is most common in smaller dogs like the Dachshund. It is distressing to the dog, and you'll notice him scooting on the floor, or licking the area. If you get close enough, you'll notice a foul odor as well. Your vet will be able to express the glands and treat the condition, and you can learn to do it also. Perform the procedure in an area that is easily cleaned—like a grooming table. Believe me, this is not an odor that you want clinging to your carpets or furniture.

In rare cases, your veterinarian may suggest that the anal sacs be removed surgically. This won't bother your dog a bit—and you even less. If the dog does not suffer impacted anal sacs, leave them alone. Routinely expressing the sacs is asking for trouble.

Intervertebral Disk Disease

Intervertebral disk disease (IVDD), is very dangerous. To understand it, you need to know something about a Dachshund's spinal configuration. The spinal column is composed of four main regions: cervical or neck (seven vertebrae), thoracic or chest (thirteen vertebrae), lumbar or lower back (seven vertebrae), and sacral or pelvic (three vertebrae). There are also vertebrae in the tail, but I'm going to ignore them right now. Each vertebra has a hollow center that, when lined up, forms the spinal canal. In the thoracolumbar (comprised of the thoracic and lumbar) region this canal is almost completely filled by the spinal cord—there's very little "wiggle room" when an injury occurs. That's one reason why a herniation (rupture) in the thoracolumbar area is much more debilitating than those occurring in the neck region, which has more space around the spinal cord. Injuries are also much more common in the area; in fact, about 80 percent of disk ruptures occur there rather than in the neck region.

Between the vertebrae are disks, which are connected to the vertebrae by fiber-like material, and which are meant to act as cushions for the vertebrae. The disk itself is divided into two parts, the *nucleus pulposus*, the central gelatinous region, and the *annulus fibrosis*, the tough outer fibrous area that contains it. These fibers accommodate all angles of force that can be applied to the disk. The intervertebral disk can withstand a good amount of straight compression, but is not designed to deal with twisting or, to a lesser extent, bending, down the length of the spine. This is especially true when these kinds of stresses are repeated over and over. With time, the annulus fibrosis is significantly weakened and can no longer respond to the stress sufficiently. As the disk degenerates, it loses its elasticity, can no longer act as a cushion, and is predisposed to rupture.

When disk herniation occurs, material from the *nucleus pulposus* intrudes into the spinal canal. The meningeal nerves, which supply the meninges (the protective coverings for the spinal cord), become compressed and inflamed. This causes a great deal of pain.

Researchers classify disk herniation as partial or complete, both of which may occur in the Dachshund. In both cases, the rupture occurs in the area nearest the spinal cord, because that's where the outer layer is thinnest.

Slipshod English

In common parlance, we talk about "slipped" disks, but this phrase gives the wrong impression. Nothing has slipped; the disk has ruptured.

In Type 1 (complete) herniation, a large quantity of *nucleus pulposus* material escapes, usually as a result of trauma or extreme physical activity. In Type 2 (partial) herniation, there are small partial tears in the *annulus fibrosis* which allow nuclear material to bulge out, but which may not actually escape. In either case, a herniated disk can cause damage to the nervous system, including loss of function. It can compress the spinal cord or nerve roots and can interfere with the blood supply. If the material gets into an abnormal site, an immune response develops against it, resulting in an inflammatory reaction. If your Dachshund has reached seven years of age without developing IVDD, he probably won't. Dogs around the age of four are at highest risk.

Both human beings and dogs can develop intervertebral disk disease, although it tends to affect them at different places in the spine. When dogs jump down, the shock goes through their forelegs and runs down the entire length of the spinal column, compressing individual disks. However, the most common site of trauma, as I mentioned earlier, is the thoracolumbar junction. An injury can be so severe as to cause profound paralysis of the hind limbs.

Dachshunds may account for half of all canine cases of this serious and debilitating condition. The precise cause of the

problem is debated, but certainly the very low, very long structure of the dog is largely at fault. Nature can tolerate a limited
amount of tampering. This doesn't mean that all Dachshunds are
subject to the disease, but it does mean that breeding for an exaggerated body shape must cease.

Over 25 percent of all Dachshunds will experience disk problems at some point in their lives, most frequently between the
ages of three and seven years. (Any Dachshund with a back that
is not as level as possible may be at increased risk. Other, simi-
larly shaped dogs like Bassets and Welsh Corgis, are also
commonly affected, and it is a common problem in Pekinese as
well.) IVDD disk disease can result in complete or rear-end
paralysis. The paralysis is not necessarily permanent—much
depends on the *speed and adequacy* of treatment.

*Any suspected back injury should be immediately and profession-
ally attended to. Don't fool around with this.*

Treatment options have traditionally included medical therapy like corticosteroids, (usually methylprednisolone sodium
succinate—shortened to "methylpred"). This drug should be
administered within eight hours of the injury, and continued for
forty-eight hours as a constant-rate intravenous infusion. One
corticosteroid, dexamethasone, should *not* be used for this kind
of injury. It can have serious systemic side effects and may be detrimental to the spinal cord.

Other options include decompressive surgery. If the veterinarian recommends surgery, he may perform (or ask a veterinary
neurologist to perform) a myelogram (a radiogram using radio-
opaque dye in the spinal cord) to confirm the diagnosis. If surgery is performed within twenty-four hours, it is usually
completely successful—but it's not cheap. In addition, not every
case of IVDD is best resolved with surgery. This is why you need
expert, trusted help from the start.

If surgery is not on the menu, your dog will be required to rest
for a period ranging from two weeks to over four. It is essential
that you follow this protocol, and keep your Doxie confined to his
crate except for brief trips outside to eliminate. This is difficult.
You can make the period easier by placing the crate near activity
where the dog can enjoy being in the center of the action, even he
can't actually get involved. His return to normal activities should
be gradual. Follow your veterinarian's advice to the letter.

Improvements in Treating Paralysis

Researchers are experimenting with a new proto-col for paralyzed dogs—stabilization of the damaged vertebrae and a single intravenous dose of polyethyl-ene glycol (PEG). The PEG fuses cell membranes by coating them with a protective film that seals the holes caused by the trauma. Coupled with intensive rehabilitative care, the new procedure offers hope for a condition that once seemed hopeless. For more information on this innovative new procedure, go to: www.vet.purdue.edu. Another cause for hope for paralyzed dogs is a new device called an oscillating field stimulator, which has been shown to stimulate nerve regeneration in the spinal cord, allowing some paralyzed dogs to walk again. It was developed at the Purdue Center for Paralysis Research. This is a rap-idly developing field with advances being made in every area, including that of artificial disks. If your dog is stricken with IVDD, ask your orthopedic or neurological vet for the *latest* research. Don't be satis-fied with less.

In addition, chiropractic care or acupuncture may be helpful. Dogs suffering from motor losses due to this condition benefit from aquatic therapy, massage, and "towel-walking." Here you place a towel beneath the dog as a sling support to help the dog "walk" beside you. This activity helps prevent muscle atrophy and contraction of the joints. Other forms of physical therapy have also been successful, including cold therapy (cryotherapy), ultrasound, and neuromuscular stimulation. Not all veterinari-ans have the necessary knowledge or resources to get your dog on a physical therapy plan, but it's worthwhile trying to find someone who does.

One way to prevent IVDD is to keep dogs from excessive jumping. (This is one reason why agility, no matter how much fun it may be, is not always desirable for Doxies.) Keep your dog from climbing stairs or jumping on and off furniture. Most critical in keeping your dog from developing this disease is to keep your

Doxie fit and trim. Good muscle tone and a proper weight are essential.

If your Dachshund does become paralyzed, his life is not over. Many dogs do very well with carts and other devices to help their mobility. Remember that legs are designed to get a body from one place to another. If wheels can be used instead, the objective has been attained.

Legg-Perthes Disease

Legg-Perthes disease is a stifle disorder that affects many small breeds. It is still another reason why Dachshunds should be discouraged from jumping.

Lung Disease

Dogs are prone to certain kinds of diseases of the pleural cavity, notably pleural effusion, a condition in which fluid accumulates around the lungs. Several causes may be at work, including: infection, heartworm disease, cancer, heart failure, fungal infection, or rupture of the thoracic duct. Most commonly, there seems to be no obvious cause. Symptoms include rapid, shallow, or labored breathing, coughing, and an inability to work. Your veterinarian can drain the fluid from the area in a painless procedure called thoracocentesis, in which the dog does not need to be anesthetized. In cases where the cause is not known, dogs are typically put on a low-fat diet, with necessary fats added as a supplement administered directly into the bloodstream.

Lupus

Lupus (Systemic Lupus Erythematosus or SLE), is a multi-system autoimmune disease. Its cause is unknown. Some veterinarians consider it rare, but it probably goes undiagnosed a good deal of the time. The onset of lupus can be acute or very slow, and this disease is quite unpredictable. Common systems include lethargy, shifting leg lameness, anorexia, skin lesions, and a change in behavior. Joints may be swollen and painful. Lupus is usually treated with initial hospitalization, followed by corticosteroids and other drugs in an attempt to control the abnormal immune response.

Malassezia Dermatitis

This lipophilic yeast (*Malassezia pachydermatis*) is commonly found in the ears of both normal and diseased dogs, but it is not confined to the ears. The condition can make other skin and ear problems worse. Symptoms of *malassezia* include intense itching, and inflamed and thickened skin. (That's where the "pachy-derm"—or elephant—part comes in.) Your vet can treat the problem with antifungal medication shampoos.

Megaesophagus

Megaesophagus is the most common cause of regurgitation (rather than true vomiting) in both dogs and cats. It can be a disease condition itself, or it can result from esophageal obstruction or neuromuscular dysfunction. Animals with this condition regurgitate food and water, lose weight, salivate excessively, and "gurgle." Some also cough or have a nasal discharge. In many cases the condition is congenital. Dogs can be treated by altering their feeding position—they actually need to be fed in a upright or semi-upright position (admittedly hard on the back). Soft foods or gruel work best.

Patellar Luxation

Also known as slipping stifles, and loose knee, patellar luxation is a hereditary and congenital disease, involving several different genes. A dog with this condition has a kneecap that slips out of joint. It tends to rest on the inside of the knee. Dogs with patellar luxation are intermittently lame, moving with the bad leg held off the ground.

Veterinarians grade patellar luxation from 1 to 4. Grade 1 cases may be so slight as to be unnoticeable, while Grade 4 cases produce permanent lameness, with the kneecaps not in position. Serious cases require an operation, followed by six weeks of forced rest. Results are usually excellent.

Progressive Retinal Atrophy

Progressive retinal atrophy (PRA) is a disease of the retina. People get much the same disease; we call it *retinitis pigmentosa*. The retina, located inside the back of the eye, contains specialized cells called photoreceptors that absorb the light focused on them. The photoreceptors convert that light into electrical nerve signals, which are passed by the optic nerve to the brain. The retinal photoreceptors are specialized into rods, for vision in dim light (night vision), and cones for vision in bright light (day and color vision). PRA usually affects the rods first, and then the cones. Miniature Longhaired Dachshunds are especially prone to a form of this disease developing when the dog is three to five years old.

Affected dogs will adapt to their handicap as long as their environment remains constant, and they are not faced with situations requiring excellent vision. You may notice the pupils of their eyes remain dilated and increased reflectivity of the eye causes a noticeable shininess. At the same time, the lens of their eyes may become cloudy, or opaque, perhaps even resulting in a cataract. Your vet can diagnose PRA using an instrument called an indirect ophthalmoscope, (as well as eye drops). Unfortunately, there is no cure.

Pyoderma

Pyoderma is a staph infection of the skin and is the most common skin problem confronting dogs. It causes small pustules, or lesions, which can develop into scabs and crusts. Pyoderma usually, but not always, produces itching and is often a symptom of a deeper problem, perhaps an allergy. To treat pyoderma itself, treatment with oral antibiotics and frequent antibacterial shampoos over a course of three weeks is prescribed.

Ringworm

Despite the name, ringworm is a fungal infection usually characterized by a circular hair loss and scaly skin. It is not usually itchy. Most cases disappear by themselves, but more severe ones can be treated with antifungal medications. If your dog gets ringworm, have him (and all the other dogs and cats in your home) treated, and then clean your house. This includes getting the air filters changed, and disinfecting animal bedding, brushes, and combs with bleach. Ringworm spores can float around in the air for years.

The Uncommon Cold

Dogs don't catch colds, so a runny nose is likely to be an indication of some irritation.

Urinary tract problems

Urinary tract problems are common and females are at particular risk. Symptoms include straining and excessive urination. Get a urine sample and take it to your vet. The best way to accomplish this is to attach a small (very small) paper cup to the end of stretched out wire clothes hanger or other piece of wire. That way you won't have to stand right next to the dog. (Most dogs stop urinating when you try to stick a cup underneath them.)

Von Willebrand's Disease

Von Willebrand's disease is the most common bleeding disorder in dogs. It is due to a complex set of inherited defects related to the synthesis or function of vWF (the von Willebrand's factor). In case you don't know what that is, the vWF is a large glycoprotein that circulates in the plasma, and is involved with one of the early steps in clot formation. You may not even know your dog has the problem until he has surgery or after you nick the quick while clipping his toenails. Some dogs may have bleeding around the gums. In serious cases, the dog may require a concentrated form of vWF and factor VIII, another important clotting factor. Fresh plasma may also be administered. (In contrast to classic hemophilia, control of bleeding is usually achieved with one or two transfusions.)

Your Complete Veterinary First Aid Kit

You don't need a special box; anything handy will do, but a fishing tackle box works very well. On the outside of the box, write "Dog First Aid Kit" in bold letters all over the place. Put it in an obvious place, since someone else might need to find it! In fact, you might tape on your bathroom mirror: "Dog First Aid Kit is in the _____."

To the inside of the box lid, attach any special information someone might need about any conditions or allergic reactions your dog may have. Tape a special card with the name, address, and phone number of your veterinarian. Also write down the use and dosage for each medication your dog is likely to need now, so you won't have to try to figure it out during an emergency. You can use a separate card, or write it right on the bottle. Or both.

The First Aid Kit is also a good place to keep a copy of your dog's medical records, including his rabies certificate.

If you have a chance, take a Red Cross or similar course in first aid. Sometimes special clinics are given in first aid for animals. It is very helpful to learn to perform artificial respiration, mouth-to-mouth resuscitation, and the Heimlich maneuver. You never know when you might need them for animals or people.

Do not give your dog Tylenol, ibuprofin, or aspirin, all of which are dangerous to dogs.

Here it is: the ultimate Canine First Aid Kit. (Get everything on the list and you can open a clinic.)

▼ Canine first aid manual

▼ Gauze and cotton pads (to clean and cover wounds)

▼ Baking soda (for burns caused by acids)

▼ Vinegar (for burns caused by alkaloids)

▼ Bandages or New Skin (the latter is especially useful for cuts on paw pads)

▼ Antibiotic soap or Nolvasan (skin and wound cleanser)

▼ Betadine (treating wounds)

▼ Antibiotic cream

▼ Hydrocortisone cream (minor inflammation)

▼ Gentle eye wash

▼ Petroleum jelly (numerous uses)

▼ Mineral oil (numerous uses, including constipation)

▼ Aloe vera (for minor burns)

▼ Activated charcoal (for poisoning)

▼ Imodium or Kaopectate for diarrhea (1 mg. for every fifteen pounds, one to two times a day, or one tablespoon for every ten pounds every six hours.)

▼ Ipecac or 3 percent hydrogen peroxide (in order to induce vomiting)

▼ Benadryl (1 to 2 mg. per pound, every eight hours; two to four 25 mg. tablets every eight hours)

▼ Witch hazel (insect bites, minor injuries)

▼ Pepto-Bismol (digestive upsets and diarrhea; one teaspoon for every five pounds during a six-hour period)

▼ Epsom salts (for soaking wounds, especially on the feet)

▼ Milk of magnesia (constipation, administer with equal amounts of mineral oil)

▼ Saline eye solution and artificial tear gel

▼ Rubber or latex gloves (to protect your hands and prevent contamination of wounds)

▼ Styptic powder (stops minor bleeding)

▼ Thermal blanket (prevents shock by preserving the dog's body heat)

▼ Syringe (without needle), or turkey baster (to administer oral medication)

▼ Canine rectal thermometer

▼ Round-tip scissors

▼ Eye dropper

▼ Clinging wrap heat or ice pack

▼ Tweezers or hemostat

▼ Magnifying glass

▼ Soft muzzle (injured dogs tend to bite)

Alternative Concepts in Canine Health

Although no reasonable person questions the benefits of modern veterinary medicine, other paths to canine health are also available. I'll look at acupuncture and herbal treatments, but lots of others, such as acupressure, massage, Bach Flower remedies, light therapy, and homeopathy are also popular.

Acupuncture

Acupuncture began in ancient China, and is closely related to the Chinese philosophical system of balance and harmony. It should be understood that acupuncture works best in that context, not as simply another "technique." Its growing popularity in the United States, by the way, can be oddly attributed to Richard Nixon. In his trend-setting visit to China in 1973, a member of the accompanying press corps had surgery performed with acupuncture as an anesthesia. This event was widely reported, and today acupuncture is accepted as a viable veterinary practice.

The goal of Chinese acupuncture is to balance the energy force, or Qi (pronounced "chee"). In a sick animal, the two polarities of Qi, yin and yang, are unbalanced. The practitioner attempts to restore the lost balance by the careful placement of needles.

Sophie   *Photo courtesy of Daisy & Charles Buchignani*

Usually the needles are removed after being in place for ten to thirty seconds, but in some cases, needles are permanently inserted. Several treatments may be necessary. (Luckily, dogs don't seem to suffer from needle-phobia, and don't seem to experience any discomfort. I had one of my dogs treated for a degenerative disk problem with acupuncture; it was very successful.)

Western practitioners, who generally don't like the yin/yang explanation of things, are baffled by how and why acupuncture works. (Some, of course, deny that it does work.) Some scientists believe that acupuncture stimulation blocks the nerve fibers that carry pain impulses. Others believe that acupuncture dilates the restricted blood vessels that accompany many musculoskeletal disorders. Still others suggest that acupuncture stimulates selected parasympathetic and sympathetic nerves that regulate the autonomic nervous system. Of course, the answer may be that acupuncture does all these things. Or none of them.

For best results, go to a veterinarian who is accredited in acupuncture, or to a qualified animal acupuncturist. In the latter case, make sure your dog gets a thorough veterinary examination first to see if his condition warrants or will respond to acupuncture.

Penny (eight years at this picture)   *Photo courtesy of Marcia & Gary Patterson*

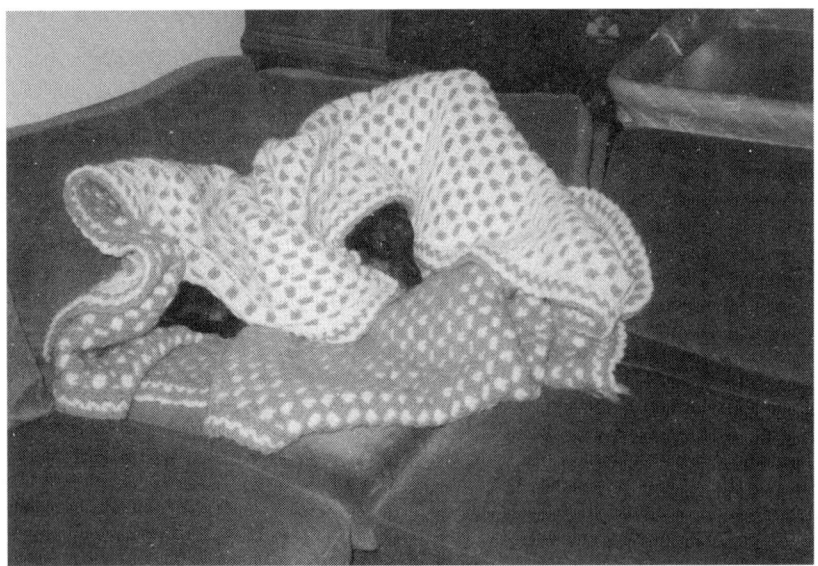

Herbs

One of the most popular methods of treating disease is by use of herbal medications. In fact, worldwide, over four billion people use herbs as a regular part of medical care. And while herbs can indeed heal, they should not be used except in consultation with your holistic veterinarian or a qualified animal herbalist.

Herbs are not always effective, and they are not always safe. (The same is true for modern drugs, of course.) The fact that herbs are "natural," says nothing about their safety. Rattlesnake venom is natural, too. The U.S. Food and Drug Administration classifies herbs (and vitamins and minerals) as dietary supplements—not as drugs—and therefore herbs are not subject to the rigorous safety tests that drugs must pass before being approved. Herbs can come in many forms and the strength of the medication can vary, depending upon which part of the plant is used, whether it is fresh or dry, whole or extracted, and whether it is prepared as a tincture or tea.

Herbal Treatment Tip

Herbs are often known by two or three different common names. And one common name can refer to several different herbs. To make sure you are using the one you want, use its official Latin name, which will consist of two parts: genus and species. Mullein, for example, is officially *Verbascum thapsus*, but it still looks like mullein to me. (It makes a wonderful ear cleaner, too.)

However, progress is being made. Good herb products carry the USP (United States Pharmacopoeia) or NF (Natural Formulary) approval, which ensure that the product has been subject to certain protocols for extracting or drying herbs. The best products, however, also carry the stamp of approval from Consumer Lab (CL). These products have a guarantee of identity, purity, consistency, and potency.

Herbs are the source of most modern medications, so it would be surprising if they didn't have any beneficial effects. They are most effective for chronic problems, but don't expect them to work miracles.

Again, don't start experimenting with these products without guidance, especially if your dog is already undergoing medical treatment. Many herbs can act adversely with drugs. Don't guess. If you do decide to use herbal supplements or herbal treatment, stick with just one or two until you can understand its effects. Herbal medications should not be confused with a potpourri.

Chapter 15
Dachshunds in Their Dotage

About seven and one-half million dogs in this country are over the age of eleven; that's about 15 percent of our pet dogs. (Some vets even specialize in geriatric care.) Dogs, like people, don't suddenly become old. Aging is a gradual process, and with proper care and attention, you can help your dog live out his golden years in comfort and peace.

It's not uncommon for well-tended Dachshunds, especially the smaller sizes, to live well into their mid- and late teens. Geriatric screening should begin about the age of nine, and older dogs should have a thorough veterinary examination twice a year. Of course, as with humans, aging is largely an individual affair, and each dog ages differently.

Exercise

Older dogs need exercise just as much as younger ones do; they just need less strenuous work. When people stop exercising their dogs, they often stop the most important interaction between them, even if the owner thinks it's for "the dog's own good." The dog then becomes depressed—a condition that can have physical roots in the lack of exercise, and psychic roots in the feeling of rejection that may develop. Daily walks improve muscle tone and bone strength (in both you and your dog). The heart, lungs, digestive system and joints all receive benefits. Moreover, the

Wolfwind's Bacardi Fizz, miniature wirehair, 11 years old
Photo courtesy of Douglas & Kimberly Cook

time and the experience go far in deepening the bond between you.

To help your dog live a long and full life, continue to work with and exercise him. He wants to feel just as much a part of your life as ever. Healthy exercise is good for his mind, body, and spirit. If possible, divide the exercise into several shorter walks rather than one long one—it's easier on those aching joints. These should be as brisk, however, as your dog can comfortably handle. The best time to exercise is before your dog eats; likewise you should refrain from feeding him until half an hour after the exercise is finished. Of course, very cold, wet, or hot weather is hard on a geriatric dog; if the weather is severe, play games indoors.

Exercise can also reveal health problems. If your dog coughs or seems out of breath even after rest following exercise, ask your vet to check his heart.

Diet

Your old dog has basically the same dietary requirements he did when he was younger—with one exception. Unless he has kidney disease, he needs more protein in his diet than he did as a young adult. (Some experts believe he needs about 50 percent more.) This news (determined in the 1990s) came as a shock to many people who believed that their older dogs needed less, not more protein. Many senior dog foods now address this need.

Senior dogs also benefit from additional levels of B-complex vitamins. This is because B vitamins help dogs manage stress, infections, and allergies, all of which are increased problems for older dogs. Older dogs may also require more vitamin E, and possibly selenium and zinc. Some people recommend adding ester-C, digestive enzymes, the 3 and 6 omega fatty acids and the coenzyme Q10 to the senior dog's diet.

Old dogs are also subject to senile friability of the nails. This just means that the nails are easily broken. Keep the nails as short as possible and add a packet or so of Knox gelatin to his diet once a day.

Vaccines

Many people stop vaccinating older dogs. They feel that the dog never goes anywhere anyhow, so why bother taking him to vet and putting him through a procedure that may be risky? However, the fact that he's cooped up may be the problem. According to one school of thought, dogs who go out and about are more likely to build up immunities against wandering pathogens. Old dogs who stay home all day may have the poorest immune systems and the least resistance to such bugs when they are exposed. All things being equal, I would vaccinate my older dogs only every three years.

Problems Common to Older Dogs

Just as we do, dogs tend to suffer from a greater number of infirmities as they age. Be watchful for the following conditions as your Dachshund obtains senior status.

Arthritis

As our dogs live longer lives, they are at increased risk of developing arthritis, and about 20 percent of all adult dogs have arthritis to some degree. Obese individuals, who carry the most weight, are more apt to be affected. For dogs (and people), the most common type of arthritis is osteoarthritis, which results from damaged cartilage. Because cartilage has no nerves, the dog feels no pain and continues to be active at first, which only accelerates the damage. Eventually, he will feel discomfort, and he may limp, show a reluctance to get up or climb stairs, develop stiffness, avoid activity, and shrink away from being touched. Arthritic dogs seem more sensitive to cold and damp weather than those who are not afflicted. Arthritis can be more troublesome to dogs than blindness or deafness, but there are ways to combat it. Many new medications, such as EtoGesic, Cosequin, and Adequan, can make a positive difference in your dog's life.

Nutraceuticals, a new class of supplements that seem to fall somewhere between conventional drugs and herbal preparations, offer important benefits to arthritic dogs. Examples include glucosamine and chondroitin. Glucosamine is a cartilage protective nutraceutical, while chondroitin sulfate is an important glycoaminoglycan (GAG), which binds water in the cartilage matrix. Adding both glucosamine and chondroitin sulfate in a single supplement is a great way to help your pet heal himself. These supplements are not simply "pain-killers." Their direct effect is both protective and restorative—leading to less pain, and to more mobility. And this will have an important effect on your dog's attitude. It is important to remember, however, that unlike traditional drug therapy, nutraceuticals work slowly (from six to eight weeks) and not all dogs respond to them. Make sure you buy a high-quality supplement, as not all nutraceuticals are created equal. Check with your veterinarian; don't just buy something over the counter—or over the Internet.

Other treatments often effective against arthritis include physical therapy, Chinese or Japanese acupuncture, chiropractic treatment, and even gene therapy. There's a whole new world out there for arthritis sufferers, and your logy, creaky, slow-to-get-up dog may get a new lease on life with one of the many new treatments available! So far, however, there is no real cure for arthritis—only relief from its more debilitating effects. (However, one tremendously promising avenue is the creation of fabricated cartilage made from different types of juvenile cartilage cells. Animal trials will shortly be underway.)

You can also supply extra bedding, and a snug place by the fire (or, as is the case in our house) the hot air vent.

Blindness

Cataracts, PRA, and glaucoma can take their toll on older pets. Even dogs not technically blind can lose visual acuity. Luckily, dogs don't depend upon their sight as much as we do. They don't care for blazing sunsets, abstract art, or a carefully orchestrated garden—except as something to dig in. If you don't rearrange the furniture, most blind dogs cope remarkably well.

You can even make your blind dog a simple piece of equipment that can save him many a bumped head. You can attach a protective aluminum or flexible plastic hoop to the front of his harness. Other people hang cachets or small scent bags to their door to help dogs find it, or spray a vanilla scent on furniture to warn dogs of its presence.

One important thing to remember is that blind dogs need training—even more than sighted dogs. Because a blind dog is at a disadvantage when it comes to sensing danger, it's critical that he respond to a command from you. "Come," "Whoa," and "Stay" are life-saving commands for any dog, but a blind dog is even more dependent on your timely intervention to save his life. And when you are working with your blind dog, you're also spending quality time together. Both of you can enjoy that. For more information on living with a blind dog check the Owners of Blind Dogs Web Site: www.blinddogs.com.

Cancer

About 50 percent of elderly dogs will develop some form of cancer. In dogs, the most common kinds of cancer are lymphoma melanoma, mammary cancer, various cancers of the head and neck regions, abdominal, and bone cancer.

Symptoms of cancer include: abnormal swellings, wounds that will not heal, bleeding or abnormal discharge, weight and appetite loss, unexplained lameness or stiffness, loss of energy, difficulty in eliminating, and behavioral changes. The most common sign is a lump, but cancer originating in the internal organs will not show this symptom. If your dog was not spayed before her first heat, mammary cancer is a real risk.

Cancer arises from "mistakes" occurring in normal cell division. These mistakes are perpetuated and develop into tumors. Sometimes, the abnormal cell division is caused by outside

Responding to Bone Cancer

At one time, the only viable treatment for bone cancer was amputation of the affected limb. Because of their structure, Dachshunds don't manage amputation as well as some other breeds. Another possibility is "graft limb salvage" in which large portions of bone are taken from a donor dog. This therapy has its drawbacks—about 44 percent of recipients develop serious infections in the grafted limb and others suffer chronic pain. In most cases the new leg doesn't work well anyhow. However, a new therapeutic technique may be on the horizon: bone transport osteogenesis (BTO). Here doctors shift bits of the patient's own bone to the defective part in order to stimulate the growth of new bone. Most of this work is being done with human trauma patients, but many oncologists are hoping the technique can also be applied to animals. Time will tell.

factors such as radiation or chemicals in the environment. Almost any cell can develop into cancer. Almost 30 percent of all cancers are skin cancers, and dogs older than six are most at risk. Any rapidly growing lump or bump, especially those that are hard and appear attached to the bone, should be removed surgically.

One exciting new possibility in cancer control is the use of the newer kinds of NSAIDs (non-steroidal anti-inflammatory drugs), the so-called COX-2 drugs. These drugs seem to have anti-carcinogenic benefits without the side effects of other cancer medications. Some of these drugs include Celebrex and Rimadyl. It is believed that they help with cancers of the bladder, kidney, and prostate as well as some types of skin cancers. The list of drugs is expected to grow as more research is done.

Cancer does not have to be hopeless. Many cases, particularly if detected in an early stage, can be successfully treated with surgery, radiation, or chemotherapy, or a combination of all three. The very word "chemotherapy" strikes fear into the hearts of some dog owners, but perhaps it shouldn't. Luckily for them, dogs seldom have the nausea or hair loss that is often a side effect of chemotherapy in humans. The chemo used for dogs is much milder than that used for people, and in human chemotherapy, doctors may use as many as ten different drugs. Usually, only three drugs are used in chemo for animals. This is because cancer is usually fairly well developed in dogs by the time it's discovered, and so the goal is not a cure, but to lengthen and enhance the quality of life. Radiation treatment, on the other hand, affects dogs and humans pretty much the same way. To learn more about canine cancer: visit the Veterinary Cancer Society's Web site at www.vetcancersociety.org. Information at this site will help you find a veterinary oncologist near you, and the site will also link you to other Web-based cancer information sites, and news and locations of clinical trials.

Cognitive Dysfunction Syndrome

It has been estimated that more than 60 percent of dogs over age eleven are to some degree affected by cognitive dysfunction syndrome. Dogs with this condition seem isolated and confused. They may forget housetraining, or bark incessantly. Cognitive dysfunction syndrome should not be treated as normal aging. It is a disease process, and there are methods to combat it. A veritable fountain of youth has been discovered in the form of Anipryl, a medication that truly seems to reverse time.

Constipation

Older dogs may have reduced bowel activity, which can lead to constipation. A laxative may be helpful in these cases. Check with your veterinarian about appropriate treatment.

Coughing

Coughing is a common problem in senior dogs. This is because old lungs tend to produce more mucus, which can lead to bronchitis. The smaller the dog, the more serious the problem, since his airways are more easily blocked than those of larger canines. (For similar reasons, a child's cold seems worse than yours.)

More seriously, night coughing can be an early sign of heart problems. Medications are available to keep fluid accumulation down.

Deafness

While dogs depend upon their hearing, the loss of it is usually so gradual the dog (and you) aren't usually aware that it's happening. There's even an upside to deafness. My old Ruby's increasing deafness has at last brought her peace from the noise of the dreaded vacuum cleaner—she sleeps right through it. She doesn't hear the letter carrier's arrival any more either, which is a great relief to him and me.

Deaf dogs can live happy and useful lives, and can be trained with hand signals. For guidance in training your deaf dog, get a copy of *Hear, Hear! A Guide to Training A Deaf Puppy*. It's available through www.dogwise.com or you can call (800) 776-2665.

Another ear condition, old dog vestibular disease, stems from an inner ear problem. Dogs with this disease typically shake their heads; they may circle around or even lose their balance and fall. Old dog vestibular disease can often be treated with anti-motion sickness medications and antibiotics and treated dogs usually recover well.

Dental Disease

Curiously, dental disease, which may seem the most minor of old age diseases, has the potential to be the most debilitating. And the incidence of dental disease increases as dogs get older. A dental problem can manifest itself as bad breath (halitosis), inflammation of the gums (gingivitis), or inflammation and tissue damage of the bone (periodontal disease). If not treated, the tartar that forms on most older dog's teeth can led to bacterial infection that may attack the heart valves and kidneys—or even make arthritis worse. Miniature Dachshunds are most severely affected because their jaws are small and their teeth tend to be crowded more tightly together.

Heart Problems

A very common disease affecting smaller old dogs involves degeneration of the heart valves. The most susceptible of these valves is the atrioventricular valve, which separates the upper chamber (atrium) from the lower one (ventricle). When a dog has this condition, the blood flows improperly between the two chambers, causing an overload on the heart. Serious cases can result in congestive heart failure. Good care involves frequent checkups by your veterinarian.

Incontinence

Spayed older females frequently lose muscle control and "leak," especially at night. Several inexpensive medications are available to control this problem. In addition, older dogs have fewer nephrons (the urine-forming units in the kidney) and thus experience progressive loss of kidney function. Dogs with kidney failure should have less protein in their diets than formerly.

Hospice Care

Most of us are well aware of the good work hospice does for human beings, to comfort the living and dying, and to make the passage from life to death as easy and fulfilling as possible. Fewer of us are aware that there is hospice care available for animals as well, and more and more people are turning to it as an alternative to euthanasia. The aim of hospice falls between a vain struggle for a cure for an incurable disease and euthanasia. Its goal is to provide a quiet, dignified dying process for the both the pet and the owner. Some hospice facilities rely upon traditional painkilling medications; others aim for a more holistic approach. But both have the same goal, dealing with day-to-day symptoms of pain and distress, while allowing the animal to find his own way—and time—to die.

Unlike most human hospice care, veterinary hospice care is home-based. This means that pet-owners have the responsibility and honor of caring for their pets in the last weeks and months of their life, a task to be approached with the compassion and sense of awe that attended your earliest days together. Hospice care is not for everyone, but if you'd like to learn more, contact the Nikki

Woody didn't find the glasses particularly helpful.

Photo courtesy of John & Margie Flynn

Foundation for Pets at (707) 557-8595 or e-mail Marocchino@ aol.com. You can also visit the organization's Web site at www.csum.edu/pethospice/

Saying Goodbye

Dogs die, even the best of them. Especially the best of them, it seems. We all know this, but that doesn't make it any easier. It's never the right time for a dog to pass away, and nowadays, most dogs need our help. Typically, the dog becomes sicker and sicker, and although he's on medication, the good days get fewer and further between.

Eventually, we make the heart-breaking appointment with the vet—or, as happens frequently today, we ask the vet to come to us. There is nothing that makes any of this any easier. Preparing, not preparing, talking about it, not talking about it—nothing seems to help but the gentle support of our friends and the silent strength of our other pets.

Much has been written about the advantages and disadvantages of staying with your dog through the entire euthanasia procedure, or waiting until he is asleep and then saying goodbye, or even leaving him in the hands of his old friend the vet. You alone know what's best for you and him. It is *not* true that the dog will necessarily suffer more if you don't stay. Some people simply can't handle the experience without falling to pieces before it even starts. Your evident distress doesn't help your dog. Only you know what is right for you and your Doxie. Go with your heart and don't feel guilty about your choices. Your Doxie will understand.

Afterward, you will grieve. Some people like to give their pets funerals and beautiful burial spots; others remember them in different ways. Many vow never to have another dog as long as they live. Some call a breeder or a rescue the next day. Again, unerringly, you will make the right decision for you. And someday, perhaps tomorrow, perhaps years from now—but surely someday—a certain pair of bright, black eyes will glance up at you—and you'll lose your heart all over again.

Appendix A
Resources: Books, Web Sites, Associations, and Institutions

Dachshund Resources

Clubs

Dachshund Club of America
Andra O'Connell, Secretary
1793 Berme Road
Kerhonkson, NY 12446
Web site: www.dachshund-dca.org

National Miniature Dachshund Club
Marlies Noll, Secretary
31030 108th Street
Princeton, MN 55371-4646
Web site: www.dachshund-nmdc.org

Breeder Referral

Standard Dachshunds
Jere Mitternight, Chair, Breeder Referral
Dachshund Club of America
Telephone: (504) 835-1025

Miniature Dachshunds
Emma Jean Stephenson, President
National Miniature Dachshund Club

Telephone: (724) 846-6745
Email: emmajean@timesnet.net

Rescue

Dachshund Club of America
Emma Jean Stephenson, Rescue Coordinator
Telephone: (724) 846-6745
Email: emmajean@timesnet.net

Breed Books

Dunbar, Ian, Ph.D., ed., *The Essential Dachshund.* New York: Howell Book House, 1999.

Gordon, Ann. *The Dachshund: A Dog for Town and Country.* New York: Howell Book House, 2000.

Hutchinson, Dee and Bruce Hutchinson. *The Complete Dachshund.* New York: Howell Book House, 1997.

Ladd, Kate. *A New Owner's Guide to Dachshunds.* Neptune, NJ: TFH Publications, 1996.

Videos

American Kennel Club, *The Dachshund* (#WT 408)
AKC Video Fulfillment Department
5580 Centerview Drive
Raleigh, NC 27609-0643
Telephone: (919) 233-9767
Web site: www.akc.org

Mind's Eye Productions, *Selecting and Caring for your Pet Dachshund*
Telephone: (800) 570-DOGS
Web site: www.petvideo.com

Journals

Dog World Magazine
3 Burroughs
Irvine, CA 92618
Telephone: (949) 855-8822
Web site: www.dogworldmag.com

Dog Fancy
3 Burroughs
Irvine, CA 92618
Telephone: (949) 855-8822
Web site: www.animalnetwork.com

The Whole Dog Journal
Nancy Kerns, Editor in Chief
P.O. Box 420234
Palm Coast, FL 32142
Telephone: (800) 829-9165
Email: wholedogjl@palmcoastd.com

For Canada: Box 7820 STN Main
London, ON NY5 5WI

Your Dog: A Magazine for Caring Dog Owners
Tufts University of Veterinary Medicine
P.O. Box 420234
Palm Coast, FL 32142
Telephone: (800) 829-5116

Therapy Dogs

Delta Society Pet Partners Program
289 Perimeter Road E.
Renton, WA 98055
Telephone: (800) 869-6898, (206) 226-7357
Email: deltasociety@cis.compuserve.com

Therapy Dogs International
88 Bartley Road
Flanderd, NJ 07836
Telephone: (973) 252-9800
Email: tdi@gti.net
Web site: www.tdi-dog.org

Pets and People: Companions in Therapy and Service
P.O. Box 4266
Meridian, MS 39307
Telephone: (601) 483-8970

General

The Purina Company has a great pet care Web site, www.purina.com/dogs. Especially good is the section that answers your questions about your dog's behavior. I also recommend visiting: www.petplace.com.

American Kennel Club
5580 Centerview Drive
Raleigh, NC 27606
Telephone: (919) 233-3725
Web site: www.akc.org

United Kennel Club
100 E. Kilgore Rd.
Kalamazoo, MI 49002
Telephone: (616) 343-9020
Web site: www.ukcdogs.com

Szabo, Julia and Mary Tyler Moore, *Animal House Style: Designing a Home to Share with Your Pets*, New York: Bulfinch Press, 2001 (for sage advice and beautiful photographs on how to make life with your canine more comfortable).

Health

Acupuncture and Acutherapy
Canine Acupressure Therapists, Amy Snow and Nancy Zidonis:
Telephone: (888) 841-7211
Email: acupressure4all@earthlink.net.
Web site: www.animalacupressure.com

Snow, Amy and Nancy Zidonis. *The Well-Connected Dog: A Guide to Canine Acupressure.* Larkspur, CO: Tallgrass Publishers, 1999.

Arthritis
Beale. Brian D.V.M. *The Arthritis Cure for Pets: How to Halt, Reverse, and Even Cure Your Pet's Osteoarthritis.* New York: Little, Brown, and Company, 2000.

Epilepsy
Canine Epilepsy Network Web site:
www.canine-epilepsy.net

First Aid
Copeland, Sue and John A. Hamil, DVM, *Hands-On Dog Care: The Complete Book of Canine First Aid.* Phoenix, AZ: Doral Publishing, Inc., 2000.

Holistic
www.naturalpetvet.com is a Web site devoted to holistic medicine and natural treatments. The site provides information about essential oils and herbal extracts that can be used to treat your pet holistically, or call: (877) PESDOC.

> Flower Essence Society
> P.O. Box 459
> Nevada City, CA 95959
> Telephone: 800-736-9222
> Voice mail: 530-265-9163
> Fax: 530-265-0584
> Email: Mail@flowersociety.org
> Web site: www.flowersociety.org

> American Holistic Veterinary Medical Association
> 2218 Old Emmorton Road
> Bel Air, MD 21015
> Telephone: (410) 569-0795
> Fax: (410) 569-2346
> Email: ahva@compuserve.com
> Web site: www.altvetmed.com/ahvmadir.html

Hamilton, Don. *Homeopathic Care for Cats and Dogs: Small Doses for Small Animals.* Berkeley, CA: North Atlantic Books, 1999.

Kidd, Randy. *Dr. Kidd's Guide to Herbal Dog Care.* Pownal, VT: Storey Books, 2000.

Jones, Linda Tellington-Jones and Sybil Taylor, *The Tellington TTouch: A Revolutionary Natural Method to Train and Care for Your Favorite Animal.* New York: Penguin Books, 1992

Pitcairn, Richard and Susan Pitcairn. *Dr. Pitcairn's Complete Guide to Natural Health for Dogs and Cats,* by Richard and Susan Pitcairn. Emmaus, PA: Rodale Press, 1995.

Massage

Furman, C. Sue. *Canine Massage: A Balancing Act.* Wolfchase Press, 2000.

Hannay, Pamela. *Shiatsu for Dogs.* J.A. Allen & Co. Ltd., 1998.

Nutrition

Cusick, William D. *Canine Nutrition: Choosing the Best Food for Your Breed.* Phoenix, AZ: Doral Publishing, Inc., 1997.

Duno, Steve. *Plump Pups and Fat Cats: A Seven-Point Weight Loss Program for Your Overweight Pet.* New York: St. Martin's Press, 1999.

Gianfrancesco, Cheryl. *Doggie Desserts: Homemade Treats for Happy, Healthy Dogs.* Phoenix, AZ: Doral Publishing, Inc., 2001.

Morgan, Diane. *Feeding Your Dog for Life.* Phoenix, AZ: Doral Publishing, Inc., 2002.

Traditional

American Veterinary Medical Association
1931 N. Meacham Road, Suite 100
Schaumberg, IL 60173
Telephone: (847) 925-8070
Web site: www.avma.org

International Alliance for Animal Therapy and Healing,
Ardsley, NY
Telephone: (914) 378-5295
Web site: www.IAATH.com

Products

Ark Natural Products for Pets
6166 Taylor Road, No. 105
Naples, FL 34109
Telephone: (800) 926-5100, (941) 592-9388
Web site: www.arknaturals.com

Training

Association of Pet Dog Trainers
P.O. Box 385
Davis, CA 95617
Telephone: (800) PET-DOGS

Bulanda, Susan. *Ready! The Step by Step Training of the Search and Rescue Dog.* Phoenix, AZ: Doral Publishing, Inc., 1995.

Dodham, Nicholas. *Dogs Behaving Badly: An A-to-Z Guide to Understanding and Curing Behavioral Problems in Dogs.* New York: Bantam Books, 1999.

Haithcox, Anet. *A-1 K-9.* Phoenix, AZ: Doral Publishing, Inc., 2002.

Lachan, Larry and Frank Mickadeit. *Dogs on the Couch: Behavior Therapy for Training and Caring for your Dog.* New York: Overlook, 1999.

Owens, Paul with Norma Ecroate. *The Dog Whisperer: A Compassionate, Nonviolent Approach to Dog Training.* Avon, MA: Adams Media Corp., 1999.

Pryor, Karen. *Don't Shoot the Dog: The New Art of Teaching and Training*, Revised edition. New York: Bantam Books, 1999.

Travel, Kennels, and Sitters

AAA Publishing. *Traveling with your Pet: The AAA Petbook.* Heathrow Publishing.

Barish, Eileen. *Vacationing with Your Pet*, 4th ed. Petfriendly Publications, Scottsdale, AZ. 1999.

National Association for Professional Pet Sitters Referral Network
Telephone: (800) 296-PETS
Web site: www.petsitters.org

Pet Sitters International will give you tips and provide references for finding a petsitter in your area. Check out their Web site: www.petsit.com.

United States Department of Agriculture (USDA)

The USDA produces a brochure, "Traveling with your Pet" (#1536) that gives helpful advice and explains airline regulations concerning pet travel.

Telephone: (800) 545-USDA to obtain a copy.

www. petswelcome.com is an up-to-date Web site listing travel spots and hotels that welcomes pets.

Index